The Legacy of the Great War

PEACEMAKING, 1919

Edited by

William R. Keylor

Boston University

Houghton Mifflin Company   Boston   New York

Editor-in-Chief: Jean L. Woy
Associate Editor: Leah Strauss
Senior Project Editor: Janet Young
Editorial Assistant: Carolyn Wagner
Associate Production/Design Coordinator: Deborah Frydman
Assistant Manufacturing Coordinator: Andrea Wagner
Marketing Manager: Sandra McGuire

Cover Design: Sarah Melhado
Cover Art: Versailles Treaty. Lloyd George, Clemenceau, Wilson in
          Paris during peace negotiations, 1919. The Bettmann
          Archive, New York.

Printed in the U.S.A.

Library of Congress Catalog Number: 97-72503

ISBN: 0-669-41711-4

123456789-DH-01 00 99 98 97

ONE WEEK LOAN

PROBLEMS IN EUROPEAN
CIVILIZATION SERIES

To James T. Dutton

Contents

IV The Colonial Settlement 169

V The Abortive Quest for Human Rights 223

Preface

In the thirty-seven years since Professor Ivo J. Lederer edited a volume in this series entitled *The Versailles Settlement: Was It Foredoomed to Failure?*, the historiography of the Paris Peace Conference of 1919 has undergone a radical transformation. The British and French archives for the period, which (unlike the American records) had been closed to researchers, were declassified and opened in the 1960s and 1970s. In the course of the past two decades, a number of studies based on this documentary record have led to a fundamental reassessment of the peace settlement after the Great War, which so profoundly shaped the future of the century that is approaching its end.

The collection in this volume comprises selections from some of the significant contributions to this recent scholarly literature. It also includes a number of primary sources to bring the reader into direct contact with some of the important debates that enlivened the unprecedented exercise in global diplomacy that transpired in Paris during the first half of 1919. In assembling the primary and secondary sources that follow, I was guided by the conviction that while the peace settlement after the Great War applied primarily to the continent of Europe, the new international order that it fashioned had important consequences for the peoples of Asia, Africa, and the Middle East as well.

The Introduction summarizes the historiography of the Peace Conference, from the early reflections of supporting actors in the drama, such as John Maynard Keynes, Ray Stannard Baker, and Harold Nicolson, to more recent scholarly studies based on newly opened archives. Part I focuses on the daunting task that confronted the peacemakers as they sought (with the advice of a formidable throng of specialists) to delineate the new frontiers of Europe amid the clash of nationalist aspirations and strategic interests. Part II addresses the various projects for promoting the postwar security that surfaced in Paris, including President Wilson's plan for a League of Nations, Marshal Ferdinand Foch's proposal for creation of a buffer state in the Rhineland, and the novel experiment in deterrence represented by the ill-fated Anglo-American pledge to defend France against unprovoked German aggression. Part III examines the controversial topic of reparations, which has been subjected to a searching reexamination by historians dissatisfied with the conventional wisdom of Keynes and his school. Part IV treats the peace settlement in Africa, Asia, and the Middle East and identifies the first faint signs of anti-imperialist sentiment in the world beyond Europe. Part V explores the abortive attempts in Paris to establish procedures for preventing the maltreatment of individuals based on their race, religion, or ethnicity.

The idea for this volume was hatched in a conversation—one of many that we have had in the course of what we playfully call our "power lunches"—with Dr. Lancelot Farrar. He and his wife, Marjorie, both distinguished scholars of the Great War, have been a frequent source of intellectual stimulation and good fellowship. I profited greatly by attending an international conference at the University of California at Berkeley in 1994, held by the German Historical Institute on the occasion of the 75th anniversary of the signing of the Treaty of Versailles. I am particularly grateful to the following people who have contributed significantly to my understanding of various aspects of the Versailles settlement over the years: Lloyd Ambrosius, Denise Artaud, Joel Blatt, Michael Carley, Carole Fink, André Kaspi, Tony Lentin, Sally Marks, Steve Schuker, Alan Sharp, Georges-Henri Soutou, and David Stevenson.

James Miller supervised this project in its early stages with his customary skill, and Leah Strauss proved a worthy successor after assuming editorial control. Janet Young and Carolyn Wagner skillfully guided the manuscript through its final stages at Houghton Mifflin. My wife, best friend, and favorite conversation partner, Dr. Rheta Grenoble Keylor, has been a constant source of love and support. My children, Daniel and Justine Keylor, cheerfully tolerated my nocturnal wanderings to the bookshelf and the word processor.

W. R. K.

Chronology of Events

Background

1914	1 August	Germany declares war on Russia
	3 August	Germany declares war on France, invades Belgium
	4 August	Great Britain declares war on Germany
	23 August	Japan declares war on Germany, lands forces on Shantung peninsula of China to attack German possession at Tsingtao
	5 October	England and France declare war on Turkey
	7 November	German fortress at Tsingtao capitulates to Japanese
1915	18 January	Japan issues "twenty-one demands" to China
	26 April	Great Britain, France, Russia, and Italy conclude secret Treaty of London promising Italy territorial gains in exchange for its intervention
	23 May	Italy declares war on Austria-Hungary
	24 October	British pledge to Sharif Hussein of the Hejaz to support Arab state south of Anatolia as reward for an Arab rebellion against Turkish Empire
1916	16 May	Sykes-Picot Agreement divides Turkish Empire into British and French spheres of influence
	5 June	Beginning of Arab revolt against Turkey in the Hejaz
1917	1 February	Germany resumes unrestricted submarine warfare
	3 February	United States breaks diplomatic relations with Germany
	15 March	Tsar Nicholas II abdicates, ending the Romanov dynasty in Russia
	6 April	United States Congress declares war on Germany
	2 November	Balfour Declaration on "Jewish home" in Palestine
	7 November	Bolshevik Revolution in Russia

1918	8 January	Wilson's "Fourteen Points" address
	3 March	Germany and Russia sign Treaty of Brest-Litovsk
	21 March	Ludendorff offensive in France begins
	5 April	Japanese forces land in Vladivostok
	4 June	American second division helps French army break German advance at Château Thierry, representing first substantial military action by U.S. troops
	23 June	British forces land in Murmansk
	18 July	Allied counteroffensive ordered by Marshal Foch
	4 October	German and Austrian governments appeal to President Wilson for armistice on basis of fourteen points; exchange of notes between Washington and Berlin begins
	14 October	Turkish government appeals for armistice
	30 October	Turkish armistice signed; Allied prime ministers accept fourteen points (with reservations) as basis of armistice with Germany
	3 November	Austro-Hungarian armistice signed
	8 November	German delegation arrives at Forest of Compiègne
	9 November	German Emperor abdicates, German Republic declared in Berlin
	11 November	German armistice signed
	18 November	Wilson announces intention to attend peace conference in person
	27 November	W. E. B. Du Bois submits memorandum to Wilson on African self-determination
	4 December	Wilson and American delegation sail for Europe
	14 December	Wilson arrives in Paris
	23 December	Maxim Litvinov announces he is authorized by Soviet government to negotiate with Allied powers
	25 December	Wilson embarks on tour of Great Britain and Italy

Peacemaking in Paris

1919	7 January	Wilson returns to Paris to prepare for conference
	8 January	Wilson completes preliminary draft of League of Nations Constitution (Covenant)
	10 January	Foch note to Allied governments proposing permanent military occupation of Rhineland and creation of independent Rhenish buffer state

14–16 January	William Buckler, sent by Wilson, negotiates with Litvinov in Stockholm
18 January	First plenary session of Peace Conference opens at French Foreign Ministry ("Quai d'Orsay"); Wilson completes second draft of League Covenant
20 January	Clemenceau, in three memoranda written by Tardieu, endorses Foch's Rhineland proposals
22 January	Council of Ten approves Wilson–Lloyd George invitation to delegates from all factions in Russian Civil War to conference at Prinkipo Island in Sea of Marmara in Turkey
25 January	Conference unanimously approves resolution for establishment of a League of Nations and creates a commission to draft its constitution (Covenant); conference establishes Commission on the Reparation of Damage to draft reparation clauses of peace treaties
2 February	Hurst-Miller draft of League Covenant completed
3 February	First meeting of League of Nations Commission
4 February	Reparation Commission creates subcommissions
6 February	Prince Feisal presents case for independence for Arabic-speaking population of the Middle East
11 February	French delegation to League of Nations Commission introduces amendment proposing League military force; consideration of amendment is postponed
13 February	Japanese delegation to League of Nations Commission introduces "racial equality amendment" to League Covenant; consideration of the amendment is postponed
14 February	Draft of League of Nations Covenant approved by Third Plenary Session of peace conference; Wilson departs for United States to address urgent domestic problems
19 February	Assassin wounds Clemenceau in Paris
19–21 February	Pan-African Congress meets in Paris
24 February	Wilson arrives in United States
3 March	Republican Senator Henry Cabot Lodge publicizes "round robin" signed by enough senators to defeat peace treaty containing League Covenant

4 March	Wilson speech in Metropolitan Opera House proclaiming that League Covenant cannot be separated from peace treaty
4 March	Lenin founds Third (Communist) International in Moscow
5 March	Wilson sails for Europe
9–14 March	U.S. State Department official William Bullitt meets with Bolshevik officials in Petrograd and Moscow
13 March	Wilson lands in Brest to learn that Colonel House has tentatively approved—against the president's wishes—the French proposal for an independent Rhineland Republic as a buffer state
14 March	Wilson returns to Paris by train. Wilson and Lloyd George spell out opposition to French demand for independent Rhenish buffer state, offer Clemenceau compensatory pledges to guarantee France against unprovoked aggression from Germany
17 March	France accepts Anglo-American security pledges, abandons demand for separate Rhenish buffer state, proposes temporary rather than permanent military occupation of Rhineland, reiterates demand for annexation of Saar
22 March	League of Nations Commission reconvenes to consider amendments to Covenant
24 March	Council of Four begins meeting at Wilson's house
25 March	Lloyd George submits Fontainebleau Memorandum to Council of Four proposing more lenient terms
26 March	Bullitt conveys to Lansing Lenin's offer of an armistice and territorial concessions
27 March	British representative Lord Sumner proposes that pensions be included in reparation bill
1 April	Wilson accepts British proposal to include pensions
4 April	Council of Four approves German-Czechoslovak frontier
5 April	Council of Four accepts Norman Davis's proposal that Germany be held responsible for war and resulting damage (origin of "war guilt clause")
10 April	Council of Four accepts German-Polish frontier

	11 April	At its final meeting League of Nations Commission approves American-sponsored amendment recognizing Monroe Doctrine, rejects French amendment for a League military force, and rejects Japanese racial equality amendment
	13 April	Council of Four adopts compromise for the Saar
	22 April	Council of Four adopts compromise for the Rhineland
	28 April	League of Nations Covenant presented in final form
	29 April	German delegation arrives at peace conference
	7 May	Draft peace treaty submitted to German delegation
	1 June	Rhenish separatists proclaim "Rhineland Republic," which quickly collapses
	21 June	Crews scuttle German fleet interned at Scapa Flow in Scotland
	28 June	Treaty of Versailles with Germany signed; Anglo-American security pacts with France signed; Rhineland agreement signed; Minority Treaties signed

Aftermath

	7 July	Germany ratifies Versailles treaty
	10 September	Treaty of Saint-Germain-en-Laye with Austria signed
	13 October	France ratifies Versailles treaty
	15 October	Great Britain and Italy ratify Versailles treaty
	30 October	Japan ratifies Versailles treaty
	19 November	U.S. Senate fails to ratify Versailles treaty in first vote
	27 November	Treaty of Neuilly with Bulgaria signed
1920	10 January	Treaty of Versailles enters into force
	19 March	Second and final rejection of peace treaty by U.S. Senate; Franco-American security pact not acted upon, so Anglo-French security pact lapses
	4 June	Treaty of Trianon with Hungary signed
	16 July	Spa Protocol on Reparations adopted
	10 August	Treaty of Sèvres with Turkey signed
1921	5 May	London Schedule of Payments for reparations issued

1922	26 December	Reparations Commission declares German default
1923	11 January	Franco-Belgian forces begin occupation of Ruhr
	14 July	Treaty of Lausanne with Turkey signed
1924	9 April	Dawes Plan on reparations issued
	16 August	London Reparations Conference ends after adopting Dawes Plan
1925	27 August	French troops evacuate Ruhr
	1 December	Locarno treaties signed
1926	31 January	First Rhineland zone evacuated
1927	31 January	Allied inspection of German disarmament ends
1929	7 June	Young Plan on reparations announced
	29 October	Crash on New York Stock Exchange begins
	30 November	Second Rhineland zone evacuated
1930	17 May	Young Plan on reparations enters into effect
	30 June	Third and final Rhineland zone evacuated
	14 September	German Reichstag elections return 107 Nazis
1931	6 July	Hoover Moratorium on reparations and war debt payments goes into effect for one year
1932	9 July	Lausanne Conference ends after agreeing to de facto abolition of reparations
1933	30 January	Adolf Hitler becomes Chancellor of Germany
1935	13 January	Plebiscite in Saar votes for reunion with Germany
	9 March	Germany announces existence of air force in violation of Versailles treaty
	16 March	Germany announces conscription and 36-division army in violation of Versailles treaty
	18 June	Anglo-German Naval Treaty signed, allowing Germany to violate Versailles treaty naval disarmament clauses
1936	7 March	Hitler remilitarizes the Rhineland in violation of Versailles treaty and Locarno treaties
1938	12 March	Germany annexes Austria in violation of Versailles treaty
1938	29 September	Munich Conference and Agreement

1939	15 March	Germany invades Czechoslovakia and transforms Bohemia and Moravia into a German protectorate in violation of Versailles treaty and Four Power ("Munich") Agreement
	1 September	Germany invades Poland
	3 September	Great Britain and France declare war on Germany

Principal Proper Names

Abdullah: Second son of Sharif Hussein of Mecca in the Hejaz region of the Arabian peninsula, who became Emir of Transjordan in 1922.

Allenby, General Sir Edmund: British Commander in Chief of Egyptian Expeditionary Force, 1917–1919; British High Commissioner in Egypt, 1919–1925.

Atatürk, Mustafa Kemal: Commander of Turkish forces at Gallipoli; President of Turkish Republic, 1923–1938.

Baker, Ray Stannard: Journalist, head of American Press Bureau at the peace conference; author of an early study of the peace conference.

Balfour, Arthur James: British Foreign Secretary, 1916–1919.

Baruch, Bernard M.: Chairman of the War Industries Board in the United States; economic adviser to the American peace delegation.

Beneš, Edvard: Plenipotentiary Czechoslovak delegate to the peace conference; foreign minister of Czechoslovakia, 1918–1935; President, 1935–1938; 1945–1948.

Benson, Vice Admiral William S.: Naval adviser to the American peace delegation.

Bernstorff, Johann Heinrich, Count von: German Ambassador to the United States, 1908–1917.

Berthelot, Philippe: Political adviser to the French peace delegation.

Bliss, General Tasker H.: American representative on the Supreme War Council, 1917–1918; plenipotentiary American delegate to the peace conference.

Borden, Sir Robert: Canadian Prime Minister, 1911–1920; plenipotentiary Canadian delegate to the peace conference.

Botha, General Louis: Prime Minister of the Union of South Africa, 1910–1919; plenipotentiary South African delegate to the peace conference.

Bourgeois, Léon: French delegate to the League of Nations Commission.

Bowman, Isaiah: American geographer; member of the Inquiry.

Brockdorff-Rantzau, Count Ulrich von: Head of the German peace delegation.

Buckler, William: American diplomat sent to Stockholm in January 1919 to negotiate with Bolshevik representative Maxim Litvinov.

Bullitt, William C.: American State Department official sent to Moscow for secret talks with Bolshevik leaders in February–March 1919.

Cambon, Jules: Chairman of commissions dealing with Greek, Czech, and Polish questions at the peace conference; French plenipotentiary delegate.

Cecil, Lord Robert: British delegate to the League of Nations Commission; one of the authors of the League of Nations Covenant.

Chinda, Viscount Sutemi: Plenipotentiary Japanese delegate to the peace conference.

Churchill, Winston Leonard Spencer: British Secretary of State for War, 1918–1921.

Clemenceau, Georges: French Prime Minister, 1917–1920; leader of the French delegation to and presiding officer at the peace conference.

Clémentel, Etienne: French Minister of Commerce and Industry; economic adviser to the French peace delegation.

Cunliffe, Baron Walter: British delegate to the Reparation Commission.

Davis, Norman H.: American delegate to the Reparation Commission.

De Bon, Admiral Ferdinand: Naval adviser to the French peace delegation.

Denikin, General Anton: Head of anti-Bolshevik forces in southern Russia, 1918–1919.

Derby, Lord Edward: British Ambassador to France during the peace conference.

Dmowski, Roman: Chairman of the Polish National Committee in Paris.

Dorten, Hans Adam: Leader of the French-supported separatist movement in the Rhineland.

Du Bois, William Edward Burghardt: Director of Publicity and Research for the National Association for the Advancement of Colored People; organizer of the Pan-African Congress in Paris during the peace conference.

Dulles, John Foster: Legal counsel to the American delegates on the Reparation Commission; nephew of Secretary of State Lansing.

Erzberger, Matthias: Leader of the Center Party in the Reichstag; head of the German delegation that signed the armistice.

Feisal I: Third son of Sherif Hussein of Mecca; advocate of Arab interests at the peace conference; King of Iraq, 1921–1933.

Foch, Marshal Ferdinand: Commander in Chief of Allied armies, 1918–1919; plenipotentiary French delegate to the peace conference.

Grayson, Rear Admiral Cary T.: President Wilson's close friend, confidant, and personal physician.

Haller, General Joseph: Commander of the Polish National Army.

Hankey, Lieutenant Colonel Sir Maurice: Head of the British secretariat at the peace conference; secretary for the Council of Four.

Haskins, Professor Charles H.: Harvard University historian; chief adviser on European affairs to the American peace delegation.

Headlam-Morley, James: Technical adviser on political affairs in the British peace delegation.

Hoover, Herbert C.: Organizer of food relief for Belgium, 1915–1917; United States Food Administrator, 1917–1919; economic adviser to the American peace delegation.

House, Edward M.: Plenipotentiary American delegate to the peace conference; American delegate to the League of Nations Commission.

Hughes, William M.: Prime Minister of Australia, 1915–1923; plenipotentiary Australian delegate to the peace conference.

Hurst, Cecil J. B.: Legal adviser to the British peace delegation; one of the authors of the League of Nations Covenant.

Hussein, Sharif of Mecca and King of the Hejaz: Leader of the Arab revolt against the Ottoman Empire in 1916; founder of Hashemite dynasty whose sons became the rulers of Iraq and Transjordan.

Hymans, Paul: Belgian Foreign Minister, 1918–1920; plenipotentiary Belgian delegate to the peace conference.

Jusserand, Jean Jules: French Ambassador to Washington, 1903–1924.

Kerr, Philip: Private secretary to Lloyd George, 1916–1921; member of the secretariat of the British peace delegation.

Keynes, John Maynard: Financial adviser to the British peace delegation; author of first book critical of the peace settlement.

Klotz, Louis-Lucien: French Minister of Finance; French plenipotentiary delegate to the peace conference; French delegate to and chairman of the Reparation Commission.

Kolchak, Admiral Alexander: Leader of anti-Bolshevik forces in Siberia, 1918–1920.

Koo, Vi Kyuin Wellington: Chinese plenipotentiary delegate to the peace conference.

Lamont, Thomas W.: Financial adviser to the American peace delegation; American delegate to the Reparation Commission.

Lansbury, George: Member of the left wing of the British Labour Party.

Lansing, Robert: United States Secretary of State, 1915–1920; plenipotentiary American delegate to the peace conference.

Larnaude, Fernand: Legal adviser to the French peace delegation; French delegate to the League of Nations Commission.

Lawrence, Colonel Thomas Edward: British officer who fought with the Arab army against the Turks; counselor and interpreter for Prince Feisal at the peace conference; nicknamed "Lawrence of Arabia."

Lenin, Vladimir Ilich: leader of the Bolshevik Revolution; head of the Soviet Union, 1917—1924.

Litvinov, Maxim: Bolshevik official who negotiated with Allied representatives during the peace conference; later foreign commissar of the Soviet Union, 1930–1939.

Lloyd George, David: British Prime Minister, 1916–1922; British plenipotentiary delegate, head of the British peace delegation.

Lodge, Senator Henry Cabot: Republican Chairman of the U.S. Senate Foreign Relations Committee, 1919–1924.

Lord, Robert H.: Harvard historian; adviser on Polish affairs to the American peace delegation.

Loucheur, Louis: French Minister of Industrial Reconstruction; economic adviser to the French peace delegation; French delegate to the Reparation Commission.

McMahon, Sir Henry: British High Commissioner in Egypt who promised Sharif Hussein of Mecca British support for the creation of an Arab state in Ottoman territory after World War I.

Makino, Baron Nobuaki: Plenipotentiary Japanese delegate to the peace conference.

Mangin, General Charles: French military commander in Mainz during the peace conference who supported the Rhenish separatists.

Mantoux, Paul: French interpreter for the Council of Four at the peace conference whose notes are the best sources of its deliberations.

Mezes, Sidney: Director of the staff of technical experts (the Inquiry) attached to the American peace delegation.

Miller, David Hunter: Legal adviser to the American peace delegation; one of the authors of the League of Nations Covenant.

Nansen, Fridtjof: Norwegian explorer and humanitarian; organizer of the abortive project for food relief to Russia.

Nicolson, Harold: Adviser on southern European affairs to the British peace delegation; author of a book highly critical of the peace settlement.

Noulens, Joseph: French diplomat who led the interallied mission to Poland, 1919.

Orlando, Vittorio: Italian Prime Minister, 1917–1919; Italian plenipotentiary delegate, head of the Italian peace delegation.

Paderewski, Ignace Jan: Polish pianist, Prime Minister, Foreign Minister, and plenipotentiary delegate to the peace conference, 1919.

Pershing, General John J.: Commander in Chief of the American Expeditionary Force, 1917–1919.

Pichon, Stephen: French Foreign Minister, 1917–1920; plenipotentiary French delegate to the peace conference.

Poincaré, Raymond: President of the French Republic, 1913–1920.

Saionji, Marquis Kimmochi: Plenipotentiary Japanese delegate to the peace conference.

Scheidemann, Philipp: First Chancellor of the German Republic.

Smuts, General Jan Christiaan: Prime Minister of the Union of South Africa, 1919–1924; plenipotentiary delegate to the peace conference; one of the authors of the League of Nations Covenant.

Sonnino, Baron Sidney: Italian Foreign Minister, 1914–1919; plenipotentiary Italian delegate to the peace conference.

Sumner, Lord John: Legal adviser to the British peace delegation and British delegate to the Reparation Commission.

Tardieu, André: French High Commissioner in the United States, 1917–1918; plenipotentiary French delegate to the peace conference.

Tumulty, Joseph: Secretary to President Woodrow Wilson, 1911–1921.

Vénisélos, Eleutherios: Greek Prime Minister, 1917–1920; plenipotentiary Greek delegate to the peace conference.

White, Henry: Plenipotentiary American delegate to the peace conference; only Republican member of the American peace delegation.

Wilson, Field Marshal Sir Henry: Chief of the Imperial General Staff (of the British Empire), 1918–1922; chief military adviser to the British peace delegation.

Wilson, Woodrow: President of the United States, 1913–1921; American plenipotentiary delegate, head of the American peace delegation.

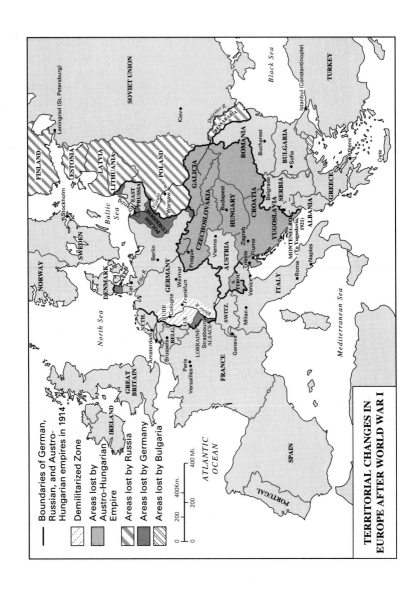

TERRITORIAL CHANGES IN EUROPE AFTER WORLD WAR I

Boundaries of German, Russian, and Austro-Hungarian empires in 1914

Demilitarized Zone

Areas lost by Austro-Hungarian Empire

Areas lost by Russia

Areas lost by Germany

Areas lost by Bulgaria

0   200   400 Km.
0   200   400 Mi.

SOVIET UNION

Leningrad (St. Petersburg)

Kiev

Dniester R.

BESSARABIA

ROMANIA

Bucharest

BULGARIA

Sofia

Black Sea

Istanbul (Constantinople)

TURKEY

GREECE

Athens

Crete

Mediterranean Sea

FINLAND

ESTONIA

LATVIA

LITHUANIA

POLAND

EAST PRUSSIA

Vistula R.

Warsaw

Bzura R.

POLISH CORRIDOR

GALICIA

CZECHOSLOVAKIA

Budapest

HUNGARY

Vienna

AUSTRIA

Prague

CROATIA

Zagreb

Trieste

Fiume

YUGOSLAVIA

Belgrade

SERBIA

MONTENEGRO
(To Yugoslavia, 1921)

ALBANIA

Tyrol

Venice

Rome

Naples

ITALY

Milan

SWITZ.

Geneva

Berlin

Weimar

Frankfurt

Rhine R.

GERMANY

Cologne

RUHR

Kiel

Elbe R.

DENMARK

SWEDEN

Stockholm

NORWAY

Baltic Sea

North Sea

NETH.

Amsterdam

Brussels

BELG.

LUX.

LORRAINE

Strasbourg

ALSACE

Paris

Versailles

FRANCE

GREAT BRITAIN

IRELAND

ATLANTIC OCEAN

SPAIN

PORTUGAL

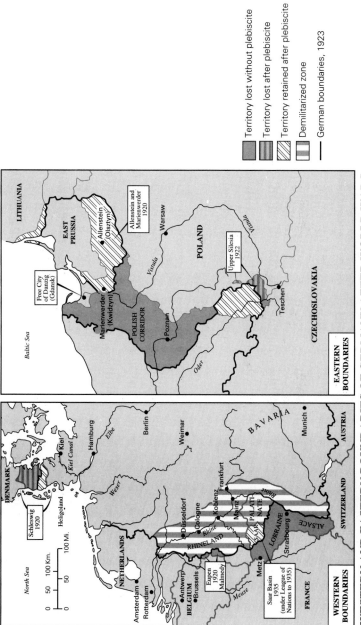

WESTERN AND EASTERN BOUNDARIES OF GERMANY AFTER WORLD WAR I

Territory lost without plebiscite
Territory lost after plebiscite
Territory retained after plebiscite
Demilitarized zone
German boundaries, 1923

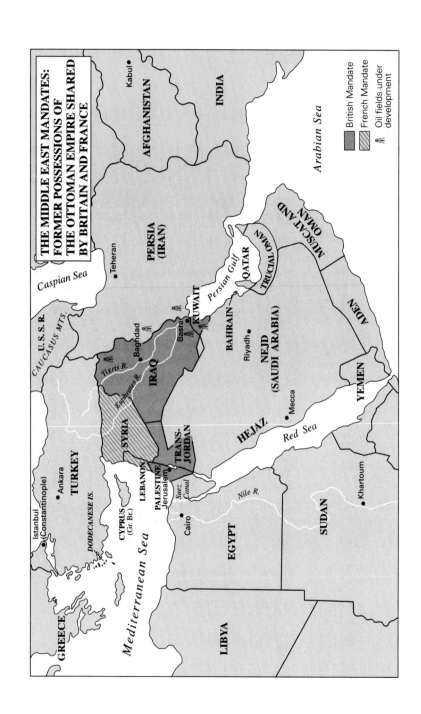

THE MIDDLE EAST MANDATES:
FORMER POSSESSIONS OF
THE OTTOMAN EMPIRE SHARED
BY BRITAIN AND FRANCE

British Mandate

French Mandate

Oil fields under
development

Arabian Sea

Kabul

AFGHANISTAN

INDIA

Caspian Sea

PERSIA
(IRAN)

Teheran

U.S.S.R.

CAUCASUS MTS.

Persian Gulf

QATAR

OMAN

TRUCIAL OMAN

MUSCAT AND OMAN

Tigris R.

Baghdad

Basra

KUWAIT

BAHRAIN

Riyadh

NEJD
(SAUDI ARABIA)

ADEN

Euphrates R.

IRAQ

YEMEN

SYRIA

TRANS-
JORDAN

Mecca

HEJAZ

Red Sea

TURKEY

Ankara

Istanbul
(Constantinople)

DODECANESE IS.

CYPRUS
(Gr. Br.)

LEBANON

PALESTINE
Jerusalem

Suez Canal

Nile R.

Khartoum

GREECE

Mediterranean Sea

Cairo

EGYPT

SUDAN

LIBYA

THE PACIFIC MANDATES:
FORMER GERMAN COLONIES
SHARED BY JAPAN, AUSTRALIA,
AND NEW ZEALAND

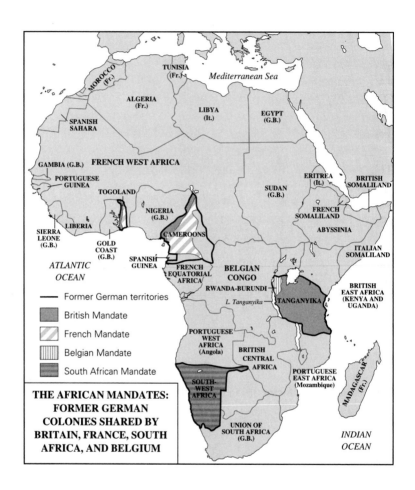

TUNISIA (Fr.)

Mediterranean Sea

MOROCCO (Fr.)

ALGERIA (Fr.)

LIBYA (It.)

EGYPT (G.B.)

SPANISH SAHARA

GAMBIA (G.B.)   FRENCH WEST AFRICA

PORTUGUESE GUINEA

TOGOLAND

ERITREA (It.)

BRITISH SOMALILAND

SUDAN (G.B.)

NIGERIA (G.B.)

FRENCH SOMALILAND

SIERRA LEONE (G.B.)

LIBERIA

CAMEROONS

ABYSSINIA

GOLD COAST (G.B.)

SPANISH GUINEA

ITALIAN SOMALILAND

ATLANTIC OCEAN

FRENCH EQUATORIAL AFRICA

BELGIAN CONGO

RWANDA-BURUNDI

L. Tanganyika   TANGANYIKA

BRITISH EAST AFRICA (KENYA AND UGANDA)

— Former German territories

PORTUGUESE WEST AFRICA (Angola)

British Mandate

French Mandate

BRITISH CENTRAL AFRICA

Belgian Mandate

South African Mandate

SOUTH-WEST AFRICA

PORTUGUESE EAST AFRICA (Mozambique)

MADAGASCAR (Fr.)

THE AFRICAN MANDATES: FORMER GERMAN COLONIES SHARED BY BRITAIN, FRANCE, SOUTH AFRICA, AND BELGIUM

UNION OF SOUTH AFRICA (G.B.)

INDIAN OCEAN

Introduction:
The Versailles Settlement in
Historical Perspective

The peace conference that terminated the Great War counts as a unique episode in the history of international relations. Never before or since have so many prominent statesmen convened for such an extended period of time to address such a complex set of political, economic, and security issues. The highest-ranking representatives of twenty-seven countries, accompanied by hundreds of political advisers, military aides, economic experts, translators, geographers, historians, and journalists, converged in the city of Paris two months after the armistice of November 11, 1918, to devise a peace settlement that would redraw the map of Europe and revise political and economic arrangements in much of the rest of the world.

The leaders of the four countries whose armies had defeated the Central Powers—President Woodrow Wilson of the United States, Prime Minister David Lloyd George of Great Britain, Premier Georges Clemenceau of France, and Prime Minister Vittorio Orlando of Italy—put aside their domestic political duties and remained at the conference site for six months during the winter and spring of 1919 to codify the rules that would govern the postwar international order. The fruits of their deliberations would appear in the form of peace treaties with the five defeated powers that were signed and sealed in various suburbs of Paris: the Treaty of Versailles with Germany (June 28, 1919), the Treaty of Saint-Germain-en-Laye with Austria (September 10, 1919), the Treaty of Neuilly with Bulgaria (November 27, 1919), the Treaty of Trianon with Hungary (June 4, 1920), and the Treaty of Sèvres with Turkey (August 10, 1920).

Some of the controversies that preoccupied the participants in that conference have long since vanished from public consciousness. The acrimonious contest between victorious France and defeated Germany for predominance on the continent has evolved into a cooperative economic and security partnership that serves as the linchpin of an emerging supranational European entity. The Anglo-French rivalry over the spoils of the defunct Ottoman Empire in the Middle East, and Japan's

bold assertion of its imperial prerogatives in the former German possessions in the Far East, have become nothing more than antiquarian re-
minders of a bygone era when colonialism still thrived in the world. The
struggle between Italy and the newly created state of Yugoslavia over
contested territory along the Adriatic coast faded into insignificance long
ago. Geographical terms that in 1919 were laden with such potent sym-
bolic significance that the very mention of them could provoke outbursts
of emotion—the Rhineland, the Ruhr, Shantung, Fiume—elicit only
indifference or unfamiliarity in our own time.

Yet many of the decisions rendered in Paris in 1919 decisively
shaped the history of international relations for the remainder of the
twentieth century. The revival of ethnic and religious strife in Eastern
Europe and the Balkans after the collapse of communism recalled the
blood feuds that raged in those regions during the peace conference of
1919. A number of episodes that seemed insignificant at the time turned
out to be harbingers of future trends that would dominate the headlines
of the world press for years to come: the ardent, incompatible aspirations
of Zionism and Arab nationalism in the Middle East; the plaintive pleas
of the Chinese delegation for the liberation of their country from foreign
domination; the petition submitted to President Wilson by the young
Vietnamese nationalist later known by the pseudonym Ho Chi Minh
championing the cause of self-determination for his people; the
respectful request from the black American advocate W. E. B. Du Bois
that the concerns of the African people be addressed by the architects of
the postwar world order; the futile bid by the Japanese delegation to insert the principle of racial equality into the constitution of the League of
Nations. These and other attempts by second- or third-rank powers and
by the disenfranchised spokesmen for what later would be called the
Third World to influence the handful of great powers that forged the
postwar international order did not succeed. But the things that did not
get done at the conference are as worthy of study as the things that did,
because of the clues that they yield about the emerging forces that would
reshape the world in the future.

Notwithstanding the almost superhuman labors of the diplomats, and
the formidable resources of scholarly expertise that they had at their disposal, the postwar international system created in 1919 unraveled within
twenty years. The "war to end all wars" would be succeeded by an even
more deadly and destructive global conflict. The unexpectedly rapid collapse of the Versailles system has resulted in an exceedingly negative evaluation of the peace deliberations that produced it. The historiography of

the Paris Peace Conference is dominated by works that criticize the peace-makers of 1919 for sowing the seeds of the war that began in 1939. Two interrelated themes underlie this critical assessment of the Versailles peace. The first is the claim that by single-mindedly pursuing their own parochial national interests, the victorious European allies betrayed the lofty ideals associated with the "new diplomacy" of President Woodrow Wilson and therefore deprived the postwar international order of its moral justification. The second is the claim that by rejecting a peace of recon-ciliation in favor of imposing a punitive, "Carthaginian" settlement on Germany the victors virtually guaranteed that the defeated power would repudiate the new international order and do everything in its power to dismantle it.

This type of criticism had begun to appear shortly after the end of the conference in the writing of disillusioned participants. The first such denunciation flowed from the pen of John Maynard Keynes, a young financial expert who had angrily resigned from the British peace delega-tion in protest against what he considered to be the peace treaty's exces-sive harshness toward Germany. Begun even before the ink was dry on the Versailles treaty, completed in four months of frenetic writing, and rushed into print in December 1919 only two months after the final chapters reached the publisher, Keynes's work sold like a potboiler and was promptly translated into a dozen languages.[1] Long before its author became the founder of the dominant school of modern economic theory that bears his name, Keynes's polemical assessment of the peace settle-ment had become one of the most influential works in the twentieth century. Its devastating character sketch of Wilson as an ingenuous visionary hoodwinked by the wily Welsh wizard Lloyd George and brow-beaten by the tough old tiger Clemenceau haunted the American pres-ident for the tragic remainder of his life.

Too ill to compose an apologia for his diplomatic handiwork after his physical collapse in the autumn of 1919, Wilson entrusted that task to his former press secretary in Paris, the writer and muckraking jour-nalist Ray Stannard Baker. Relying on privileged access to the confiden-tial documents that the president had brought home with him from the peace conference, Baker produced a two-volume work in 1922 that was serialized in several American newspapers and became an instant best seller. Baker's book differed from Keynes's in that it gave Wilson credit

---

[1] For bibliographical references to works cited in the Introduction, see Suggestions for Further Reading.

for having secured his colleagues' acceptance of the meritorious provisions of the peace treaty, but it confirmed Keynes's unflattering portrayal of the British and French prime ministers as practitioners of an avaricious, aggressive, imperialistic diplomacy that had encumbered the peace treaty with its many flaws.

A decade later another disenchanted participant weighed in with a devastating indictment of the Versailles peace. Harold Nicolson, who had served as a technical adviser to the British delegation on East European and Balkan affairs in Paris, concentrated his fire on what he judged to be the defective decision-making procedures at the conference. Whereas Keynes evoked the sordid spectacle of European statesmen cynically manipulating the gullible American president and Baker portrayed an honorable champion of justice and right courageously defending his principles, Nicolson recounted a melancholy tale of disorder, disorganization, and perfunctory policy making by befuddled officials who lacked adequate information and sufficient time for reflection. The accusatory tone of his memoir further tarnished the reputation of the peace settlement that had already been gravely undermined by the exposés of Keynes and Baker. It is noteworthy that Nicolson's critique of the Versailles settlement appeared in the year 1933, just as Adolf Hitler assumed power in Germany and began to plot the destruction of the new international order that it had created.

This unbridled criticism of the Versailles peacemaking process by discontented former participants exercised an important influence on public opinion and policy making in Europe during the 1930s. Among the many motivations behind the policy of appeasement that was pursued during that decade was the growing conviction, particularly in the English-speaking countries, that Germany had been unfairly treated at Versailles and that European peace could best be preserved by redressing the defeated power's legitimate grievances. The two most deeply felt of those grievances related to the reparation and territorial sections of the peace treaty. A number of "revisionist" historical studies appeared in the 1920s that disputed the claim that Germany was responsible for planning and launching a war of aggression, asserting that the other belligerents bore an equal if not greater share of the blame. This historiographical argument undermined the reparation section of the treaty, which was based on the presumption of Germany's responsibility for the war, thereby reinforcing Keynes's earlier criticism of reparations on technical economic grounds. By the time that Germany's reparation obligation (which had been revised downward periodically throughout the 1920s) was effectively canceled at the Lausanne Conference in 1932, few observers outside of the recipient countries still believed in either the morality or the wisdom of such compulsory transfers of national wealth.

With reparations already a dead letter by the time Hitler came to power, the new German leader directed his energies toward challenging the territorial provisions of the peace settlement. The Führer placed the defenders of the territorial status quo in an embarrassing position by astutely invoking the Wilsonian principle of national self-determination, which, as numerous non-German critics had already demonstrated, had not been scrupulously applied in the peace treaties. He concentrated his fire on the most flagrant violations of this principle: the prohibition against the political unification of Germany and Austria; the inclusion within Czechoslovakia of over three million German-speaking inhabitants of the defunct Habsburg Empire; and detachment of the predominantly German city of Danzig from Germany together with the annexation by Poland of a "corridor" through German territory.

All three of these territorial arrangements represented instances in which the peacemakers had elected to subordinate the principle of national self-determination to other priorities: to prevent the imbalance of power that would result from Germany's acquisition of the resources, territory, and population of Austria; to provide Czechoslovakia with defensible frontiers that were inconveniently located within the German-speaking borderlands of Bohemia; and to enhance Poland's opportunity for economic development by providing it with special rights in the Baltic port of Danzig and access to it through territory annexed from Germany. In the year 1938 the Nazi leader succeeded in revising the first two of these territorial arrangements peacefully through a combination of intimidating and self-righteous appeals to the principle of national self-determination. By the time he attempted to revise the third a year later, Hitler's arguments had lost their credibility and did not prevent Great Britain and France from going to war on behalf of the much maligned Versailles system.

The victorious allies who gathered at Yalta and Potsdam in 1945 to fashion a new international order displayed little inclination to consult the precedents of the peace conference after the last war, so thoroughly had the Versailles settlement been discredited. It is ironic that the peace settlement of 1919, which had been roundly denounced during the interwar period for betraying the principle of national self-determination in the territorial settlement and imposing harsh and economically unsound reparation terms on defeated Germany, would be succeeded by a peace settlement in 1945 whose provisions were much more deserving of criticism on both grounds.

Josef Stalin, whose country had suffered the most from Germany's aggression and had played the principal role in Germany's defeat, had no interest in applying the abstract moral or economic principles that the Big Four had been condemned for sacrificing in 1919. The Soviet Union would extract all moveable economic assets from its occupation zone in Germany without bothering to consult a reparation commission or to evaluate Germany's capacity to pay. The principle of national self-determination as a guideline for the delineation of postwar frontiers had long since been prudently shelved, save for those ritualistic effluvia of neo-Wilsonian rhetoric in the Atlantic Charter and the Declaration on Liberated Europe. Poland and Czechoslovakia would peremptorily annex German territory without feeling bound by the obligation to determine the wishes of the people concerned. No special treaties would be drafted to protect minority populations left stranded within the frontiers of newly enlarged states after the territorial changes in East-Central Europe. The German-speaking inhabitants of western Poland and the Sudetenland of Czechoslovakia would be unceremoniously expelled from their ancestral lands in what was euphemistically referred to as a "compulsory population transfer."

*   *   *

In the years after the Second World War, the historiographical reassessment of the Versailles settlement was profoundly influenced by the ideological conflict between the United States and the Soviet Union. In a massive study evocatively entitled *Politics and the Diplomacy of Peacemaking: Containment and Counterrevolution at Versailles,* Professor Arno Mayer of Princeton University traced the origins of the Cold War of his own day to the ideological confrontation between what he called the "forces of movement" and the "forces of order" at the end of the Great War. In the former category he included Socialists, labor leaders, and liberals who were tempted by the reformist idealism of Wilson and the revolutionary Marxism of Lenin as alternative panaceas for the socioeconomic chaos that engulfed the postwar world. In the latter category he included imperialists, monarchists, and reactionaries of various types who were intent on preserving the existing political hierarchies and socioeconomic inequalities.

In Mayer's narrative, anxiety about the Russian revolution dominated the peace conference and decisively shaped the peace settlement. As Bolshevik-style insurrections erupted in Germany and Hungary and labor unrest broke out in other countries, the Allied leaders became obsessed with the need to block the westward spread of Bolshevism by any means: the alternatives included the maintenance of Allied military forces in Russian ports, support of the White Russian forces and neighboring nations such as Poland that fought the Bolsheviks, and the use of food and other economic resources to alleviate the suffering of the European populations in order to inoculate them against the revolutionary disease. Other works by G. Gordon Levin and John M. Thompson published in the 1960s complemented Mayer's analysis by emphasizing the extent to which the American ideology of Wilsonian liberalism was designed to win the support of the war-ravaged populations of Europe that were disillusioned with the old order and susceptible to the siren song emanating from Moscow. By emphasizing the distorting role of anti-Bolshevism as a motivating force at the end of the Great War, these new works added a new dimension to the negative evaluation of the Versailles settlement.

During the 1970s and 1980s the first significant set of positive assessments of the peace conference began to appear. These "revisionist" studies reflected the results of research conducted in the French government archives, which, unlike the documentary collections of the other major countries that participated in the Versailles conference, had long been inaccessible to scholars. The diplomatic records of the French Foreign Ministry had emerged from the Second World War in terrible disarray. Many had been burned in the courtyard of the Quai d'Orsay in the spring of 1940 to prevent them from falling into the hands of the invading German armies. Others were misplaced during the hectic days of the liberation in 1944. The private papers of several important French participants in the peace deliberations had been sequestered by their heirs. By the early 1970s a team of archivists had painstakingly reassembled the surviving foreign ministry records while a number of private collections began to turn up in Parisian repositories.

Exploiting these newly accessible sources, a number of historians published works that challenged the uniformly negative evaluation of the peace settlement that had been bequeathed by Keynes, Nicolson, Mayer, and others. The works of Charles Maier, Sally Marks, Marc Trachtenberg, and Stephen A. Schuker presented a more balanced assessment of the much maligned reparation section of the Versailles treaty. In the meantime, American historians, returning to records that had long been in the public domain, offered new insights about the role of Woodrow Wilson in America's disengagement from the peace settlement. Lloyd Ambrosius toppled Wilson from the pedestal on which

Baker and subsequent American historians had placed him by contrast-ing his lack of realism with the more sensible policies pursued both by Wilson's Allied antagonists in Europe and by his Republican critics at home. As a result of this recent scholarship, the universally negative as-sessment of the Versailles legacy that had characterized the historio-graphical consensus for many years was tempered by a greater appreciation of the achievements of the peacemakers in 1919.

*   *   *

This anthology includes a mixture of primary and secondary sources. Save for the earlier piece by Keynes, the selections from secondary sources are all taken from recent archival-based historical studies that have enriched our understanding of the peacemaking process. Most of the primary sources derive from two useful collections of documents that have appeared in recent years under the stewardship of Professor Arthur Link of Princeton University. The first is the multivolume edition of the Woodrow Wilson papers, nine volumes of which contain primary source materials relating to the peace conference. The second source is available because of the fortuitous good fortune that Italian Prime Minister Vittorio Orlando, though fluent in French, could not speak or understand Eng-lish. When he and the leaders of the United States, Great Britain, and France closeted themselves in the library of President Wilson's Parisian residence to confer as the "Council of Four," they were obliged to sum-mon a French interpreter named Paul Mantoux to translate back and forth from French to English. The notes of these confidential delibera-tions that Mantoux retained, which have been recently translated and published by Link and his colleagues, provide the most accurate record of this crucial exercise in peacemaking. They may be supplemented by the minutes taken by the British secretary, Sir Maurice Hankey, who was invited to attend the sessions several weeks after they had begun.

The first section of this anthology focuses on the territorial settle-ment. Arthur Walworth explores the conflict between the Wilsonian prin-ciple of national self-determination and the aspirations of several European powers at the peace conference. In summarizing the debates over the drawing of Germany's frontiers, he demonstrates how the peace-makers strove to modify that abstract principle—which, if scrupulously applied, would have redounded to Germany's benefit because of the pres-ence of large German-speaking minorities in several other countries—to take account of the competing strategic, economic, and historical claims advanced by the representatives of France, Poland, and Czechoslovakia.

The next selection is the famous "Fontainebleau Memorandum" that Lloyd George dispatched to Wilson and Clemenceau as the "Big Four" began to meet privately in Wilson's house to speed up the peace conference. The British prime minister had originally displayed a vindictive attitude toward defeated Germany, particularly in the matter of reparations, during his postwar election campaign of December 1918 and in the early stages of the peace conference. But his mounting anxiety about the prospect of a Bolshevik-style revolution in Germany in reaction to a harsh peace treaty prompted him to advocate a lenient territorial settlement that would reconcile the German people to their postwar status. After an intensive meeting of British officials at a hotel in the forest of Fontainbleau outside of Paris, Lloyd George's secretary, Philip Kerr, drafted a memorandum that made the case for a peace of reconciliation.

As the selection from the minutes of the Council of Four indicates, Clemenceau resolutely opposed Lloyd George's proposals (endorsed in general by President Wilson) for a moderate territorial settlement. Whereas the American president argued ingenuously that "we must avoid giving our enemies even the impression of injustice," the crusty old French statesman refused to rely on abstract notions of justice or German good will as the basis of the postwar international order. Instead, he insisted that the only means of guaranteeing the security of Germany's neighbors was to deprive the former enemy of territory and resources that would enhance its war-making potential. To the pleas emanating from Wilson and Lloyd George for a spirit of reconciliation toward Germany, Clemenceau had a ready response: "America is far away, protected by the ocean. Not even Napoleon himself could touch England. You are both sheltered; we are not."

The peace treaties of 1919 violated the principle of national self-determination by assigning territories inhabited by German or German-speaking people to Poland and Czechoslovakia and by forbidding the political unification of German-speaking Austria and Germany for strategic or economic reasons. Adolf Hitler, an Austrian who enlisted in the German army in 1914, became chancellor of Germany in 1933 on a program of revising the "unjust" frontiers that had been imposed on Germany at the peace conference. In selections from his speeches before the outbreak of the Second World War, the Führer summarizes his objections to the Versailles territorial settlement. In so doing, he disingenuously invokes the Wilsonian principle of national self-determination to justify the destruction of Czechoslovakia and Poland.

In the final offering from the section on the territorial settlement, David Stevenson addresses the anomalous position of one of the belligerents that played no role in the peace conference. A former ally in the war against the Central Powers whose new Bolshevik leaders had signed a separate peace with Germany in March 1918, Russia was excluded from the deliberations in Paris by the resolutely anti-Bolshevik Allied leaders. While Allied military forces that had been dispatched to Russian ports during the war tacitly assisted counterrevolutionary "White" armies against the Bolsheviks during the peace conference, Wilson and Lloyd George made half-hearted attempts to open negotiations with Soviet officials that might lead to military disengagement and a settlement of financial claims. Stevenson highlights the inability of the peacemakers to decide between the two opposing alternatives of diplomatic negotiation with the Bolsheviks (advocated by Lloyd George) and all-out military intervention against them (favored by Marshal Foch and the British secretary of state for war, Winston Churchill). The result of this vacillating policy toward the Russian Civil War was a Bolshevik victory in the Russian Civil War coupled with long-standing resentment at the Western powers for their support of the counterrevolutionaries.

The second section deals with the alternative strategies for securing a lasting peace that emerged from various sources during the peace conference. Because of America's superior financial resources, the belated but critical role of American military power in tipping the balance against Germany, and the enormous prestige that the American president enjoyed among the European public, President Wilson was able to win Allied acceptance of his pet project for a world organization devoted to the peaceful resolution of international disputes. Lloyd Ambrosius traces the complex negotiations in Paris that produced the constitution (or "Covenant" as it was to be called) of a League of Nations that would enforce collective security in the postwar world. Ambrosius demonstrates how the American president's plan reflected the influence of two members of the British Empire delegation, Lord Robert Cecil and the South African statesman Jan Smuts. Wilson did not favor endowing the new organization with effective means to deter or cope with aggression. When the French delegation introduced a plan to strengthen the principle of collective security by authorizing the League to impose sanctions on an aggressor and to enforce them with an international military force under the command of a permanent general staff, Wilson defeated the proposal because it would have impinged on the national sovereignty of the member states. The League would consequently develop into a forum for debate without military sanctions or an effective enforcement mechanism.

Once it became evident that the Anglo-American plan for the League of Nations would not include military sanctions to deter aggression, French Prime Minister Georges Clemenceau pressed for an alternative source of security against Germany in the form of an independent buffer state in the Rhineland under French military control. The proposal to sever this territory from Germany directly contradicted Wilson's principle of national self-determination and antagonized Lloyd George, who denounced it as an "Alsace-Lorraine in reverse" that would ensure perpetual German opposition to the peace settlement. In the next selection Walter A. McDougall analyzes the negotiations over the future political status of the Rhineland, which became so acrimonious they almost led to a breakup of the peace conference. McDougall describes how Clemenceau eventually abandoned the Rhine frontier in exchange for a number of concessions from Wilson and Lloyd George, a compromise that provoked bitter recriminations from Marshal Ferdinand Foch, President Raymond Poincaré, and other French officials who feared that Germany's retention of the Rhineland posed a grave threat to their country's postwar security.

One of the most neglected but important features of the peace settlement after the Great War was the unprecedented commitment by Great Britain and the United States to intervene on France's behalf in the event of unprovoked aggression from Germany. These pledges were offered by Wilson and Lloyd George as an alternative guarantee of French security in order to induce Clemenceau to sacrifice France's demand for an independent Rhineland. In separate contributions Antony Lentin and I explore the strange fate of these Franco-British and Franco-American pacts, which were originally regarded as critical components of the peace settlement. We show how this innovative regional security arrangement—in many respects constituting a precedent for the North Atlantic Treaty Organization after World War II—vanished because of the failure of the United States Senate to approve the agreement and because of Lloyd George's shrewd precautionary maneuver to relieve Great Britain of its continental commitment should the United States renege on its transatlantic pledge.

The third section addresses the famous (or infamous) subject of reparations. The first selection summarizes the critique of the reparation provisions of the Versailles treaty that John Maynard Keynes had popularized in his influential book, *The Economic Consequences of the Peace.*

Keynes warned that the vindictiveness of the reparation clauses would plunge Germany into economic chaos, guarantee that country's perpetual hostility to the new international system, and stifle the postwar recovery of Europe as a whole. As previously noted, Keynes's elegantly argued case against the Versailles treaty shaped the postwar world's increasingly critical evaluation of the peace settlement. It popularized the view that Germany had been unjustly treated at the peace conference, and it paved the way for a series of drastic reductions in the reparation bill that Germany was required to pay.

Relying on evidence from the belatedly opened French archives, Marc Trachtenberg forcefully contested the traditional account of the conflict between Clemenceau's "Carthaginian" policy and Wilson's quest for a peace of reconciliation. He argues that France's reparation policy at the peace conference did not differ significantly from that of the United States and holds Great Britain primarily responsible for preventing agreement on a moderate reparation figure. Trachtenberg contends that the French government originally anticipated financial assistance from the United States rather than reparation payments from Germany to finance France's postwar economic recovery. It was only after learning that there would be no earlier version of the Marshall Plan for Europe, he contends, that the French delegation to the peace conference endorsed Britain's inflated reparation demands. Relying on German archival sources, Trachtenberg also calls attention to clandestine bids by the French foreign ministry to establish contact with the German government and to pursue a policy of Franco-German economic collaboration that would liberate France from dependence on her fickle "Anglo-Saxon" allies. All in all, this version of the reparation settlement diverges sharply from the conventional portrait of a vindictive, "Carthaginian" policy.

Sally Marks sets out to expose what she regards as a number of popular "myths" about the reparation settlement. In the next selection she challenges the conventional wisdom, derived largely from Keynes's original critique, concerning a number of important features of the reparation sections of the peace treaty: article 231 (the notorious "war guilt" clause); the much-debated question of Germany's capacity to pay; and the periodic revisions (always downward) of the reparation obligation in the 1920s. In the end Marks concludes that the reparation settlement ultimately failed not because of Germany's inability to raise the amounts required, but rather because the German people had never accepted the legitimacy of the obligation, the German government continually attempted to sabotage the payment procedures, and the victorious Allies were unwilling or unable to compel compliance.

While redrawing the map of Europe, the peacemakers also had to decide the fate of the German colonial empire in Africa and Asia and of the non-Turkish portion of the Ottoman Empire in the Middle East. The fourth section addresses the consequences of the peace settlement of 1919 for the world beyond Europe. When the victorious powers prepared to acquire the colonial possessions of their defeated enemies as the spoils of victory, President Wilson demurred on the grounds that such a transaction violated the spirit of his "new diplomacy." The South African statesman Jan Smuts shrewdly secured the president's endorsement of a scheme whereby the allies could obtain de facto control of the former German and Turkish possessions without bearing the stigma of colonialism: acting as trustees of the League of Nations, they would administer these territories as "mandates" while preparing the indigenous populations for eventual independence. In the first selection in this section, Alan Sharp demonstrates that the mandatory system served as little more than a convenient "fig leaf" to enable the victors to acquire the spoils of war.

As the peacemakers prepared to redistribute the non-Turkish territory of the defeated Ottoman Empire, they had to contend with a series of conflicting pledges and agreements that had been negotiated during the war. The British government had promised to support the creation of both a large Arab state in the Middle East that Arab nationalists believed would include the biblical land of Palestine and a "national home for the Jewish people" in the same region. In the meantime, the secret Sykes–Picot Agreement partitioned the Ottoman Empire into British and French spheres of influence. Representatives of the Zionist movement petitioned the peace conference to redeem the British pledge for the "Jewish home" in Palestine. In the second selection in this section, American Jewish leaders seek President Wilson's support for the plan, while Prince Faisal, son of Emir Hussein of the Hejaz (who had received the promise of British support for an Arab state), pleads the Arab case.

The third excerpt in this section addresses the subject of imperialism and anti-imperialism in Asia by focusing on the acrimonious dispute that erupted between the Japanese and Chinese delegations at the peace conference. Soon after hostilities broke out in Europe during the summer of 1914, Japan declared war on Germany and seized German-owned islands in the northern Pacific and the German concession on the Shantung peninsula of China. As one of the five principal powers at the peace conference, Japan claimed the right to retain control of Shantung. In response, the articulate young Chinese representative, V. K. Wellington Koo, vigorously asserted his country's claim to full sovereignty over her own province. As selections from the official transcript and from Arthur Walworth's study reveal, the Allied leaders (while sympathetic to China's position on grounds of principle) refrained from opposing Japan's claim to Shantung for fear that its representatives would abandon the peace conference and repudiate the League of Nations. The peace conference's failure to support China's right to self-determination sparked an outburst of anti-foreign and anti-imperialist fervor in that country that poisoned China's relations with the great powers for many years to come.

While China's bid to free itself from foreign interference was being thwarted, the issue of Africa's right to control its own affairs was never even broached. Shortly after the armistice an African-American intellectual named William Edward Burghardt Du Bois sent a memorandum to President Wilson urging the American president to apply his celebrated principle of national self-determination to the people of Africa and asking him to meet with black leaders to discuss the subject of European colonialism on that continent. Wilson ignored Du Bois's message and never responded to the request for a meeting. Du Bois thereupon convened a Pan African Congress in Paris during the peace conference that was attended by fifty-seven black delegates from the United States, Europe, Africa, and the West Indies. The first faint expressions of anti-imperialist sentiment that emanated from this gathering had no effect whatsoever on the peace conference. Not only did Great Britain and France retain control of their African empires, but they acquired the former German possessions in Africa as mandates under the League of Nations.

Though the term *human rights* did not enter the vocabulary of diplomacy until after the Second World War, there were a few notable attempts in 1919 to insert in the peace agreements guarantees against discrimination on racial, religious, or ethnic grounds. The first of these pertained to the newly enfranchised peoples of Eastern and Central Europe. The attempt to apply the principle of national self-determination in this region was complicated by the uneven distribution of ethnic and religious groups there. The impossibility of forming ethnically or religiously homogeneous nation-states out of the multinational empires of

Germany, Austria-Hungary, and Russia resulted in the creation of several states that contained large ethnic and religious minorities. In order to protect these vulnerable populations from maltreatment by the majority-controlled governments, the peace conference drafted a number of treaties stipulating guarantees of minority rights that were to be enforced by the League of Nations. The selection by Carole Fink demonstrates how the minority treaties represented a bold but ultimately unsuccessful attempt to protect citizens of a sovereign state whose ethnic identity or religious practices differed from those of the majority.

The final selection indicates that the Western statesmen who dominated the Paris Peace Conference had no intention of applying the principle of human rights to the non-Western world. During the deliberations of the League of Nations Commission, the Japanese delegation startled the American and European representatives by introducing an amendment to the League Covenant affirming the principle of racial equality in international relations. The article by Paul Gordon Lauren explains why this seemingly innocuous proposal provoked an intense reaction in countries populated primarily by white people. Their delegates in Paris bristled at the suggestion that the nonwhite races of the world were equal to their own, and expressed concern that such a provision might be exploited by the government in Tokyo to challenge the legality of the stringent restrictions on Japanese immigration and property ownership that had been adopted in Canada, Australia, and the western states of America. President Wilson, a southerner who had introduced racial segregation in federal employment in Washington, joined with the British Empire delegation to defeat the Japanese amendment. This dispute left a residue of bitterness in Japan, as well as in other parts of the non-Western world, and tarnished Wilson's reputation as a champion of justice and right.

The "Big Four" take a break from their deliberations outside Woodrow Wilson's house in Paris. Left to right: David Lloyd George, Vittorio Orlando, Georges Clemenceau, and Woodrow Wilson. (The National Archives)

I Redrawing the Map of Europe

Arthur Walworth

The Establishment of the German Frontiers

Arthur Walworth, a free-lance historian who has written extensively on Woodrow Wilson, summarizes in the following selection the complex set of issues that confronted the peacemakers as they sought to delineate the western and eastern borders of Germany. The clash of competing national interests is evident as the countries bordering on Germany struggle to expand their territory and power at its expense.

From *Wilson and His Peacemakers: American Diplomacy at the Paris Peace Conference, 1919*, by Arthur Walworth, pp. 255–276. Copyright © 1986 by W. W. Norton & Company, Inc. Reprinted by permission of W. W. Norton & Company, Inc. Footnotes omitted.

In March, when The Four formed the habit of meeting for secret talks, questions of national boundaries were considered not only by them, but by the territorial commissions and by the council of foreign ministers.

Neither the speeches of Wilson nor House's commentary on the Fourteen Points drew precise lines for the frontiers of postwar Germany. According to the commentary, occupied areas were to be "restored," and Alsace-Lorraine was to be "restored completely to French sovereignty" in order "to right the wrong done to France by Prussia in 1871." No definite plan had been advanced for the future of many borderlands. Yet the studies that the Inquiry had carried out for the past year made it possible for the Americans to take part intelligently in the work of the territorial commissions not only with respect to Germany's eastern and western frontiers, but also with respect to questions that affected its boundaries on the north with neutral Denmark and the Netherlands. Nevertheless, when the time came to apply academic wisdom to the drafting of articles for a peace treaty, no one could say with authority how much German territory could be conceded to claimants on several fronts without causing the fall of the new Weimar Republic. Territorial specialists such as Haskins and Lord tended to sympathize with the national claims that they had studied; and their prime concern was for a satisfied France and a strong Poland rather than for a sound government in Germany.

The English-speaking political chiefs, however, had profound respect for the opinion of the German people. Lloyd George, fearing there would be an explosion in Germany if they took too much of its territory and wealth, dismissed Foch's fervent pleas by declaring that Foch, a great general, was "just a child" in his thinking on political questions. Wilson, supporting Lloyd George, said in a session of The Four on March 27: "We do not want to destroy Germany and we could not do so. Our greatest mistake would be to furnish her with powerful reasons for seeking revenge at some future time. Excessive demands would be sure to sow the seeds of war." In modifying frontiers and changing national sovereignties, he said, they must not give their enemies "even an impression of injustice."

The demand for the creation of strong and friendly states to stand between Germany and Russia increased as the prospect of rapprochement with the Soviet regime grew dimmer. Foch included Poland with Czechoslovakia and Romania in a projected *cordon sanitaire*. However, the "liberated" peoples could not be expected to form an effective barrier so long as they themselves engaged in petty wars in defiance of the edict that the Peace Conference had issued. Hostilities became chronic, and the Supreme

Council, finding that it had little control over military and political developments in areas to the south and east of Poland, left in abeyance the fixing of frontiers there.

It would obviously be difficult to reconcile the principle of self-determination with Wilson's promise to Poland of "free and secure access" to the Baltic Sea. The Poles, desiring a good harbor and access to it by rail, demanded both banks of the Vistula and the port of Danzig, once a great medieval city under the protection of Polish kings. After the partition it was a part of Prussia, developed industrially by a population in which German blood predominated overwhelmingly. The Danzigers made it known by violent demonstrations that they wished to retain their German nationality.

During the president's absence from Paris the French had pressed measures to further their policy of strengthening Poland. Their purpose was supported when in February, Bowman and Lord reached accord with their British associates. The Black Book of the Inquiry strongly supported the claims of Polish nationalists.

The question of Poland's western and northern frontiers was taken up in March by the Paris Committee on Polish affairs, and Bowman was appointed to serve on a subcommittee that was to prepare recommendations. In the subcommittee, of which French general Le Rond was chairman, the German-Polish frontier from Czechoslovakia to the Baltic was discussed. A most competent scholar, Bowman did not appear to negotiate effectively in defense of the American principle of self-determination, and in some instances he conceded priority to considerations of economics and administration rather than to that of ethnography. While opposing limitations upon the sovereignty of Germans in East Prussia, Bowman fully supported the contention that Poland should have Danzig. In this he had the approval of House and therefore, Bowman doubtless supposed, that of Wilson.

Actually, however, the president had not committed himself specifically on the question of Danzig. Pressed by Dmowski at Washington, Wilson had asked whether Poland's purposes would not be served if the lower Vistula was neutralized and Danzig made a free port; and the Pole had replied that this arrangement would give his people full liberty to breathe, but with a German hand on their throat. When on February 23 House reported to his chief that the British experts, though not their government, had joined with the American specialists in accepting most of the Polish claims, there was no response from the White House. Therefore, House had allowed Clemenceau and Lloyd George to understand that the American delegates thought that Danzig should become a part of Poland.

In its report to the full commission on March 6 the subcommittee proposed the inclusion of Danzig in Poland, a plebiscite for Allenstein, and a definite line for the German-Polish frontier elsewhere except in western East Prussia. The next day an alteration placed more Germans in Poland than Bowman desired. Thus violence was done to the principle of self-determination to an extent that alarmed Lloyd George and disturbed Wilson. It could be expected that Germany would object strenuously to the isolation of East Prussia as well as to the loss of Danzig. The report of the commission provided for a corridor to the Baltic that would result in Polish rule over many people of German blood in the city of Danzig and in the land along the Vistula.

In the session of the Supreme Council on March 19 Jules Cambon, the chairman of the Polish commission at Paris, explained that its report gave more weight to economic and strategic necessities than to ethnography and that it had been found impractical to adhere everywhere to the ideal of self-determination. He asked that the council hear comment by French general Le Rond, who for the most part supported Poland's claims while tempering the most extravagant of them. However, Wilson very politely objected that Poland's western frontier was "a political matter and not a military one." When he suggested that the discussion should proceed without military men, the generals left the room.

Lloyd George objected particularly to the transfer of Marienwerder, a district on the right bank of the Vistula in which the population was largely German. Such an arrangement, he warned, might sow "the seed of future war." He suggested that they ask the commission to reconsider, with a view to the exclusion from Poland of territory that was historically and ethnically Prussian. He asked a disturbing question: If, as was proposed, more than 2 million Germans were to be included in Poland, and if they rebelled against their rulers and were supported by a future government of Germany, would the great Western powers go to war to maintain Polish rule over them?

Wilson, caught in the conflict between the promise of free access to the sea and that of self-determination, called for a balancing of the antithetical considerations. Alluding to the difficulty experienced by the Poles in the past in governing themselves, and prophesying that religious differences would create factions in the future, he said that the state they were creating in Poland inevitably would be weak. He tried to palliate violence to self-determination by suggesting that there would be compensating instances in which areas historically Polish would be left within Germany. The inconclusive discussion resulted only in agreement to instruct the commission to reconsider in the light of what was said. The next day, however, the advisory body voted to stand by its original recommendations in every respect, and it stated the reasons for assigning to Poland the region through which the Warsaw-Mława-Danzig railway passed.

When the subject came up again in the Supreme Council of Ten, Lloyd George gave voice to his growing fear that Germany would not sign a treaty that included the settlement recommended. A formula proposed by Wilson was adopted, reserving the question "for final examination in connection with subsequent boundary determinations affecting Germany." Actually, the Germans were infuriated by the possibility of losing Danzig, and it seemed possible that they would be driven to overthrow their new government, just as the Hungarians had revolted in protest when the Peace Conference gave a slice of their territory to Romania.

Linked with the question of the disposal of Danzig was the problem of repatriating Haller's Polish army, which was in France and which Foch wished to use in his grand plan for resisting Soviet aggression. There was an immediate need for assurance from Germany that these troops, as well as American foodstuffs, could move safely through Danzig to Poland. Foch had advocated the transport of Haller's army, and House had supported the marshal. At the time of the January renewal of the armistice, Wilson and Lloyd George had turned down Foch's proposal. However, both Foch and Noulens, the French chairman of the commission sent to Warsaw by the Peace Conference, pressed for the shipment of Haller's troops and the end of German rule in Danzig, where an American destroyer was anchored and stood ready to supply marines to aid the German military authorities in preserving order. The Warsaw commission, asked by the Supreme Council at Paris during Wilson's absence to study the question of loading Haller's troops on trains in a German-controlled Danzig, demanded of German negotiators that they guarantee the security of Haller's troops, and it was hinted that the city probably would be occupied by Polish forces or by those of the Associated powers. To this demand the Germans did not respond, having been directed from Berlin to profess a lack of instructions. Remembering riots that were precipitated by Paderewski's appearance in Poznań, they feared a similar uprising on the part of the Polish minority in Danzig if Haller entered the city. They wished to bring the matter before the Armistice Commission at Spa, where they counted upon the sympathy of American and British military men to check French designs.

When Noulens turned to Foch for action, and the tense situation at Danzig threatened to bring the armistice to a violent end, Foch put the question before the Supreme Council of the Peace Conference on March 17. Actually, the credibility of the German government's peace policy was at stake. Nationalistic demonstrations within Germany impelled the officials toward violation of the armistice; but realizing the futility of outright resistance, Erzberger, who spoke for Germany in the armistice talks, suggested an ingenious way out of the dilemma. He proposed that Haller's troops travel by rail across Germany from one of the Rhine bridgeheads that were under occupation. To transmit this proposal to Wilson he used the military channel that had been established by Colonel Conger at Spa with a German at Berlin, Major Loeb. Erzberger's message, which included a temperate statement of Germany's position on issues of the peacemaking, was in the hands of the American peace commission on March 31.

The American military men realized fully that the German government was under pressure from Right and Left and was, as General Bliss put it, "fighting for its life," and might be overwhelmed if it consented to the transport of Haller's army through Danzig. "It seems a pity," Bliss wrote to the president, "that she [Germany] cannot in any way be heard while the peace terms are being discussed." He recommended that the idea of moving the Polish troops across Germany by rail should be taken up by Foch with the Germans immediately. Hoover, who had been directing shipments of food through Danzig since mid-February with German cooperation, warmly supported the plan for keeping Haller's army out of Danzig and thus averting a risk of violence. He opposed ceding the city to Poland.

After Foch brought the matter before the Supreme Council on March 17, Wilson and Lloyd George persistently questioned the arbitrary actions of French diplomats and military men, who had committed the peacemakers to a position in respect of Danzig that would be difficult to disavow without loss of prestige. Finally, on the morning of April 1 Wilson, warned by his advisers that the Berlin government might not sign a treaty of peace, put Erzberger's proposal before Clemenceau and Lloyd George. It appeared to offer not only a means of countering the French and Polish intention to take Danzig from Germany; it was also a practical answer to the difficulty raised by a lack of ships. Therefore, Wilson was willing to accept the German suggestion that the troops be moved by rail from the Rhine, provided that a contingent should be allowed to pass through Danzig as a symbol of their right to do so. The Supreme Council instructed Foch to go personally to discuss the possibility of rail transport with the German armistice commissioners at Spa. Wilson warned that no guarantee was to be given as to the future status of Danzig, and he urged the marshal to adopt the tone of a diplomat rather than that of a soldier. Accordingly, Foch negotiated an understanding that both maintained the right of the Allies, acting under Article 16 of the armistice, to route Haller's troops through Danzig, and also took advantage of the German proposal to move them by rail. It was agreed that the United States would provide its share of the supervisory officers that would be needed. The problem was finally solved in part by the transport of the army across Germany in three hundred trains provided by the Allies. Thus the German government won the acclaim of its nation's press for a diplomatic success. The use made of Haller's repatriated troops, however, was the subject of further controversy at Paris.

The question of the future of Danzig, which the long negotiations over the transport of Haller's army had kept urgent, was discussed at great length near April 1 by the Supreme Council. For support of his proposal that Danzig be a free port and the Poles have transit rights, Lloyd George read a memorandum from General Smuts, whose opinion he could count on to influence Wilson. "The fact is," Smuts wrote, "the Germans are and have been and will continue to be the *dominant factor* on the Continent of Europe, and no permanent peace is possible which is not based on that fact." At the same time, on the other hand, Wilson was pressed by Clemenceau to give due regard to the lessons of history and to the unquenchable national spirit of the Poles. The old veteran of Europe's wars urged Wilson to accept the fact that Europeans were "a tough bunch" and had to be handled with gauntlets of steel. He despaired of bringing the American prophet to see what he regarded as inescapable realities, but he hoped that Colonel House was right in saying that their differences could be "ironed out."

Wilson, perhaps influenced by his desire to endow the league of nations with responsibilities, inclined toward Lloyd George's position. It seemed to him that France was intent upon weakening Germany by giving Poland territory to which it had no right. He was impressed by the similarity of the situation to that at Fiume, where, he told Bowman, the real struggle between high principles and national demands would come. He feared that consistency would require him to give Fiume to Italy if he gave Danzig to Poland. On April 1 he told Mezes that he was willing to make Danzig and the surrounding German-speaking territory "free or international or independent," with transportation and customs in the hands of the Poles. The administration was to be under a local body, supervised by a high commission of the League of Nations. The Poles were to have a corridor along the Vistula, but Marienwerder as to be disposed of by a plebiscite—an arrangement that House's advisers saw to be equivalent to turning it over to Germany.

After he received these instructions from the president Mezes conferred immediately with Lloyd George's adviser, James Headlam-Morley. Without consulting any representative of France, they prepared a paper for the afternoon session of the Supreme Council providing for the cession of Danzig and certain areas along the Vistula to the League of Nations, which would determine the exact boundaries and deliver the territory to Poland on condition that relative autonomy was assured.

Wilson presented this new project to his European colleagues together with other possible solutions, and he commented on their advantages and disadvantages. Lloyd George then spoke in favor of the "free cities idea" for Danzig under the League. This would give British merchants and shippers an opportunity to develop profitable trade. When he urged that Marienwerder be left in East Prussia, Wilson, who preferred a plebiscite, said that he would like to refer the question for further study by experts.

The next day the president conferred with Mezes and Headlam-Morley, and on April 3 he presented to the Council of Four a proposal that was agreed upon. The conditions were those that he had proposed to Mezes two days before. Clemenceau assented reluctantly, remarking that he did not want to break with the Poles and they were "not always easy to handle." Lloyd George came away from the meeting boasting that he had won Wilson over by persuading him that the desired plan was in reality his own, a stratagem that House had often found effective. The matter was not finally settled, however, until April 18, after Paderewski came to Paris to plead the Polish case.

The president of the United States, acting in the role of arbiter without prejudice, could hardly expect that Polish patriots who had worshiped him as a liberator, or indeed their kin in the United States, would receive his Jovian dispensation with glee. Wilson found it difficult to regard the Poles as less chauvinistic than the Germans in view of reports to the effect that the troops of General Haller, which were now to be transported to Poland by rail, would be sent to fight the Ukrainians at Lemberg.

The drawing of a frontier between Germany and Czechoslovakia brought up the same questions of principle that proved vexing in arranging the boundaries of Poland. The American Black Book called for a border that would follow "the historical frontiers of the Bohemian crownlands," and took the position that the resulting inclusion of 2.5 million Germans in Czechoslovakia would be justified by economic advantages that they would share with the racial majority in the new state. Wilson did not repudiate this position.

Although House had let Foreign Minister Beneš understand that Wilson would acquiesce in a historic frontier, the American members of the Commission on Czechoslovak Affairs, to whom the question was referred on February 5, were by no means willing to concede all that the Czechs asked. They stated in the first meeting, and kept constantly before the commission, a principle that went into its final report: i.e., "the incorporation within Czechoslovakia of so large a number of Germans involved certain disadvantages to the future of the new State." While recognizing the importance of defensible frontiers and economic unity, they argued that the restlessness of alien minorities within Czechoslovakia would imperil its constitutional processes and indeed its national existence. The delegates of the United States, however, were isolated and outvoted by Europeans.

The commission, accepting the historic frontiers between Bohemia and Germany and between Slovakia and Poland, rejected Czechoslovak claims to Lusatia and to a corridor to Yugoslavia. It drew a Slovak-Hungarian boundary closely following the request of Beneš, and approved a provision, promoted by Ruthenian immigrants in the United States, for the inclusion of Ruthenia in Czechoslovakia and for its autonomy. The recommendations of the commission were approved by the central territorial committee on March 25 and were taken up by the Council of Foreign Ministers on April 1.

In the sessions of the territorial committee and in those of its subcommittee the American delegates advocated the award to Germany of the salients of Rumburg and Eger (Cheb), where the population was almost entirely of German blood. The Europeans, however, did not accept this opinion; but they did report the American dissent to the Council of Foreign Ministers.

In the meeting of the Council of Foreign Ministers on April 1 the American secretary of state conducted himself in a way that served only to antagonize the Europeans and to discourage concessions on their part. Instead of working informally with Balfour, who hoped for a clarification of policy, Lansing made an ill-calculated effort to champion Wilsonian principles. The delegates of the United States, he said, objected to the whole method of drawing frontier lines on strategic principles, and any delineations made with a view to military strength and in contemplation of war were directly contrary to the whole spirit of the League of Nations. Jules Cambon, presiding over the commission, was wearied by what he later called the *Pharasaïsme* of the American, but he refrained from embittering the debate by any reference to the policy of the United States in respect of racial minorities in California and Puerto Rico. Balfour, lacking precise instructions from Lloyd George, stood aside. The meeting ended in a deadlock. The American experts were not consulted by Wilson, and their dissents fared no better in a session of The Four on April 4 in which House took Wilson's place.

The question of the western frontiers to be imposed on Germany was a matter of life or death to the people of France and Belgium, who demanded assurance that the German invasions of the past not be repeated. They found no adequate satisfaction in the Covenant of the League of Nations, which lacked adequate sanctions and might not be ratified by the American Senate. Neither the Covenant's provision against aggression nor the treaties of guarantee that were offered by Wilson and Lloyd George to Clemenceau and upon which the French premier put his primary reliance reassured French militarists.

Wilson's Point Eight provided that the wrong done to France in 1871 should be righted, and House had interpreted this in the prearmistice meetings to mean that the seized provinces of Alsace and Lorraine were to be "restored completely to French sovereignty." Thus it was clear that the Rhine would be the frontier as far north as the River Lauter. However, the future of the left bank, from the Lauter up to the Dutch border, raised complications that became embarrassing to the peacemakers.

North of the Lauter, the area occupied by the victorious armies included about 7 million inhabitants and stretched from the western boundary of Germany to the Rhine, with bridgeheads across the river at Cologne (Köln), Koblenz, and Mainz. It was composed of several districts that had a long history of divisions and reunions and had been united under France only for a score of years before 1814. Its people had a distaste for government from without and a leaning toward self-rule. In considering French plans for this area the American specialists found it "not always possible to distinguish what was imperialistic by nature from what was necessary to the restoration and protection of France."

French troops had taken over the southern region bordering France and were thus in a strategic position to control traffic across the frontier to the advantage of their nationals. The American Third Army, constituting less than a third of the occupying forces, was stationed in the central area and at the bridgehead at Koblenz. Its objective was stated in a directive of the Fourth Division: "We are to help build a new government to take the place of the one we have destroyed; we must feed those whom we have overcome; and we must do all this with infinite tact and patience, and a keen appreciation of the smart that still lies in the open wound of their pride." It was the purpose of the American military authorities to conform with Foch's policy of preserving normal civil life.

Early in 1919, however, rifts had developed in the common front. General Pershing, who had lost French confidence to such an extent that just before the armistice his removal from his command had been requested by Clemenceau, was deeply offended when Foch arbitrarily reduced the area of the American zone. Moreover, controversy between these commanders over the rate of repatriation of American troops became so heated that it was carried to the Supreme Council for adjudication. There was discord also over responsibility for occupation of the Duchy of Luxembourg.

Concern for the economic welfare of German citizens in the Rhineland was stirred by certain commercial operations that were carried on under French military protection. Under the authority of a commission that was set up in Luxembourg to license commerce, the trade of the Rhineland was being reoriented toward France. French businessmen, eager to make up for the lean years of the war at the expense of the enemy, were able under the protection of Foch's high command to disregard German import tariffs and to get licenses at Mainz that were valid in all occupied zones. Although the influx of French goods provided immediate comfort for those who could pay for them, the prospect for protecting any local production that could support an enduring economy was darkening. The German populace, which at first had welcomed the American army as the least unfriendly of the victors, was disappointed by its failure to check French designs.

In the American zone the commanding officer announced that the offensive licenses were merely "advisory." However, complaints were made to the Supreme Economic Council, which was created to deal with such matters; and Pershing protested to House. Wilson was aware of the situation before he left Paris in February and doubtless recalled the behavior of Yankee carpetbaggers after the Civil War, which he had witnessed as a boy. He had warned House by cable that Foch was acting "under exterior guidance of the most unsafe kind."

On March 6 the office of the War Trade Board at Paris, following an example set by the British Foreign Office, sent a civilian to replace American army officers on the supervising commission. This representative was able to make little progress against the prevailing French policy. Nevertheless, a prospect of relief from exploitation appeared when on March 17 the Supreme Council decided that an inter-Allied commission of control should supplant the High Command. It was not until late in April, however, just before German delegates were given the terms of peace at Versailles, that an effective American protest took shape. Controversy continued into May and June.

As a substitute for the permanent separation of the left bank from Germany, the president, immediately after his return to Paris, had joined Lloyd George in offering to France a binding promise of immediate military aid in the event of an unprovoked attack. (The prime minister had suggested earlier to House that France should be given this guarantee until the League of Nations proved its worth.) On March 17, however, Wilson received a French note that, while acknowledging the value of the guarantee proposed, nevertheless insisted on the necessity for something more; for it was "really not possible for France to give up a certain safeguard for the sake of expectations." If attacked, the nation would have to defend itself alone until its allies from overseas could bring their strength to bear. Past experience had made it clear that the French armies must control the Rhine in order to be able to resist invasion immediately and effectively. Clemenceau now conceded, however—as Tardieu had earlier—that the peace treaty might set a time limit to the occupation of German territory. He sent a copy of the note of March 17 to House, hopeful that the colonel might persuade Wilson to modify his views.

However, the president was irritated by the French refusal to accept the proffered treaty of guarantee as sufficient. "I know the bitter feeling which the president had against England and the British government," Edith Benham wrote on the day the note was delivered, "and now that is all gone and the bitterness is transferred to the French government, but not the French people." For a month after the president's return to Paris, the future of the Rhineland remained undecided.

A further division of opinion arose in respect of the Saar valley, where there were rich deposits of noncoking coal. The political status and the supervision of the region, as well as the question of the place of its resources in the industry of Europe, were the subject of controversy. In 1917 the Quai d'Orsay had informed the British Foreign Office that

France would insist on the return of Alsace and Lorraine with the boundary that had existed prior to the European settlement of 1815. Actually, however, the French coveted an area that included rich mines beyond the boundary of 1814. Clemenceau, wary of a German monopoly of Saar coal and pressed by his people to seek compensation for the wrecking and flooding of the mines in occupied France, had discussed the matter frankly with House prior to the Armistice of Rethondes.

The Germans, whose empire was said to have been "built more truly on coal and iron than on blood and iron," argued that the Saar valley was inhabited mostly by Germans and had been theirs for a millennium, except for a few years prior to 1815 when it was part of France. Nevertheless, Professor Haskins, the chief American expert on the question, giving less attention to historic than to economic and strategic considerations, early came to the conclusion that the French claim was valid. But Wilson, upon his return to Paris in March, was troubled by the palpable threat to his cherished principle of self-determination. It was becoming apparent that some ingenious form of political administration must be invented that would prevent German interference with French operation of the mines and would at the same time protect the population, predominantly German from alien rule.

When the matter was taken up by The Four on March 28, Lloyd George, who in his Fontainebleau memorandum had just proposed that France be granted the frontier of 1814, shifted his position. He now would go only so far as to give the Saar an autonomous government, with French ownership of the mines. But to this Wilson would not agree. As the president saw it, "To grant a people independence they do not request is as much a violation of the principle of self-determination as forcibly handing them over from one sovereignty to another." He recognized no principle but the consent of the governed, and would not consider French ownership of the mines, but only an arrangement for the delivery of coal by Germany to France.

Feeling ran high in this meeting on March 28. In an interchange not recorded in the minutes, Clemenceau complained that Wilson was pro-German; the president, obviously hurt, asked whether he should not return to the United States. Whereupon Clemenceau walked out of the room without a further word. At noon Wilson said to his advisers: "I do not know whether I shall see M. Clemenceau again. I do not know whether he will return to the meeting this afternoon. In fact, I do not know whether the Peace Conference will continue." However the president, urged by House to yield a little so that his position would be supported by the British, asked his scholarly advisers to work with their British colleagues toward some settlement that would not require any annexation by France.

After a ride in the Bois with Dr. Grayson, during which Wilson confessed that he had been "insulted grossly" and feared he could not control his temper when he returned to the fray that afternoon, he addressed the three premiers in an impassioned plea that Grayson thought the most eloquent that Wilson had ever made. The president said that he had come to Europe with the conviction that if the work performed at this conference was well performed, all the future generations would honor their names as world benefactors; that this task in which they were engaged was the most solemn task that could enlist the thought and energy and patience of men; that it would be easy enough merely to punish Germany, merely to wreak vengeance for wrongs done; that he himself had no illusions as to what Germany had done—she had in the fury of her war madness put herself outside the pale of civilization; he was not doubting that; but he believed they had a greater mission than the mere punishment of Germany; Germany should be made to pay for what she had done and pay to the last farthing; they were arranging for all that in the terms which they were drawing up and had been drawing up in this room for weeks and months past; but if they should crush Germany, wreck her economically, they would assuredly turn the ultimate sympathies of the world toward Germany; the terms laid upon Germany should be stern—justice is stern—but they should be terms which the unenraged generations of the future could read and say: "This is justice, not vengeance." "This is no time to see red," said the president. He insisted that they in that room, charged with responsibility for the future as well as the present, must rid themselves of the passions and the rancors of the moment and look to the future, to the children and to the generations unborn, in whose name and for whose sake they were striving to establish a peace which could outlast all men's hot anger, recriminations, bloodthirstiness, and cries of vengeance.

The prophet stood as he delivered this exhortation. At one point Clemenceau moved as if to rise from his chair, and with a backward sweep of his hand Wilson said fiercely: "Sit down. I didn't interrupt you this morning when you were speaking." The Tiger slunk back, but later, when the speech ended, he got to his feet, his dark eyes burning under the white brows. When he stretched out his arms toward the president, no one knew what might happen; but the tension ended when he took Wilson's hand in his, softly patted it, and said: "You are a good man, and a great one."

Haskins thought the president too severe, and impervious to his French environment. Fearing a complete rupture, he worked with Headlam-Morley to draft a basis for compromise. The Council of Four, accepting their work, entrusted the task of devising practical political arrangements to Haskins, Headlam-Morley, and Tardieu. These men already had met unofficially and had gone far toward an understanding. During the month of April they gave advice that helped Wilson and Lloyd George to agree upon a compromise with Clemenceau. . . .

The fixing of definite boundaries of Germany was essential both to the stabilization of the governments of Europe and to the keeping of peace among them. Moreover, it had a bearing on the will and the ability of the Germans to make reparation for the damages of the war.

The procedures that the English-speaking delegates had improvised and that for a time had seemed to delay definite conclusions were beginning, at the end of March, to shape a territorial settlement that could be presented to the enemy with some confidence that it would be accepted. In certain cases, however, final arrangements would have to await the outcome of plebiscites under the supervision of the League of Nations.

The Americans at Paris often found themselves called upon to compose conflicts of policies of the Allied powers that reflected immediate national interests that in many cases grew out of deep historical roots and that sometimes conjured up prospects of future wars. The delegates of the United States, heeding scholarly advice, weighed the arguments of the various interested parties, giving due regard to strategic, economic, and political consequences. They found it not always practical to adhere to the principle of self-determination.

The immediate necessity of controlling the power of the enemy, complicated as it was by the menace of general anarchy and a possible alliance of the vanquished peoples with Moscow, as well as by nationalistic chauvinism, led the plenipotentiaries of the United States, in pursuit of their commitment to peace and justice for all peoples, to take part in the peacemaking in regions of Europe in respect of which their own people had little interest and only superficial knowledge. The involvement in the affairs of remote lands, which had begun before the opening of the Peace Conference as a result of *ad hoc* missions of relief and intelligence, now extended to negotiations at the highest level. It seemed likely that the American government would be brought into the politics of Europe to a degree that the American people and their Congress might not accept.

The British Case for a Moderate Territorial Settlement

In the following selection the British prime minister submits an urgent plea to the other members of the "Big Four" to reverse course and adopt a conciliatory policy toward Germany in the territorial settlement. After having been the foremost advocate of stiff terms concerning the German navy, the German colonial empire, and reparations, Lloyd George suddenly and unexpectedly became the principal advocate of a peace of reconciliation. This important document is customarily referred to as the "Fontainebleau Memorandum" because it was composed in a hotel in the Forest of Fontainebleau outside Paris.

SECRET   Paris. March 25, 1919.

Some considerations for the Peace Conference
before they finally draft their terms.

[I] When nations are exhausted by wars in which they have put forth all their strength and which leave them tired, bleeding and broken, it is not difficult to patch up a peace that may last until the generation which experienced the horrors of the war has passed away. Pictures of heroism and triumph only tempt those who know nothing of the sufferings and terrors of war. It is therefore comparatively easy to patch up a peace which will last for 30 years.

What is difficult, however, is to draw up a peace which will not provoke a fresh struggle when those who have had practical experience of what war means have passed away. History has proved that a peace

"Some Considerations for the Peace Conference Before They Finally Draft Their Terms," March 25, 1919, Arthur S. Link, ed., *The Papers of Woodrow Wilson*, Princeton University Press, Vol. 56 (1987), pp. 259–265. Copyright © 1987 by Princeton University Press. Reprinted by permission of Princeton University Press. Footnotes omitted.

which has been hailed by a victorious nation as a triumph of diplomatic skill and statesmanship, even of moderation in the long run has proved itself to be shortsighted and charged with danger to the victor. The peace of 1871 was believed by Germany to ensure not only her security but her permanent supremacy. The facts have shown exactly the contrary. France itself has demonstrated that those who say you can make Germany so feeble that she will never be able to hit back are utterly wrong. Year by year France became numerically weaker in comparison with her victorious neighbour, but in reality she became ever more powerful. She kept watch on Europe; she made alliance with those whom Germany had wronged or menaced; she never ceased to warn the world of its danger and ultimately she was able to secure the overthrow of the far mightier power which had trampled so brutally upon her. You may strip Germany of her colonies, reduce her armaments to a mere police force and her navy to that of a fifth rate power; all the same in the end if she feels that she has been unjustly treated in the peace of 1919 she will find means of exacting retribution from her conquerers. The impression, the deep impression, made upon the human heart by four years of unexampled slaughter will disappear with the hearts upon which it has been marked by the terrible sword of the great war. The maintenance of peace will then depend upon there being no causes of exasperation constantly stirring up the spirit of patriotism, of justice or of fair play to achieve redress. Our terms may be severe, they may be stern and even ruthless but at the same time they can be so just that the country on which they are imposed will feel in its heart that it has no right to complain. But injustice, arrogance, displayed in the hour of triumph will never be forgotten or forgiven.

For these reasons I am, therefore, strongly averse to transferring more Germans from German rule to the rule of some other nation than can possibly be helped. I cannot conceive any greater cause of future war than that the German people, who have certainly proved themselves one of the most vigorous and powerful races in the world should be surrounded by a number of small states, many of them consisting of people who have never previously set up a stable government for themselves, but each of them containing large masses of Germans clamouring for reunion with their native land. The proposal of the Polish Commission that we should place 2,100,000 Germans, under the control of a people which is of a different religion and which has never proved its capacity for stable self-government throughout its history must, in my judgment, lead sooner or later to a new war in the East of Europe. What I have said about the Germans is equally true of the Magyars. There will never be peace in South Eastern Europe if every little state now coming into being is to have a large Magyar Irredenta within its borders. I would therefore take as a guiding principle of the peace that as far as is humanly possible the different races should be allocated to their motherlands, and that this human criterion should have precedence over considerations of strategy or economics or communications which can usually be adjusted by other means. Secondly, I would say that the duration for the payments of reparation ought to disappear if possible with the generation which made the war.

But there is a consideration in favour of a long-sighted peace which influences me even more than the desire to leave no causes justifying a fresh outbreak 30 years hence. There is one element in the present condition of nations which differentiates it from the situation as it was in 1815. In the Napoleonic war the countries were equally exhausted but the revolutionary spirit had spent its force in the country of its birth and Germany had satisfied the legitimate popular demands for the time being by a series of economic changes which were inspired by courage, foresight and high statesmanship. Even in Russia the Czar had effected great reforms which were probably at the time even too advanced for the half savage population. The situation is very different now. The revolution is still in its infancy. The extreme figures of the Terror are still in command in Russia. The whole of Europe is filled with the spirit of revolution. There is a deep sense not only of discontent, but of anger and revolt amongst the workmen against pre-war conditions. The whole existing order in its political, social and economic aspects is questioned by the masses of the population from one end of Europe to the other. In some countries, like Germany and Russia, the unrest takes the form of open rebellion, in others like France, Great Britain and Italy it takes the shape of strikes and of general disinclination to settle down to work, symptoms which are just as much concerned with the desire for political and social change as with wage demands.

Much of this unrest is healthy. We shall never make a lasting peace by attempting to restore the conditions of 1914. But there is a danger that we may throw the masses of the population throughout Europe into the arms of the extremists whose only idea for regenerating mankind is to destroy utterly the whole existing fabric of society. These men have triumphed in Russia. They have done so at a terrible price. Hundreds and thousands of the population have perished. The railways, the roads, the towns, the whole structural organisation of Russia has been almost destroyed, but somehow or other they seem to have managed to keep their hold upon the masses of the Russian people, and what is much more significant, they have succeeded in creating a large army which is apparently well directed and well disciplined, and is, as to a great part of it prepared to die for its ideals. In another year Russia, inspired by a new enthusiasm may have recovered from her passion for peace and have at her command the only army eager to fight, because it is the only army that believes that it has any cause to fight for.

The greatest danger that I see in the present situation is that Germany may throw in her lot with Bolshevism and place her resources, her brains, her vast organising power at the disposal of the revolutionary fanatics whose dream it is to conquer the world for Bolshevism by force of arms. This danger is no mere chimera. The present government in Germany is weak; it has no prestige; its authority is challenged; it lingers merely because there is no alternative but the spartacists, and Germany is not ready for spartacism, as yet. But the argument which the spartacists are using with great effect at this very time is that they alone can save Germany from the intolerable conditions which have been bequeathed her by the war. They offer to free the German people from indebtedness to the Allies and indebtedness to their own richer classes. They offer them complete control of their own affairs and the prospect of a new heaven and earth. It is true that the price will be heavy. There will be two or three years of anarchy, perhaps of bloodshed, but at the end the land will remain, the people will remain, the greater part of the houses and the factories will remain, and the railways and the roads will remain, and Germany, having thrown off her burdens, will be able to make a fresh start.

If Germany goes over to the spartacists it is inevitable that she should throw in her lot with the Russian Bolshevists. Once that happens all Eastern Europe will be swept into the orbit of the Bolshevik revolution and within a year we may witness the spectacle of nearly three hundred million people organised into a vast red army under German instructors and German generals equipped with German cannon and German machine guns and prepared for a renewal of the attack on Western Europe. This is a prospect which no one can face with equanimity. Yet the news which came from Hungary yesterday shows only too clearly that this danger is no fantasy. And what are the reasons alleged for this decision? They are mainly the belief that large numbers of Magyars are to be handed over to the control of others. If we are wise, we shall offer to Germany a peace, which, while just, will be preferable for all sensible men to the alternative of Bolshevism. I would, therefore, put it in the forefront of the peace that once she accepts our terms, especially reparation, we will open to her the raw materials and markets of the world on equal terms with ourselves, and will do everything possible to enable the German people to get upon their legs again. We cannot both cripple her and expect her to pay.

Finally, we must offer terms which a responsible Government in Germany can expect to be able to carry out. If we present terms to Germany which are unjust, or excessively onerous, no responsible Government will sign them; certainly the present weak administration will not. If it did, I am told that it would be swept away within 24 hours. Yet if we can find nobody in Germany who will put his hand to a peace treaty, what will be the position? A large army of occupation for an indefinite period is out of the question. Germany would not mind it. A very large number of people in that country would welcome it as it would be the only hope of preserving the existing order of things. The objection would not come from Germany, but from our own countries. Neither the British Empire nor America would agree to occupy Germany. France by itself could not bear the burden of occupation. We should therefore be driven back on the policy of blockading the country. That would inevitably mean spartacism from the Urals to the Rhine, with its inevitable consequence of a huge red army attempting to cross the Rhine. As a matter of fact, I am doubtful whether public opinion would allow us deliberately to starve Germany. If the only difference between Germany and ourselves were between onerous terms and moderate terms, I very much doubt if public opinion would tolerate the deliberate condemnation of millions of women and children to death by starvation. If so the Allies would have incurred the moral defeat of having attempted to impose terms on Germany which Germany had successfully resisted.

From every point of view, therefore, it seems to me that we ought to endeavour to draw up a peace settlement as if we were impartial arbiters, forgetful of the passions of the war. This settlement ought to have three ends in view. First of all it must do justice to the Allies, by taking into account Germany's responsibility for the origin of the war, and for the way in which it was fought. Secondly, it must be a settlement which a responsible German Government can sign in the belief that it can fulfil the obligations it incurs. Thirdly, it must be a settlement which will contain in itself no provocations for future wars, and which will constitute an alternative to Bolshevism, because it will commend itself to all reasonable opinion as a fair settlement of the European problem.

[II] It is not, however, enough to draw up a just and far-sighted peace with Germany. If we are to offer Europe an alternative to Bolshevism we must make the League of Nations into something which will be both a safeguard to those nations who are prepared for fair dealing with their neighbours, and a menace to those who would trespass on the rights of their neighbours, whether they are imperialist empires or imperialist Bolshevists. An essential element, therefore, in the peace settlement is the constitution of the League of Nations as the effective guardian of international right and international liberty throughout the world. If this is to happen the first thing to do is that the leading members of the League of Nations should arrive at an understanding between themselves in regard to armaments. To my mind it is idle to endeavour to impose a permanent limitation of armaments upon Germany unless we are prepared similarly to impose a limitation upon ourselves. I recognise that until Germany has settled down and given practical proof that she has abandoned her imperialist ambitions, and until Russia has also given proof that she does not intend to embark upon a military crusade against her neighbors, it is essential that the leading members of the League of Nations should maintain considerable forces both by land and sea in order to preserve liberty in the world. But if they are to present an united front to the forces both of reaction and revolution, they must arrive at such an agreement in regard to armaments among themselves as would make it impossible for suspicion to arise between the members of the League of Nations in regard to their intentions towards one another. If the League is to do its work for the world it will only be because the members of the League trust it themselves and because there are no rivalries and jealousies in the matter of armaments between them. The first condition of success for the League of Nations is, therefore, a firm understanding between the British Empire and the United States of America and France and Italy that there will be no competitive building up of fleets or armies between them. Unless this is arrived at before the Covenant is signed the League of Nations will be a sham and a mockery. It will be regarded, and rightly regarded as a proof that its principal promoters and patrons repose no confidence in its efficacy. But once the leading members of the League have made it clear that they have reached an understanding, which will both secure to the League of Nations the strength which is necessary to enable it to protect its members and which at the same time will make misunderstanding and suspicion with regard to competitive armaments impossible between them its future and its authority will be ensured. It will then be able to ensure as an essential condition of peace that not only Germany, but all the smaller States of Europe undertake to limit their armaments and abolish conscription. If the small nations are permitted to organise and maintain conscript armies running each to hundreds of thousands, boundary wars will be inevitable and all Europe will be drawn in. Unless we secure this universal limitation we shall achieve neither lasting peace, nor the permanent observance of the limitation of German armaments which we now seek to impose.

I should like to ask why Germany, if she accepts the terms we consider just and fair, should not be admitted to the League of Nations, at any rate as she has established a stable and democratic Government. Would it not be an inducement to her both to sign the terms and to resist Bolshevism? Might it not be safer that she should be inside the League than that she should be outside it?

Finally, I believe that until the authority and effectiveness of the League of Nations has been demonstrated, the British Empire and the United States ought to give to France a guarantee against the possibility of a new German aggression. France has special reasons for asking for such a guarantee. She has twice been attacked and twice invaded by Germany in half a century. She has been so attacked because she has been the principal guardian of liberal and democratic civilisation against Central European autocracy on the continent of Europe. It is right that the other great Western democracies should enter into an undertaking which will ensure that they stand by her side in time to protect her against invasion, should Germany ever threaten her again or until the League of Nations has proved its capacity to preserve the peace and liberty of the world.

[III] If, however, the peace conference is really to secure peace and prove to the world a complete plan of settlement which all reasonable men will recognise as an alternative preferable to anarchy, it must deal with the Russian situation. Bolshevik imperialism does not merely menace the states on Russia's borders. It threatens the whole of Asia and is as near to America as it is to France. It is idle to think that the Peace Conference can separate, however sound a peace it may have arranged with Germany, if it leaves Russia as it is today. I do not propose, however, to complicate the question of the peace with Germany by introducing a discussion of the Russian problem. I mention it simply in order to remind ourselves of the importance of dealing with it as soon as possible.

Georges Clemenceau

The French Response

French Prime Minister Georges Clemenceau responded with ill-concealed indignation to Lloyd George's "Fontainebleau Memorandum" urging a moderate territorial settlement. Refusing to allow his battered country to be held hostage to Germany's good intentions, he demanded a territorial settlement that would render the defeated enemy incapable of again threatening French security.

March 27, 1919, 11 A.M.

Mr. Lloyd George. Have you read the memorandum which I sent you regarding the general peace terms?

M. Clemenceau. I intend to reply to it in writing; but it must first be translated into French for the President of the Republic.

President Wilson. I hope you agree in principle with Mr. Lloyd George on the moderation which must be shown towards Germany. We don't wish to destroy Germany, nor could we do so; our greatest error would be to give her powerful reasons for wishing one day to take revenge. Excessive demands would most certainly sow the seed of war.

Everywhere we are compelled to change boundaries and national sovereignties. Nothing involves greater danger, for these changes run contrary to long-established customs and change the very life of populations whilst, at the same time, they affect their feelings. We must avoid giving our enemies even the impression of injustice. I don't fear future wars brought about by the secret plottings of governments, but rather conflicts created by popular discontent. If we ourselves are guilty of injustice, such discontent is inevitable, with the consequences it entails. Hence our desire to negotiate with moderation and fairness.

Mr. Lloyd George. I have a historical precedent to cite. In 1814, after the defeat of Napoleon, Prussia, whose chief representative in this

"Conversations between President Wilson and MM. Clemenceau, Lloyd George, and Orlando," March 27, 1919 in *The Deliberations of the Council of Four (March 24–June 28, 1919): Notes of the Official Interpreter* (Trans. and ed. by Arthur S. Link), Princeton University Press, Vol. 1 (1992), pp. 31–38. Copyright © 1992 by Princeton University Press. Reprinted by permission of Princeton University Press. Footnotes omitted.

case was Blücher, wanted to impose crushing terms upon France. Wellington, who had good sense, took an opposite position and was supported by Castlereagh, who had earlier been one of France's bitterest enemies. Both felt it would be a great error to seek to destroy France, whose presence was necessary for civilization and European stability. Such was the position taken by the representatives of England towards France; and if their opinion had not prevailed, France would have been half destroyed, with no other result than to deliver all of Europe to the Germanic powers.

Germany has learned a lesson as hard as any in history. The fall of the Napoleonic empire in 1814 cannot be compared, for the campaign in France was a glorious conclusion to Napoleon's wars; whilst last November the Germans capitulated without even attempting a last stand.

M. Clemenceau. I said yesterday that I agree completely with Mr. Lloyd George and President Wilson about the manner in which to treat Germany. We must not abuse our victory; we must treat peoples with consideration and fear provoking a surge of national consciousness.

But I venture a fundamental objection. Mr. Lloyd George is excessively afraid of the consequences if the Germans should refuse to sign the treaty. I remind you that the Germans surrendered without even waiting for our troops to enter Germany, no doubt fearing the atrocious reprisals of which we were incapable. This time we must expect them to stand out: they will argue, they will dispute every point, they will talk of refusing to sign, they will play up incidents such as the one which has just taken place in Budapest and those which may occur tomorrow in Vienna; they will contest or refuse all they can refuse. You read the interview with Count Bernstorff in yesterday's newspapers: he speaks with the arrogance of a victor. But we mustn't fear them any more than is necessary. We must be aware of possible danger; but, after having obtained victory at the price of so many sacrifices, we must also, assure ourselves of its fruits.

After all, the resistance of the Germans hasn't always been what we expected. You took their entire war fleet from them; yet they were very proud of it, and their Emperor had told them, "Our future is on the sea." We had envisaged the possibility of a desperate opposition on the part of the Germans once they were deprived of their fleet; you remember the observations made by Marshal Foch on this subject when we were drafting the terms of the Armistice. In fact, nothing happened. We are now seizing their merchant fleet—in order to feed them, it is true. But they have foreseen the possibility that they wouldn't be fed, for the *Berliner Tageblatt* reports today that, in that event, Germany would manage to live despite the blockade.

I come to President Wilson's precept, which I accept, but which I apply to the Germans only with certain reservations. We must not—says President Wilson—give the Germans a feeling of injustice. Agreed, but what we find fair here in this room will not necessarily be accepted as such by the Germans.

There is surprise that France is opposed to the immediate admission of Germany to the League of Nations. Only yesterday, I received a new report of the atrocities committed in France. Unfortunately, we have come to know the Germans at our own expense; and we know they are a people who submit themselves to force in order to impose their own force upon the world. I remind Mr. Lloyd George of a conversation I had with him at Karlsbad seven or eight years ago: I conveyed to him my uneasiness over the future of Europe, and I mentioned the German threat. Mr. Lloyd George hoped that Germany would be wise; unfortunately, he has had his eyes opened.

The Germans are a servile people who need force to support an argument. Napoleon said before his death: "Nothing permanent is founded upon force." I am not sure of that; for it is enough to look at the great nations of Europe and the United States itself to have doubts. What is true is that force can't establish anything solid unless it is in the service of justice. We must do everything we can to be just towards the Germans; but, as for persuading them that we are just towards them, that is another matter. I believe we can do something to spare the world from German aggression for a long time; but the German spirit will not change so quickly. Look at the German Social Democrats, who called themselves the brothers of our Socialists and yours: we have seen them in service of the Imperial government, and today they serve Scheidemann, surrounded by the old Imperial bureaucracy, with Rantzau at its head.

Notice that no one in Germany makes a distinction between the just and the unjust demands of the Allies. There is no resistance stronger than that which shows itself against assigning Danzig to Poland. However, to make amends for the historical crime committed against the Polish nation, we are compelled, in bringing that country back to life, to give her the means to live. We must not forget the crimes committed in particular by Germany against Poland, following the great crime of her partition in the nineteenth century, and by scientific methods, so to speak. We remember the children whipped for having prayed to God in Polish, peasants expropriated, driven from their lands to make room for occupants of the Germanic race.

Perhaps each of us has similar expropriations on his conscience, in a more or less distant past; but here we have deeds that took place under our very eyes, and those who have committed them are before us. The Social Democrats are with them, for they supported their government during four years of war.

I pay tribute to Mr. Lloyd George's spirit of fairness, when he expresses the desire to give Poland as few German subjects as possible. But I do not accept the sentence in which he says that, on the question of communications between Danzig and the interior, we must leave aside all strategic considerations. If we followed this advice, we would leave a sad legacy to our successors. We must accept the inevitable difficulties in the principle of self-determination if we wish to safeguard this principle itself.

An example haunts my mind: that of Austria. We speak of everyone disarming: I want it very much; believe me, the spirit of conquest, which was once the spirit of the French people, is dead forever. But if we reduce our armaments, and if, at the same time, Austria adds seven million inhabitants to the population of Germany, the power of our German neighbors will increase in a manner very threatening to us. Is it a flagrant insult to the rights of peoples to say to the Austrians: "We only ask you to remain independent. Do what you wish with this independence; but you must not enter into a German bloc and participate in a plan for German revenge"?

My principles are your own; I am only arguing about their application. May I say to President Wilson: don't believe that the principles of justice which satisfy us will also satisfy the Germans. I know them; I have forced myself to go to Germany nearly every year since 1871. I wanted to know the Germans, and, at certain times, I hoped that mutual understanding could be reached between our two peoples. I can tell you that their idea of justice is not our own.

After the greatest effort and the greatest sacrifices of bloodshed that history has ever seen, we must not compromise the result of our victory. The League of Nations is offered to us as a means of giving us the security we need. I accept this instrumentality, but should the League of Nations be unable to give military sanctions to its decrees, that sanction would have to be found from another quarter. I note that, on the sea, that sanction is already in effect: Germany has no more fleet. We must have an equivalent on land. I don't have preconceived opinions about the methods to employ. I implore you to understand my state of mind about this, just as I am making an effort to understand yours. America is far away, protected by the ocean. Not even Napoleon himself could touch England. You are both sheltered; we are not.

No man is further than I from the militaristic spirit. I am ready to do anything to arrive at a solution which would be better than the military solution But we cannot forget that, in our great crisis, the military did much to save us. Let's not make the error of not taking their advice at a moment like this. On the day of danger and of trial, they would say to us: "It is not our fault if you didn't listen to us."

One last word. We are right to fear Bolshevism amongst the enemy and to avoid provoking its development; but we must not spread it amongst ourselves. There is a sense of justice amongst allies which must be satisfied. If this sentiment was outrageously thwarted, either in France or England, great danger would result. It's good to want to spare the conquered; but we must not lose sight of the victors. If a revolutionary movement was to appear somewhere because our solutions appear unjust, let it not be in our own countries. I wish to give only a simple indication here.

Mr. Lloyd George. I am in agreement on many points with M. Clemenceau, but certain of the positions he takes seem to me full of peril. I know something about the Bolshevik danger in our countries; I have fought it myself for several weeks now, and I congratulate my colleagues for having had less trouble with it than I do. I combat Bolshevism, not by force, but by searching for a means to satisfy the legitimate aspirations that have given birth to it.

The result is that trade unionists like Smillie, the secretary-general of the miners, who could have become formidable, end up by helping us to avoid a conflict. The English capitalists—thank God—are frightened, and that makes them reasonable. But concerning the peace terms, what could provoke an explosion of Bolshevism in England would not be the reproach of having asked too little from the enemy, but of having asked too much. The English worker doesn't want to crush the German people with excessive demands. It's rather amongst the upper classes that you will find an unlimited hatred of the German. Moreover, a marked change of attitude has taken place in this regard since Germany gave up its old political system. If our terms seem too moderate, I will have great difficulties in Parliament, but they won't come from the common people.

I do not agree with what M. Clemenceau has said about the opinions of the military. Their assistance is essential in time of war. But in matters of state, they are the last people I would consult. I admire and like Marshal Foch very much; but on political questions, he is a child. I wouldn't take his advice about how to insure the greatest possible security to nations. Let's remember that Moltke, who was undoubtedly an eminent military leader, perhaps led Bismarck in 1871 further than he would have gone himself. In the end, Germany fell victim to the idea of a strategic frontier, which led it to mutilate France.

Likewise, we had a school of officers who sought to give the Indian Empire what was called a scientific frontier. Gladstone did not believe in scientific frontiers. But Disraeli, in the name of this doctrine, allowed the occupation of Afghanistan, from which we were eventually obliged to withdraw under disastrous conditions. Since then, Afghanistan, respected by us, has become a most useful buffer state. This leads us to the discussion between Wellington and Blücher about which I spoke a moment ago.

I received a letter from General Smuts, who is an impartial soul and whose loyalty to us I insist upon recalling. He is one of the best generals who fought against us in the Boer War. He invaded the Cape Colony with a few hundred men; he had thousands at the time he surrendered to us. During the present war, I have only to recall the role which he played in helping us to suppress the uprising fomented by Germany in South Africa.

His letter, as he himself says, is unpleasant. He talks much about Danzig; he believes that the terms we wish to impose are the opposite of what a statesman should impose. I admit my own grave fears concerning Danzig. We're going to give Poland two million Germans. The Poles will govern badly and will take a long time to conduct business in the western manner. There will be disturbances; the Germans in Poland, if they revolt, will be defeated. If Germany wants to intervene, will you send troops to keep the Germans of Poland under the yoke? The Poles, it is true, will tell us: what good is it to have given us these territories if you don't help us to defend them? I'm certain that public opinion, both in America and in England, would not support us if we intervened in such circumstances. The League of Nations, the treaty which we will sign, will be likewise flouted. I do not believe in a treaty whose future execution could not be assured. If you are not determined to assure the execution of this clause, what good is it to place it in your treaty?

Whatever happens, we are going to impose a very hard peace on Germany: she will have no more colonies, no more fleet; she will lose six or seven million inhabitants, a great part of her natural resources—nearly all her iron, a notable portion of her coal. Militarily, we are reducing her to the status of Greece and, from a naval point of view, to that of the Argentine Republic. And on all these points, we are entirely in agreement. Moreover, she will pay, according to the estimates, five or ten billion pounds sterling. Setting our terms at the lowest level, they will be such as no civilized nation has ever been compelled to accept. If you add to all this terms of minor importance, which could be considered unjust, it will perhaps be the straw that breaks the camel's back.

What did France resent most: the loss of Alsace-Lorraine or the obligation to pay five billions in indemnity? I already know your answer. What struck me most on my first trip to Paris was the statue of Strasbourg in mourning. Germany must not be able to erect such statues in her cities through any fault of ours.

M. Clemenceau. Nor do I want that.

Mr. Lloyd George. The Germans have certain fine qualities of character. They fought very bravely. I believe they will accept all the rest, including a very heavy indemnity; but what will wound them most is the idea of abandoning millions of Germans to Polish domination. It has been very painful for France to see Frenchmen pass under German domination; but the French would at least consider the Germans their equals. It's not the same with the Poles in the mind of the Germans. It's this type of feeling that might prevent them from signing the peace treaty.

I would prefer a solution making Danzig a free port and leaving the Poles in Poland and the Germans in Germany. General Smuts writes very aptly: "Poland cannot exist without the good will of Germany and of Russia." When we all go home, the Poles will stay there by themselves, isolated in the middle of enemies who surround them on all sides.

M. Clemenceau. What's your conclusion?

Mr. Lloyd George. My conclusion is that we must not create a Poland alienated from the time of its birth by an unforgettable quarrel from its most civilized neighbor.

Do not believe that our most extreme democrats don't understand the necessities of the present situation. In a conversation I had yesterday with Lansbury, one of our most notorious pacifists, I told him I would be ready to promise France that, in case of German aggression, we would place all our forces at her disposal. Lansbury told me that he approved. But we must avoid sowing the seeds of war ourselves.

> —*The letter from General Smuts is read. He greatly fears the imposition on Germany of excessive terms and is alarmed about what is being said about Danzig and the left bank of the Rhine, as well as about the figures for indemnities, and maintains that it is in collaboration with Germany, and not against her, that it will be possible to keep new nations such as Poland and Bohemia alive. "Germany," writes General Smuts, "will remain, despite everything, a dominant element in continental Europe, and it would be folly to believe that we can reconstruct the world without her assistance."*

M. Clemenceau. I am willing to believe that General Smuts, who has proved his loyalty to England, does not speak merely as a friend of Germany. But I want the French point of view also to be taken into account.

Adolf Hitler

The Versailles Territorial Settlement and Nazi Revisionism

Adolf Hitler, born and raised in Austria and a decorated veteran in the German army during the Great War, had developed by the mid-1920s an ambitious plan for German hegemony in Europe that he would energetically pursue after becoming chancellor in 1933. In issuing his territorial claims against neighboring states, Hitler usually concealed this grandiose scheme for the subjugation of Europe by focusing, as in the following excerpts from his speeches in the late 1930s, on the German grievances against the Versailles territorial settlement's violation of the principle of national self-determination.

From Adolf Hitler, *My New Order* (Raoul de Roussy de Sales, ed. New York: Octagon Books, 1973), pp. 505–507, 635–638, 693–695. Reprinted by permission of Octagon Books.

Speech of September 12, 1938

Nuremberg

Since the days when we took over the Government the united front around Germany is standing against us. Today we again see plotters, from democrats down to Bolsheviks, fighting against the Nazi State. While we were struggling for power, and particularly in the decisive final struggle, they formed a united bloc against us.

We are being insulted today, but we thank God that we are in a position to prevent any attempt at plundering Germany or doing her violence. The State that existed before us was plundered for fifteen years. But for this it was praised as being a brave and democratic State.

But it becomes unbearable for us at a moment when a great German people, apparently defenseless, is delivered to shameless ill-treatment and exposed to threats. I am speaking of Czechoslovakia. This is a democratic State. It was founded on democratic lines by forcing other nationalities, without asking them, into a structure manufactured at Versailles. As good democrats they began to oppress and mishandle the majority of the inhabitants. They tried gradually to enforce on the world their view that the Czech State had a special political and military mission to perform in the world. Former French Air Minister Cot has only recently explained this to us. According to his opinion, the task of Czechoslovakia is in case of war to bombard German towns and industrial works.

This mission, however, is in direct contrast to the vital interests, to the wishes, and to the conception of life of a majority of the inhabitants of this State. But the majority of the inhabitants had to be quiet, as any protest against their treatment was regarded as an attack on the aims of this State and therefore in conflict with the Constitution. This Constitution, as it was made by democrats, was not rooted in the people but served only the political aims of those who oppressed the majority of the inhabitants. In view of these political aims, it had been found necessary to construct this Constitution in a manner giving the Czechs a predominant position in the State.

He who opposes such encroachment is an enemy of the State and, according to democratic conceptions of the State, an outlaw. The so-called nation of the Czechs has thus been selected by Providence, which in this case made use of those who once designed Versailles, to see that no one rose against this purpose of the State. Should, however, some one belonging to the majority of the oppressed people of this nation protest against this, the nation may knock him down with force and kill him if it is necessary or desired. If this were a matter foreign to us and one that did not concern us, we would regard this case, as so many others, merely as an interesting illustration of the democratic conception of people's rights and the right of self-determination and simply take note of it.

But it is something most natural that compels us Germans to take an interest in this problem. Among the majority of nationalities that are being suppressed in this State there are 3,500,000 Germans. That is about as many persons of our race as Denmark has inhabitants. These Germans, too, are creatures of God. The Almighty did not create them that they should be surrendered by a State construction made at Versailles to a foreign power that is hateful to them, and He has not created 7,000,000 Czechs in order that they should supervise 3,500,000 Germans or act as guardians for them and still less to do them violence and torture. The conditions in this nation are unbearable, as is generally known. Politically more than 3,500,000 people were robbed in the name of the right of self-determination of a certain Mr. Wilson of their self-determination and of their right to self-determination. Economically these people were deliberately ruined and afterward handed over to a slow process of extermination.

These truths cannot be abolished by phrases. They are testified to by deeds. The misery of the Sudeten Germans is without end. They want to annihilate them. They are being oppressed in an inhuman and intolerable manner and treated in an undignified way. When 3,500,000 who belong to a people of almost 80,000,000 are not allowed to sing any song that the Czechs do not like because it does not please the Czechs, or are brutally struck for wearing white stockings because the Czechs do not like it, and do not want to see them, and are terrorized or maltreated because they greet with a form of salutation that is not agreeable to them, although they are greeting not Czechs but one another, and when they are pursued like wild beasts for every expression of their national life, this may be a matter of indifference to several representatives of our democracies or they may possibly even be sympathetic because it concerns only 3,500,000 Germans. I can only say to representatives of the democracies that this is not a matter of indifference to us.

And I say that if these tortured creatures cannot obtain rights and assistance by themselves, they can obtain both from us. An end must be made of depriving these people of their rights. I have already said this quite clearly in my speech of February 22.

It was a short-sighted piece of work when the statesmen at Versailles brought the abnormal structure of Czechoslovakia into being. It was possible to violate the demands of millions of another nationality only so long as the brother nation itself was suffering from the consequences of general maltreatment by the world.

To believe that such a regime could go on sinning without hindrance forever was possible only through a scarcely credible degree of blindness. I declared in my speech of February 22 before the Reichstag that the Reich would not tolerate any further continued oppression of 3,500,000 Germans, and I hope that the foreign statesmen will be convinced that these were no mere words. . . .

Speech of April 28, 1939 to the German Reichstag

Berlin

Members of the German Reichstag! The President of the United States of America has addressed a telegram to me with the curious contents of which you are already familiar. Before I, the addressee, actually received the document the rest of the world had already been informed of it by radio and newspaper reports; and numerous commentaries in organs of the democratic world press had already generously enlightened us as to the fact that this telegram was a very skillful, tactful document destined to impose upon the States in which people govern, the responsibility for warlike measures adopted by the plutocratic countries.

In view of these facts I decided to summon the German Reichstag so that you gentlemen might have the opportunity of hearing my answer first, and of either confirming that answer or rejecting it. In addition, I considered it desirable to keep to the method of procedure initiated by President Roosevelt and to inform the rest of the world on my part and by our means of my answer.

But I should like also to take this opportunity of giving expression to feelings with which the tremendous historical happiness of the month of March inspires me. I can give vent to my deepest feelings only in the form of humble thanks to Providence, who called upon me and vouchsafed to me, once an unknown soldier of the great war, to rise to be the leader of my so dearly loved people. . . .

I have worked only to restore that which others once broke by force. I have desired only to make good that which satanic malice or human unreason destroyed or demolished. I have therefore taken no step which violated the rights of others, but have only restored that justice which was violated twenty years ago.

The present Greater German Reich contains no territory which was not from the earliest times part of this Reich, not bound up with or subject to its sovereignty. Long before an American continent had been discovered—to say nothing of settled—by white people, this Reich existed, not merely in its present extent but with the addition of many regions and provinces which have since been lost.

Twenty-one years ago, when the bloodshed of war came to an end, millions of minds were filled with the ardent hope that a peace of reason and justice would reward and bless the nations which had been visited by the fearful scourge of the Great War. I say "reward" for all these men and women, whatever the conclusions arrived at by historians, bore no responsibility for these fearful happenings.

And if in some countries there still were politicians who even at that time could be charged with responsibility for this, the most atrocious massacre of all time, yet vast numbers of combatant soldiers of every country and nation were at most deserving of pity but were by no means guilty.

I myself, as you know, had never played a part in politics before the war, and only, like millions of others, performed such duties as I was called upon to fulfill as a decent citizen and soldier. It was therefore with an absolutely clear conscience that I was able to take up the cause of freedom and the future of my people, both during and after the war.

And I can therefore speak in the name of millions and millions of others equally blameless when I declare that all those who had only fought for their nation in loyal fulfillment of their duty were entitled to a peace of reason and justice, so that mankind might at last set to work to make good by joint effort the losses which all had suffered.

But the millions were cheated of this peace; for not only did the German people or other people fighting on our side suffer through the peace treaties, but these treaties had an annihilating effect on the victor countries.

For the first time appeared the misfortune that politics should be controlled by men who had not fought in the war. The feeling of hatred was unknown to soldiers, but not to those elderly politicians who had carefully preserved their own precious lives from the horror of war and who now descended upon humanity in the guise of insane spirits of revenge.

Hatred, malice and unreason were the intellectual forebears of the Treaty of Versailles. Living space and States with history going back a thousand years were arbitrarily broken up and dissolved. Since time immemorial men who belong together have been torn asunder; the economic conditions of life have been ignored, while the peoples themselves have been converted into victors and vanquished, into masters possessing all rights and slaves possessing none. . . .

However, when this new world order turned out to be a catastrophe, the democratic peace dictators of American and European origin were so cowardly that none of them ventured to take the responsibility for what occurred. Each put the blame on the others, thus endeavoring to save himself from the judgment of history.

However, the people who were maltreated by their hatred and unreason were, unfortunately, not in a position to share with those who had injured them in this escape. . . .

One of the most shameful acts of oppression ever committed is the dismemberment of the German nation and the political disintegration of her living space—which has, after all, been hers for thousands of years—was provided for in the dictate of Versailles.

I have never, gentlemen, left any doubt, that in point of fact it is scarcely possible anywhere in Europe to arrive at a harmony of State and national boundaries which will be satisfactory in every way.

On one hand, migration of peoples which gradually came to a standstill during the last few centuries and development of large communities, on the other, have brought about a situation which, whatever way they look at it, must necessarily be considered unsatisfactory by those concerned.

It was, however, the very way in which these national and political developments were gradually stabilized in the last century which led many to consider themselves justified in cherishing hope that in the end a compromise would be found between respect for the national life of various European peoples and recognition of established political structures—a compromise by which, without destroying political order in Europe and within the existing economic basis, nationalities could nevertheless be preserved.

This hope was abolished by the Great War. Peace—the dictate of Versailles—did justice neither to one principle nor to the other. Neither the right of self-determination nor yet political, let alone economic, necessities and conditions for European development, were respected.

Nevertheless, I never left any doubt that—as I have already emphasized—even revision of the Treaty of Versailles would also find its limit somewhere. And I have always said so with utmost frankness—not for any tactical reasons but from my innermost conviction.

As national leader of the German people, I have never left any doubt that whenever higher interests of the European comity were at stake, national interests must, if necessary, be relegated to second place in certain cases.

And—as I have already emphasized—this is not for tactical reasons, for I have never left any doubt that I am absolutely earnest in this attitude of mine. For quite a number of territories which might possibly be disputed I have, therefore, come to final decisions which I have proclaimed not only to the outside world but also to my own people, and have seen to it that they should abide by them.

I have not, as France did in 1870–71, described the cession of Alsace-Lorraine as intolerable for the future, but I have here drawn a difference between the Saar Territory and these two former imperial provinces. And I have never changed my attitude, nor will I ever do so.

I have not allowed this attitude to be modified or jeopardized inside the country on any occasion, either in the press or in any other way. *Return of the Saar Territory has done away with all territorial problems in Europe between France and Germany. I have, however, always regarded it as regrettable that French statesmen should take this attitude for granted.*

This is, however, not the way to look at the matter. It was not for fear of France that I preached this attitude. As a former soldier I see no reason whatever for such fear. Moreover, as regards the Saar Territory, I made it quite clear we would not countenance any refusal to return it to Germany.

No, I have confirmed this attitude to France as an expression of appreciation of the necessity to attain peace in Europe, instead of sowing the seed of continual uncertainty and even tension by making unlimited demands and continually asking for revision. If this tension has nevertheless now risen, the responsibility does not lie with Germany but with those international elements which systematically produce such tension in order to serve their capitalist interests.

I have given binding declarations to a large number of States.

None of these States can complain that even a trace of a demand contrary thereto has been made to them by Germany. *None of the Scandinavian statesmen, for example, can contend that a request has even been put to them by the German Government or by German public opinion which was incompatible with the sovereignty and integrity of their State.*

I was pleased that a number of European States availed themselves of these declarations by the German Government to express and emphasize their desire for absolute neutrality. This applies to Holland, Belgium, Switzerland, Denmark.

I have already mentioned France. I need not mention Italy, with whom we are united in the deepest and closest friendship, *or Hungary and Yugoslavia*, with whom we, as neighbors, have the fortune to be on very friendly terms.

On the other hand, I have left no doubt from the first moment of my political activity that there existed other circumstances which represent such a mean and gross outrage of the right of self-determination of our people that we can never accept or endorse them.

I have never written a single line or made a single speech displaying a different attitude toward the above-mentioned States. On the other hand, with reference to other cases, I have never written a single line or made a single speech in which I have expressed any attitude contrary to my actions.

1. Austria! The oldest Eastern march of the German people, was once the buttress of the German nation on the southeast of the Reich.

The Germans of this country are descended from settlers from all the German tribes, even though the Bavarian tribe did contribute a major portion. Later this Ostmark became the crown lands and nucleus of the five-century-old German Empire, with Vienna as the capital of the German Reich of that period.

This German Reich was finally broken up in the course of a gradual dissolution by Napoleon the Corsican, but continued to exist as a German federation, and not so long ago fought and suffered in the greatest war of all time as an entity which was an expression of the national feelings of the people, even if it was no longer one united State. I myself am a child of this Ostmark.

Not only was the German Reich destroyed and Austria split up into its component parts by the criminals of Versailles, but Germans also were forbidden to acknowledge that community which they had confessed for more than a thousand years. I have always regarded elimination of this state of affairs as the highest and most holy task of my life. I have never failed to proclaim this determination. And I have always been resolved to realize these ideas which haunted me day and night.

I should have sinned against my call by Providence had I failed in my own endeavor to lead my native country and my German people of Ostmark back to the Reich and, thus, to the community of German people.

In doing so, moreover, I have wiped out the most disgraceful side of the Treaty of Versailles. I have once more established the right of self-determination and done away with democratic oppression of seven and a half million Germans.

I have removed the ban which prevented them from voting on their own fate, and carrying out this vote before the whole world. The result was not only what I expected but also precisely what had been anticipated by the Versailles democratic oppressors of the peoples. For why else did they stop a plebiscite on the question of Anschluss!

2. When in the course of the migrations of peoples, the Germanic tribes began, for reasons inexplicable to us, to migrate out of the territory which is today Bohemia and Moravia, a foreign Slav people made its way into this territory and made a place for itself between the remaining Germans. Since that time the living space of this Slav people has been inclosed in the form of a horseshoe by Germans.

From an economic point of view independent existence is, in the long run, impossible for these countries except on a basis of relationship with the German nation and German economy. But apart from this, nearly four million Germans lived in this territory of Bohemia and Moravia.

The policy of national annihilation which set in, particularly after the Treaty of Versailles under pressure of the Czech majority, combined, too, with economic conditions and a rising tide of distress, led to emigration of these German elements so that Germans left in the territory were reduced to approximately 3,700,000.

The population of the fringe of territory is uniformly German, but there are also large German linguistic enclaves in the interior. The Czech nation is, in its origins, foreign to us, but in the thousand years in which the two peoples have lived side by side a Czech culture has, in the main, been formed and molded by German influences.

Czech economy owes its existence to the fact of having been part of the great German economic system. The capital of this country was for a time a German imperial city, and it contains the oldest German university. Numerous cathedrals, town halls, and palaces of nobility and citizen class bear witness to the influence of German culture.

The Czech people itself has in the course of centuries alternated between close and more distant contacts with the German people. Every close contact resulted in a period in which both the German and the Czech nations flourished: every estrangement was calamitous in its consequences.

We are familiar with the merits and values of the German people, but the Czech nation, with the sum total of its skill and ability, its industry, its diligence, its love of its native soil and of its own national heritage, also deserves our respect.

There were, in actual fact, periods in which this mutual respect for the qualities of the other nation were a matter of course.

The democratic peacemakers of Versailles can take credit for having assigned to this Czech people the special rôle of a satellite State capable of being used against Germany. For this purpose they arbitrarily adjudicated foreign national property to the Czech State which was utterly incapable of survival on the strength of the Czech national unit alone; that is, they did violence to other nationalities in order to give a firm basis to a State which was to incorporate a latent threat to the German nation in Central Europe.

For this State, in which the so-called predominant national element was actually in the minority, could be maintained only by means of brutal assault on national units which formed a major part of the population.

This assault was possible only insofar as protection and assistance was granted by European democracies. This assistance could naturally be expected only on condition that this State was prepared loyally to take over and play the role which it had been assigned at birth, but the purpose of this role was none other than to prevent consolidation of Central Europe, to provide a bridge to Europe for bolshevik aggression, and, above all, to act as the mercenary of European democracies against Germany.

Everything else followed automatically. The more this State tried to fulfill the task it had been set, the greater was the resistance put up by national minorities. And the greater the resistance, the more it became necessary to resort to oppression.

This inevitable hardening of internal antitheses led, in its turn, to increased dependence on democratic European founders and benefactors of the State. For they alone were in position to maintain in the long run the economic existence of this unnatural and artificial creation.

Germany was primarily interested in one thing only and that was to liberate nearly four million Germans in this country from their unbearable situation and make it possible for them to return to their home country and to the thousand-year-old Reich.

It was only natural that this problem immediately brought up all other aspects of the nationalities problem. But it also was natural that removal of different national groups should deprive what was left of the State of all capacity to survive — a fact of which the founders of the State had been well aware when they planned it at Versailles, since it was for this very reason that they decided on assault on other minorities and had forced these against their will to become part of this amateurishly constructed State. . . .

David Stevenson

The Empty Chair at the Peace Conference: Russia and the West

David Stevenson, a professor of international history at the London School of Economics who has written widely on the history of the First World War, recounts in the following passage the strange tale of Bolshevik Russia's exclusion from the Paris Peace Conference. Stevenson assesses the inconsistent and ambivalent policy that the Allies pursued toward Russia, which vacillated between negotiation with the Bolsheviks and active support for the counterrevolutionary forces that were attempting to overthrow them.

The Conference created a more fragile and unstable settlement than those established in 1814–15 and after 1945. This, however, resulted less from the Conference's procedural difficulties than from the intractability of the substantive dilemmas that it faced. Of these among the most crucial was the peacemakers' inability either to reach an understanding with the Bolshevik Revolution or to crush it. Negotiation failed despite the time and energy that the Supreme Council gave to it; and suppression failed although the Allies' intervention continued and even increased after the Armistice with Germany. They maintained their blockade of the Bolshevik zone, and the British gave training and vast quantities of weaponry to the White armies of General Denikin in South Russia and Admiral Kolchak in Siberia. In November 1918 British Empire forces occupied the Baku–Batum railway, and detachments remained in Baku until July 1920. The Royal Navy helped the Baltic States win independence; a Franco-Greek expedition landed in Odessa and held much of the Black Sea coast between December 1918 and April 1919. Of the earlier interventions, that in the Arctic continued until September 1919, and the Japanese abandoned Vladivostok only in 1922.

Reprinted from *The First World War and International Politics* by David Stevenson (1988; reissued 1991), pp. 237–243. Reprinted by permission of Oxford University Press. Footnotes omitted.

This policy remained in part an anti-German one. Until Berlin had ratified the peace treaty, an Eastern Front might still be needed, especially as the Kaiser's overthrow brought nearer Lenin's vision of a Russo-German revolutionary alliance. In practice the Republican authorities in Germany rejected military collaboration with the Bolsheviks, for fear of jeopardizing possible Western food relief and losing American goodwill. But the possibility remained that the far Left, which staged repeated insurrections in the spring of 1919, would oust the SPD. After the Armistice, none the less, motives other than containing Germany grew in importance as reasons for intervention. The British Government felt its past co-operation with the Whites obliged it to give them a reasonable chance of victory in the Russian Civil War. Intervention might also secure the Indian frontiers and weaken a traditional rival through the creation of independent border States. The French, by contrast, hoped at least until March 1919 to reunite Russia under White leadership and reinstate the traditional counterbalance to Germany. In addition, they wanted to protect their Ukrainian investments, and feared the Bolsheviks would try to spread their ideology across Europe by force. But Allied war aims in Russia were confused and inconsistent, and intervention continued partly through inertia. It was difficult to extricate the troops after the rivers had frozen over and the 1918–19 winter had set in; and both Lloyd George and Clemenceau had to tread with caution because of the anti-Bolshevism of their parliamentary following.

The domestic pressures on the Allied leaders, however, were conflicting. Intervention was denounced by the expanding socialist and labour movements. It clashed with the needs of Treasuries for retrenchment and of Chiefs of the General Staff—such as Sir Henry Wilson in Britain—for the dwindling troops available to be deployed elsewhere. Demobilization was also the priority for the soldiers themselves. All the occupation forces suffered from unrest and poor morale, and the French precipitately evacuated Sebastopol in April 1919 because of mutiny in their fleet offshore. On 15 March a Senate resolution in favour of pulling out all American troops was defeated only by the Vice-President's casting vote. Hence Lloyd George and, eventually, the French leaders came to fear that expanded intervention might destabilize their own societies. Foch in Paris and Churchill, as War Minister, in London wished to commit much larger forces, but they lacked Clemenceau's and Lloyd George's support. As a result, the Western Governments intervened sufficiently to reinforce the Bolsheviks' suspicion of their intentions, but insufficiently to drive them from power.

The two main attempts at compromise between the Allies and the Bolsheviks were the Prinkipo conference proposal and the Bullitt mission. Prinkipo originated as a British suggestion, although one that encountered much hostility in Lloyd George's own delegation. After Wilson gave his backing Clemenceau also consented—for the sake, he said, of Allied unity—and on 22 January the Ten approved the proposal. They called for a ceasefire, and for a conference on Prinkipo island in the Sea of Marmora between representatives of all the Russian factions and the Allied Powers. A Soviet reply on 4 February accepted the invitation, and offered in exchange for peace to recognize and pay interest on Russia's foreign debts, to grant the Allies mining and forestry concessions, possibly to cede territory under Allied occupation, and to refrain from interfering in Allied internal affairs. Twelve days later, however, the Russian Political Conference, representing the Whites, rejected the Prinkipo summons.

What lay behind this sequence of events? Wilson, like Lloyd George, professed to be "repelled" by Bolshevism, but both men suspected that military intervention would consolidate rather than overthrow it, and they refused to finance intervention on a larger scale. They also had reason in advance to count on Bolshevik acceptance of the Prinkipo offer. The November Armistice had relieved the pressure on the Soviet authorities, who strengthened the Red Army for possible intervention in Germany and prepared for co-ordinated agitation in the West through the Communist International, or Comintern, founded in March 1919. But Lenin also sought a "second Brest": to buy time before the showdown with "international imperialism" by bribing the Allied capitalist interests through economic concessions. In December 1918 Litvinov, from the People's Commissariat for Foreign Affairs, had arrived in Stockholm, and in response to a personal appeal from the Soviet emissary Wilson had sent William Buckler for conversations on 14–16 January. Litvinov had offered Buckler conditions very similar to those contained in the Bolsheviks' subsequent reply to the Prinkipo appeal. Prinkipo therefore emerged both from the Anglo-Saxon leaders' assessment that intervention was not working and should be liquidated if reasonable terms were available, and from Lenin's anxiety for a breathing space, a course he could impose on his Party more easily than a year before. The convergence of interests was temporary. And it was significant, given that the Red Army was improving its position on the ground, that the Allies set the condition of a ceasefire along the present battle lines, but the Bolsheviks failed to mention this in their reply.

The Russian Political Conference rejected Prinkipo on behalf of the three main White authorities, in Siberia, North Russia, and the Ukraine. The Whites vehemently opposed a meeting with the Bolsheviks, but at this point the military balance was moving against them and they needed Allied support. Prinkipo foundered not only on the enmity between the Russian factions but also on the disunity of the Allies, and in particular on the equivocal behaviour of the French. With the Odessa expedition the French Government was involved in its most ambitious attempt to reconstruct its former influence in Russia, and Clemenceau felt—or said he felt—that his ministry would be endangered if it appeared to favour compromise. Although he judged it necessary to humour Wilson within the Supreme Council, the Quai d'Orsay and the Paris press encouraged White opposition to Prinkipo outside. As a result, the Anglo-American effort to disengage from Russia by negotiation was rendered fruitless, and Bolshevik sincerity over the armistice question remained untried.

The Bullitt mission never came even this close to success. Bullitt was a junior member of the American delegation, who travelled unofficially to Moscow and began discussions with the Bolshevik leaders on 10 March. They told him they would accept a two-week ceasefire and a peace conference if the Allies made such an offer within a month. The Allies should lift their blockade, withdraw their forces, and end assistance to the Whites. All *de facto* Governments in Russia would stay in control of their territory unless changed by the decision of the conference or by the local inhabitants. On regaining Paris, Bullitt pressed for acceptance of the Bolshevik terms, but was unable to see Wilson, and the Allies failed to reply before the time limit expired.

The mission was bedevilled by a confusion of authority. House was the driving force behind it, and he appears to have won support in principle from Wilson before the President's mid-Conference visit to Washington. But Wilson seems to have supposed that Bullitt would gather information rather than negotiate; and the French were told it was merely a fact-finding expedition. Before Bullitt's departure, however, House indicated to him that the United States was willing to grant an armistice and to press for joint Allied withdrawal if the Bolsheviks undertook not to retaliate against the Whites. Philip Kerr, of Lloyd George's secretariat, set out similar conditions on behalf of the Prime Minister and Balfour, although he stipulated that the *de facto* Governments in Russia should stay within their territories, and that the Allies would withdraw only after local Russian forces had been demobilized.

The Bolsheviks therefore offered terms similar to those that Bullitt had brought with him, and were now prepared to accept a temporary partition of Russia along the existing battle lines while the Allies disentangled themselves. But their qualifications (that *de facto* Governments could be replaced by their citizens, and that all aid to the Whites must end) betrayed their intention to return later to the attack.

Once again, Bolshevik good faith was never put to the test. For by the time Bullitt came back to Paris Wilson was losing confidence in House, and was "against taking up the question at present." House and Bullitt were isolated within the American delegation, and the Colonel and Lloyd George decided not to press the matter further in the face of public opposition in Britain and America to dealings with the Soviet regime. The existence of an apparent alternative may have facilitated the decision. On 16 April the Council of Four approved a suggestion by Hoover, the Director of the American food relief programme, for a neutral commission under the Norwegian, Nansen, that would distribute food in Russia on the conditions of a ceasefire and of commission control over the railways. The Nansen Plan was a counter-revolutionary as well as a humanitarian proposal, which House hoped would maintain the existing boundaries and alleviate the famine conditions that contributed to Bolshevik support. On 7 May the Bolsheviks replied that they were willing to talk to Nansen, but objected to the political condition of a ceasefire. By the time the Council of Four discussed this the Whites were advancing, and the Plan received no further consideration.

Each of the successive Allied projects had been less favourable to the Soviet regime. And now that the military pendulum was swinging back towards Lenin's opponents the Allied leaders abandoned negotiation in favour of a military solution that White armies, rather than their own, would impose. On 27 May the Four took a first step towards recognizing Admiral Kolchak's Government at Omsk. In return for undertakings to set up an elected regime and to acknowledge the independence of Poland and Finland as well, perhaps, as other border territories, they promised to send him volunteers and munitions and assist him in establishing an all-Russian Government. Allied policy therefore became to continue the blockade and to aid the Whites and border States, but avoid further direct intervention. By now the French Odessa expedition had ended in débâcle. Wilson withdrew his contingents from the Arctic as soon as the thaw permitted, and he continued to limit strictly the role of his forces in Siberia. During the autumn the British evacuated their forces from the Arctic, Siberia, and most of Transcaucasia, and stopped supplying Kolchak and Denikin, although they did so at a moment when Denikin's armies were advancing on Moscow and White victory seemed near. When the tide turned, and Denikin was thrown back, the British took the lead in a further realignment of policy. They agreed with France and Italy in December to continue aid to Poland and the other border States but to give nothing to the Whites beyond the consignments that had already been promised. Early in 1920 the same three Powers decided in effect to end the blockade of the Soviet zone, and the British reached an agreement on the exchange of prisoners. The undeclared Allied–Soviet war was thus ended by an undeclared peace.

With the eventual Bolshevik triumph in the Russian Civil War intervention had failed in almost all of its objectives. True, there re-emerged a Russian State free from German dominance, but this was made possible less by intervention than by the Allied victory over Germany in the West. And the severance of Russia's borderlands made it unlikely that the Bolsheviks would take up the Tsar's old function as an eastern ally against Berlin. Nor did the Allied leaders accomplish the broader, less anti-German aims for which intervention was continued after November 1918. They shrank from committing the hundreds of thousands of their own troops that would be needed to overthrow Lenin, and discovered no White forces strong enough to carry out the task. Given this, however, it is unlikely that they missed an opportunity to achieve through negotiation what was unattainable through force. An agreement with the Bolsheviks in the spring of 1919 would have secured limited economic concessions and a decent interval before the Civil War was fought to a finish anyway. But the absence of agreement greatly complicated the peacemakers' broader task. The Treaty of Versailles abrogated Brest-Litovsk, required German forces to evacuate Russia when the Allies saw fit, and reserved Russia's right to claim reparations. Otherwise the country's future remained opaque, and the peacemakers were obliged to decide the fate of Germany in ignorance of how the chaos in the east would be resolved. In addition, in the absence of a compromise with Moscow, the Conference became self-consciously a gathering of capitalist Powers, aiming not only to impose their will on the defeated enemy but also to repel a challenge to their economic and social system.

Members of the League of Nations Commission. Prominent members appear as follows: Seated, far left, Baron Nobuaki Makino of Japan; second from left, Léon Bourgeois of France; third from left, Lord Robert Cecil of Great Britain. Standing, far left, Colonel Edward House of the United States; sixth from left, Jan Christiaan Smuts of South Africa; seventh from left, Woodrow Wilson of the United States; second from right, V. K. Wellington Koo of China. (Woodrow Wilson Papers Project, Photographs Series, Mudd Library, Department of Rare Books and Special Collections, Princeton University Library)

Conflicting Strategies for Ensuring European Peace

Lloyd Ambrosius

The Drafting of the Covenant

Lloyd Ambrosius, author of several important works on Wilsonian diplomacy who teaches history at the University of Nebraska, describes in the following passage the tortuous path leading to the adoption of the League of Nations Covenant. He demonstrates how President Wilson and his allies in the British delegation beat back attempts by other powers to modify the Anglo-American plan for the world organization that Wilson regarded as the key to postwar peace and security.

From Lloyd Ambrosius, *Woodrow Wilson and the American Diplomatic Tradition: The Treaty Fight in Perspective*, 1987, pp. 64–77, 113–118, Copyright © 1987. Reprinted with the permission of Cambridge University Press. Footnotes omitted.

Prospects for establishing a league of nations seemed favorable on the eve of the peace conference. Wilson was now confident that he would succeed. To gain French support, he and Cecil met separately with Léon Bourgeois, whom Clemenceau later appointed, along with Ferdinand Larnaude, to the commission that would draft the Covenant. Bourgeois had earlier attempted to arrange a meeting with Wilson to discuss a league. The French were genuinely interested in collective security. At the peace conference's first plenary session on January 18, 1919, President Poincaré opened formal deliberations by outlining the tasks of peacemaking. In conformity with the last of Wilson's Fourteen Points, he called for "a General League of Nations which will be a supreme guarantee against any fresh assaults upon the right of peoples." Clemenceau expressed the same hope for postwar unity among the victorious powers. "Everything must yield to the necessity of a closer and closer union among the peoples who have taken part in this great war," he emphasized. "The League of Nations is here."

To coordinate British and American plans, Wilson conferred with Cecil and Smuts. Prior to this meeting, House had received a copy of the British draft convention and accompanying resolutions. After studying the British resolutions, he requested Miller to prepare a substitute. Lansing also drafted his alternative resolution, which reaffirmed his idea of a negative covenant. In view of their recommendations, House constructed his own proposal, an abbreviated version of Miller's, submitting it to Wilson along with a copy of the British draft convention. The president ignored this advice, accepting instead the British resolutions with a modification to emphasize that the League Covenant would be an integral part of the peace treaty. On January 19 he presented his draft of a covenant to Cecil and Smuts. They were both impressed with its similarity to previous British plans. Smuts was elated that his plan had been so influential but was terribly anxious because Wilson had altered his conception of mandates to include former German colonies. This alteration threatened South Africa's and Australia's claims, which he and Prime Minister William Hughes advanced. Smuts lamented that Wilson was "entirely opposed to our annexing a little German colony here or there, which pains me deeply and will move Billy Hughes to great explosions of righteous wrath." He had earlier urged Lloyd George to "smooth the way for a conciliatory policy of President Wilson towards our very far-reaching claims." Despite this contentious issue, the president achieved a broad consensus with Cecil and Smuts concerning a league. On January 20 he informed the American Commission about this substantial agreement and shared with them copies of his third draft of a covenant.

Lloyd George was still unwilling to commit his government to a particular plan. He was more interested in the general structure of Anglo-American cooperation than in the details of a new league. Smuts regretted that the prime minister was not more enthusiastic about his plan. "I believe the Americans like it more than my British friends; but it has ever been thus with the prophets," he observed with obvious pride of authorship. The prime minister told Cecil he preferred the British draft convention to Wilson's covenant. "However, he did not want to talk about the League of Nations at all, in which he takes no real interest," Cecil regretfully noted.

British and American leaders, despite their differences, collaborated to determine the nature of the future League. In the Council of Ten—heads of government and foreign ministers of Great Britain, France, Italy and the United States, and two delegates from Japan—Lloyd George and Balfour expressed their willingness to accept Wilson's covenant as the basis for discussion. In accordance with the British draft resolutions, they recommended the adoption of general principles and referral to a committee. After this session, apparently with Wilson's encouragement, Lansing prepared his own set of suggested resolutions. For the first time, he now gave tentative endorsement to a positive guarantee. The president, however, supported the British resolutions. The Council of Ten on January 22 officially called for a league of nations—that "should be open to every civilised nation which can be relied on to promote its object"—as "an integral part" of the peace treaty. Lloyd George proposed that the great powers should each appoint two representatives to the drafting commission and jointly select two delegates to represent all small states. Wilson advocated that great powers alone should draft the League Covenant, and only then give small states the opportunity to review it. In contrast, Clemenceau championed the small states' right to full participation. He eventually convinced the British and American leaders to permit small states to select a total of five delegates to serve with ten representatives of the great powers on the commission. To announce these decisions of the Council of Ten, but not to allow any votes or official action, leaders of the five principal Allied and Associated Powers agreed to convene a plenary session of the peace conference. They were clearly determined to maintain control by the great powers.

At the plenary session on January 25, Wilson outlined his league idea. He emphasized that the peace conference's purpose was not only to settle the issues of the recent war but also to lay the basis for lasting peace. He explained that the United States was less interested than other nations in specific terms of the peace settlement because the American people had never feared the war's outcome. It was their ideals that had led them to enter the war and support the future League. Reconciling the isolationist and internationalist aspects of his foreign policy, he stressed the League's importance to the United States. "We regard it," the president asserted, "as the keystone of the whole program which expressed our purpose and our ideal in this war and which the Associated Nations have accepted as the basis of the settlement." In support of Wilson, Lloyd George stated "how emphatically the people of the British Empire are behind this proposal." Bourgeois likewise voiced France's "deep enthusiasm" for a league. He observed that local conflicts inevitably threatened the whole world. "There is such an interdependence in all the relations between nations in the economic, financial, moral and intellectual spheres," he stated, "that, I repeat, every wound inflicted at some point threatens to poison the whole organs." Although generally approving the creation of a league, delegates from small states complained about their exclusion from the drafting process. Despite these grumblings, leaders of the great powers asserted their dominance in the peace conference.

This procedure elicited Lansing's strong criticism. Privately, he complained that five great powers were running the peace conference like the Congress of Vienna. He said, "the small nations have not more voice in settling the destinies of the world than they had a hundred years ago. . . . Translated into plain terms it will mean that five or six great powers will run the world as they please and the equal voice of the little nations will be a myth." The alienated secretary of state would not play a central role in the peace negotiations. Instead of Lansing, Wilson selected House to serve with himself on the commission that would draft the Covenant. House was more willing to approve the views of Wilson and Lloyd George, both of whom indeed anticipated the great powers' primacy, and especially Anglo-American control, in the future League.

House and Cecil took the initiative to prepare a joint Anglo-American plan for a league. Miller had discussed with Cecil the common characteristics of the British draft convention and Wilson's covenant. Now that the president had modified the provision for automatic war against covenant-breaking states, Miller expressed only one major criticism of the remaining features. He opposed the provision for future revision of boundaries. House instructed him to endeavor to amalgamate British and American plans into a single document. This procedure offered the advantage of avoiding any official American commitment to the resulting joint draft. As long as Lloyd George refused to obligate the British government, House wanted to preserve the same freedom for the president. Taking Wilson's third draft as the basis for discussion, Miller sought British approval with the fewest possible changes. In consultation with Smuts, and with the assistance of Lord Eustace Percy of the Foreign Office, Cecil directed the preparation of British amendments to Wilson's covenant. By January 27 he and Miller agreed on most provisions. At Cecil's request, Miller approved three important alterations so as to allow representation by British dominions and India, to limit membership in the council to the great powers, and to increase the stature of the chancellor's office. The title of this officer was later changed to secretary general. This Cecil-Miller draft resolved most, but not all, of the outstanding differences. Still undetermined were provisions for a permanent court of international justice and a system of mandates. Accompanied by Miller and Wiseman, House and Cecil reviewed this draft. They agreed that the question of mandates was the only major obstacle to complete Anglo-American accord on the future League.

The Council of Ten considered the disposal of Germany's former colonies and the establishment of a mandatory system. It had agreed on January 24 not to restore these colonies to Germany. Lloyd George endorsed the idea of mandates, for which he saw the British Empire as the model. Wanting to protect the British dominions' claims, he committed only Great Britain to this new system. He supported South Africa, Australia and New Zealand in advancing their separate demands for the conquered German colonies in South-West Africa, New Guinea and Samoa. British dominions were not alone in desiring their share of the spoils of war. The Council of Ten heard French claims to the Cameroons and Togoland in central Africa, and also Japanese demands for German islands north of the equator and German rights in the Shantung province of China. During these deliberations, Wilson attempted to convince Allied leaders that trusteeship under a league was preferable to outright annexation. "If any nation could annex territory which was previously a German Colony," he asserted, "it would be challenging the whole idea of the League of Nations." He was afraid that "if the process of annexation went on, the League of Nations would be discredited from the beginning."

As the president firmly opposed the transfer of colonies from one empire to another, Lloyd George and Smuts began to search for a compromise. Despite the reservations of Hughes and, to a lesser extent, of

Prime Minister W. F. Massey of New Zealand, Smuts prepared a series of resolutions to establish three classes of mandates. Dividing the conquered parts of the former Turkish and German empires into these classes, the resolution distinguished between ostensible levels of development of the affected peoples. The first class included parts of the Turkish Empire, which would enjoy autonomy but not full self-government. Eventual independence was offered as a possibility. The second class encompassed German colonies in central Africa, which the mandatory powers would administer in accordance with principles adopted by the league. The third class of mandates, including German colonies claimed by British dominions, would entail only minimal supervision by the league. After Lloyd George succeeded in gaining the dominions' acceptance of this compromise, Smuts solicited Wilson's approval through House. In accordance with his earlier promises to Derby, House was willing to concede these colonial claims in return for British support for a league. Wilson accepted House's advice. His decision resulted partly from his misplaced confidence in Smuts, who viewed mandates as a veil for annexation. Lloyd George enabled the president to gain a victory for the idea of mandates, while British dominions retained the substance of their colonial claims.

Once the question of mandates was resolved, American and British leaders quickly settled their remaining differences. House and Cecil continued to coordinate joint Anglo-American planning for a league. Although Lloyd George was not enthusiastic about proceeding immediately with this project, he permitted Cecil and Smuts to confer with Wilson, House and Miller on January 31. At this time the president approved the changes that Cecil and Miller had earlier incorporated into their draft. Rather than attempt to agree on elaborate plans for a permanent court of international justice, the conferees decided merely to insert a general provision calling for its later creation. They also agreed, in response to Italy's request, to modify the prohibition of conscription. General Bliss, from whom Wilson had solicited advice, had noted that abolition of conscription would give an unfair advantage to rich nations that could recruit volunteer armies by paying higher wages than poor states could afford. Recognizing that the Cecil-Miller draft, with these additional changes, required polishing, American and British leaders delegated this task to Miller and Cecil J. B. Hurst. These two legal advisers completed their assignment on February 2. In preparing this Hurst-Miller draft, they made one substantial change on their own initiative. They omitted the provision for revision which Wilson and then

Cecil had combined with the positive guarantee of political independence and territorial integrity.

Wilson now felt hopeful that he could accomplish his goal at the
peace conference. But his self-image as a lonely warrior, although justified by Lansing's continued resistance, threatened to destroy the
Anglo-American accord that House had fostered in cooperation with
Cecil. The president surprisingly denounced the Hurst-Miller draft and
began to prepare another draft of a league covenant. Except for allowing representation by small as well as great powers on the executive
council, his fourth draft was not substantially different from the Hurst-
Miller draft. He even deleted the provision for revision from the positive guarantee of political independence and territorial integrity. Cecil
strenuously objected when he learned that the president intended to
present his own latest covenant as the basis for deliberations in the drafting commission. With the support of Smuts and House, Cecil succeeded in convincing Wilson to reverse his unilateral decision and
preserve Anglo-American collaboration.

Excluded from Anglo-American preparations, French leaders
meanwhile had worked for a league of their own liking. At Clemen-
ceau's instigation, Bourgeois invited other national organizations to join
the French Association for the Society of Nations for the purpose of de-
veloping a common plan. Along with similar groups from Great Britain,
Italy, Belgium, Romania, Serbia and China, the League to Enforce
Peace participated in this project. Its executive committee had in
December 1918 already established a committee in Paris, with Oscar S.
Straus as chairman and Hamilton Holt as vice-chairman, to support
Wilson's efforts and to advise the New York office. The League to Enforce Peace received no official endorsement or encouragement from
the president. Late in January the Paris committee joined similar groups
from other countries in unanimously adopting a resolution calling for a
powerful league. This resolution, which Bourgeois submitted to Wilson
on January 31, proposed an international council to preserve liberty and
maintain order. This council would establish a permanent committee
on conciliation and also arrange for development of international legislation. The committee on conciliation could mediate any conflict between nations, or refer it either to arbitration or to an international court
of justice. The resolution required the settlement of all disputes by
peaceful methods. It obligated the league members to use "all means
within their power" to prevent any state from resorting to acts of war
which would disturb world peace. It also assigned to such a league the

responsibility for limiting and supervising the armament of each nation and for prohibiting secret treaties. Only nations which would faithfully fulfill these stringent requirements could be admitted to this proposed league. By endorsing this plan, the League to Enforce Peace showed its willingness to support a world organization with greater obligations than Wilson envisaged.

Clemenceau wanted to preserve the wartime coalition and conceived of the League as an alliance against Germany. In the Council of Ten, he repeated his belief that "if, before the war, the Great Powers had made an alliance pledging themselves to take up arms in defence of any one of them who might be attacked, there would have been no war. Today they had not only five nations in agreement but practically the whole world. If the nations pledged themselves not to attack any one without the consent of the members of the League, and to defend any one of them who might be attacked, the peace of the world would be assured. Such an alliance might well be termed a League of Nations." Wilson shared Clemenceau's goal, but not his methods. To the French Senate on January 20, he had related his vision of a league to the security of France: "The whole world is awake, and it is awake to its community of interest. . . . It knows that the peril of France, if it continues, will be the peril of the world. It knows that not only France must organize against this peril, but that the world must organize against it." On February 3, Wilson reiterated this thought to the French Chamber of Deputies. He said, "there shall never be any doubt or waiting or surmise, but that whenever France or any other free people is threatened the whole world will be ready to vindicate its liberty." These assurances, however, did not indicate any intention to establish the future League as a postwar alliance.

The French desire for an anti-German alliance challenged the Anglo-American conception of peace. While Clemenceau sought to restore the balance of power in Europe, Lloyd George and Wilson endeavored to avoid entanglement on the continent. Less concerned about the German problem, they defined their countries' aims in global terms. They identified either British or American interests with universal ideals, while the French concentrated more on the immediate requirements of national security. The ensuing conflict would complicate the negotiations to establish a league. It would, moreover, separate Wilson from some of his opponents at home. Differences between the advocates of a general system of collective security and those of a particular alliance affected not only the peacemaking in Paris but also the treaty fight in the United States.

Anglo-American cooperation limited French influence during the drafting of the Covenant. At the first meeting of the League of Nations Commission, Wilson presented the Hurst-Miller draft as the basis for deliberation. As agreed, Cecil supported him in overriding the objections of Bourgeois and other delegates that they had not yet had the opportunity even to study this Anglo-American proposal. American and British leaders were determined to maintain their control. By forcing immediate acceptance of the Hurst-Miller draft, they placed other representatives in the difficult position of attempting to achieve their goals for a league through amendments. This procedure immediately thwarted the French initiative to create a powerful international organization to preserve peace.

Foreign Minister Stéphen Pichon belatedly submitted a French plan for a society of nations. Prepared during the spring of 1918 by a commission under Bourgeois' leadership in the Ministry of Foreign Affairs, it provided for military as well as diplomatic, legal and economic sanctions. If conciliation or arbitration failed to resolve a dispute, these sanctions might be employed by an international council against any state that committed aggression. To prepare for military sanctions, the French plan called for the organization of international forces under a permanent staff. Membership in this society of nations would be restricted to states which would loyally fulfill these mutual obligations. This plan provided the basis not only for the resolution that Bourgeois had earlier submitted to Wilson on January 31 but also for subsequent French amendments to the Hurst-Miller draft. Although Bourgeois presented it to the League Commission, the French plan did not enjoy the same official status as the Anglo-American proposal in the ensuing proceedings.

French leaders were not alone in resenting American and British domination of the drafting of the Covenant. When delegates from small states had convened on January 27 to select their five representatives on the League Commission, they began to protest against their subordinate position. They demanded the inclusion of at least four more states out of their total of seventeen. In compliance with the Council of Ten's restriction, the small states elected Belgium, Serbia, Portugal, Brazil and China to the commission. But they also voted for Romania, Poland, Greece and Czechoslovakia as additional choices. In the Council of

Ten, which considered the small states' request, Wilson objected to their desire for more representation. He did not want them to enjoy equality with the great powers. On his recommendation, the Council of Ten agreed to refer this question to the League Commission for final decision. Nevertheless, he eventually lost. At its second meeting on February 4, Foreign Minister Paul Hymans of Belgium presented the small states' case. Supported by Bourgeois and the Serbian and Portuguese delegates, he secured a favorable vote in the commission. Despite Wilson's and Cecil's objections, small states gained a larger role in these proceedings.

During subsequent consideration of the Hurst-Miller draft, Hymans and other delegates from small states, aided by Bourgeois and Italian premier Orlando, pressed their demand for membership in the future League's executive council. They generally endorsed the position that Wilson had earlier taken in favor of minority representation by four small states along with the five great powers. Cecil strongly opposed such an alteration but eventually followed the president in making this concession. Nevertheless, with their majority in the executive council and the requirement for unanimity on its vital decisions, the great powers would still retain their primacy in the future League.

In defining the role of great powers in the League, Wilson focused on the positive guarantee of political independence and territorial integrity. This mutual commitment, eventually to emerge from the drafting as Article 10, was, in his opinion, "the key to the whole Covenant," Smuts regarded it as the most far-reaching part of the document. Cecil, who had only reluctantly approved it, now reverted to his earlier preference for a negative covenant. He attempted to remove the positive guarantee from the Hurst-Miller draft, leaving only the obligation for each state in the League to respect other members' political independence and territorial integrity. Cecil's attempt to weaken this article failed as other delegates joined the president in defending it. From Larnaude's French perspective, it was already too weak. This positive guarantee was "only a principle" because it failed to specify the means for its fulfillment. To clarify the procedure for responding to future aggression, Wilson proposed that the executive council should offer advice on the means to fulfill this obligation. After the League Commission approved this amendment, Cecil revived Wilson's earlier idea of periodic revision of international obligations. He later succeeded in inserting it into the Covenant. With this addition, the possibility of revision was again combined with the positive guarantee, as in Wilson's earlier drafts of the Covenant. Article 19 authorized the body of delegates to recommend reconsideration of treaties or other international conditions which might endanger world peace. The net effect of these changes was to leave the positive guarantee as ambiguous as ever. Members of the League would be obligated to protect each other from aggression, but they would retain the freedom to decide when and how to fulfill this commitment.

Despite their differences over Article 10, British and American leaders alike sought to avoid extensive obligations for their countries. The Hurst-Miller draft would require the league members to submit their conflicts to arbitration or conciliation, if the ordinary processes of diplomacy should fail. Refusal to attempt one of these methods would be regarded *ipso facto* as an act of war, leading to commercial and financial sanctions. On the executive council's recommendation, the League might even use military sanctions. These sanctions were strictly limited to the purpose of forcing the parties to a conflict to submit the issues to arbitration or conciliation. The Hurst-Miller draft did not provide for compulsory arbitration or for enforcement of even the executive council's unanimous recommendations. The key to peace was the cooling-off period for arbitration or conciliation.

Belgium tried to strengthen the Covenant. For any settlement, the Hurst-Miller draft would require a unanimous vote in the executive council, exclusive of the parties to a dispute. Hymans endeavored to remove the power of veto by a single nation in order to permit the executive council to make a recommendation by majority vote. He also wanted to obligate the league members not only to respect but also to enforce a unanimous recommendation. He further sought to empower the League to employ sanctions for the broader purpose of enforcing an arbitral award or a recommendation, rather than only for the limited purpose of requiring submission of disputes to arbitration or conciliation. Sanctions under Article 16 should apply as well to Article 10. Hymans obviously did not wish to rely on a cooling-off period, but favored enforcement of pacific settlement of disputes. All of these Belgian amendments encountered Wilson's and Cecil's opposition, while Bourgeois and various other delegates gave their support. The commission referred this matter to a committee consisting of Hymans, Bourgeois, Cecil and Greek premier Eleutherios K. Venizelos for further study. At its meeting Cecil defeated most of the Belgian amendments. The committee recommended only one change, authorizing the executive council to consider what action to take to enforce its unanimous recommendations. The League Commission approved the amendment, but its decision constituted only a temporary concession. Wilson later successfully reversed this decision, thereby preserving the Hurst-Miller draft's original provisions for pacific settlement of disputes.

Anglo-American control over the drafting limited the League's jurisdiction. Wilson and Cecil prevented what they regarded as excessive obligations. "It will be seen," Cecil later wrote, "that there is no provision for the enforcement of any decision by the Council, except so far as the provision goes which lays it down that no State is to be attacked because it carries out the Council's unanimous decision. That was the deliberate policy of the framers of the Covenant. They desired to enforce on the parties a delay of some months before any war took place, believing that during that period some pacific solution would be found. But they did not think that it would be accepted by the nations if there was an attempt to compel them to agree to a solution dictated by the Council." In accordance with this Anglo-American conception of the League, its members would be obligated only to attempt a pacific settlement of conflicts before resorting to war. The purpose of sanctions was merely to enforce a delay, not to impose a settlement. As Cecil noted, "all that the Covenant proposed was that the members of the League, before going to war, should try all pacific means of settling the quarrel."

Clemenceau endeavored to transform this Anglo-American plan into an effective alliance. Through an interview with an Associated Press correspondent, he appealed to the American people "to renounce their traditional aloofness." He cited with approval the president's words of assurance to the Chamber of Deputies that the whole world stood ready to protect the liberty of France and other free nations. Within the League of Nations Commission, Bourgeois and Larnaude attempted to amend the Hurst-Miller draft in conformity with the French plan. Bourgeois offered an amendment, like that of Hymans, which would authorized sanctions against any state that refused to accept an arbitral award or a unanimous recommendation by the executive council. He proposed another amendment to clarify conditions for admission to the League. Beyond its initial members, consisting of the Allied and Associated Powers, he wanted to restrict the League to nations with representative governments that were willing to abide by its principles, including the League's guidelines regarding their military forces. Attempting to amend the Hurst-Miller draft's provision for reduction of national armaments, Bourgeois sought to authorize the executive council to establish control over national military forces and to organize an international force. This was his most important and controversial amendment.

During the ensuing debate, Wilson and Cecil vigorously opposed this French proposal for transforming the future League into a military alliance. The president offered constitutional and political objections to an international force. Placing the American army at the League's disposal, he explained, was incompatible with both the Constitution and public opinion. "Our principal safety," he asserted, "will be obtained by the obligation which we shall lay on Germany to effect a complete disarmament." This argument failed to persuade French delegates. Larnaude countered that "the idea of an international force is bound up with the very idea of the League of Nations, unless one is content that the League should be a screen of false security." In response the president gave his most explicit commitment of American military assistance if required by future circumstances. After Bourgeois continued to press the French case, Wilson further asserted: "All that we can promise, and we do promise it, is to maintain our military forces in such a condition that the world will feel itself in safety. When danger comes, we too will come, and we will help you, but you must trust us. We must all depend on our mutual good faith."

American and British leaders resisted French requests for specific military commitments that would entangle their countries on the continent. Cecil warned a French delegate that "the League of Nations was their only means of getting the assistance of America and England, and if they destroyed it they would be left without an ally in the world." This warning reflected the attitude that House had expressed to Balfour two days earlier. The League Commission referred the French amendments to a committee that it established to review the articles of the Hurst-Miller draft which were already tentatively accepted. When this drafting committee met, Cecil bluntly threatened Larnaude that Great Britain and the United States would form an alliance, excluding France, unless French delegates abandoned their plan for an international force. He described the League as "practically a present to France," and expressed his irritation over French failure to appreciate this Anglo-American gift. As a weak substitute for the French plan, Cecil repeated his offer of the previous day to insert into the Covenant a provision for establishing a permanent commission to advise the League on military and naval affairs. The drafting committee accepted this minor concession as well as the French amendment on requirements for future admission of new members to the League. This committee took no action on the other French amendment concerning sanctions, effectively killing it.

From the French perspective, a viable league would entail specific military obligations. When the League Commission considered the drafting committee's report on February 13, French delegates continued their attempt to strengthen the document, and again failed. Bourgeois explained that "by a thoroughgoing supervision of armaments the League of Nations would discourage any attempt at war." If this international control failed to prevent aggression, French leaders wanted a league capable of responding with sufficient and timely military strength. Coordination of national forces would require an international general staff. This French plan continued to encounter British and American rejection. Cecil considered the idea of an international general staff "a perfectly fatuous proposal." He emphatically renounced it, affirming that the future League "could not be considered as an alliance against Germany. Nothing would more quickly imperil peace." As Anglo-American control continued, the commission approved only those changes recommended by the drafting committee. The Covenant would now include Cecil's weak substitute of a permanent advisory commission on military and naval affairs. French leaders failed to transform the Anglo-American plan for a league into an effective alliance for their country's defense.

Japanese delegates did not take an active part in the drafting. In the League Commission on February 13, Baron Nobuaki Makino finally raised the one issue that most interested his country. As an addition to the provision for freedom of religion, he proposed an amendment affirming racial equality. He explained that peoples of various races and nationalities could hardly be expected to assume the responsibilities of the new League unless it affirmed their equality. This Japanese demand challenged the racial prejudice of British and American leaders. Having previously received a copy of the Japanese amendment, House had attempted to prepare an acceptable substitute using language from the American Declaration of Independence. He conferred with Balfour, who rejected the idea that "all men are created equal" as an eighteenth-century proposition. The British foreign secretary said that perhaps all men in a particular nation were equal, but repudiated the notion that black Africans were equal to Europeans. Opposing any amendment that threatened to open the British Empire to Japanese immigration, he denounced as "blackmail" the intimation that Japan might refuse to join the League unless its amendment was accepted. House agreed with this denunciation, but still hoped to find an acceptable compromise. Miller, to whom he assigned the task of drafting a substitute, clearly recognized the difficulty of preparing an amendment which affirmed the principle of racial equality without its having any practical implications. The basic difficulty was that British and American leaders did not believe in this principle. House's efforts were in vain. Rather than adopt any racial equality amendment, the League Commission removed from the Covenant the carefully prepared provision for religious liberty.

Once the League Commission completed its work, Wilson presented the Covenant to the peace conference. . . . at the plenary session on February 14. . . .

Maintaining Anglo-American control over drafting of the Covenant, Wilson, House and Cecil met privately in March to consider possible amendments. The president consistently opposed any substantial change in the future League. Despite his reluctance even to appear to compromise, he recognized widespread American sensitivity on questions such as the Monroe Doctrine. Encouraged by House, Cecil took the initiative in preparing amendments. They agreed to stipulate that decisions of the executive council and the body of delegates would require unanimity unless otherwise specified. This wording coincided with their earlier interpretation of the League's procedures. Anticipating Germany's admission to the League, which Lloyd George favored, they wanted to empower the executive council to expand its membership. This provision for eventually including Germany among the great powers reflected the Anglo-American vision of a universal league rather than an alliance. In other ways as well, British and American leaders sought to limit national commitments under the Covenant. They altered Article 8 to clarify that the League could not adopt any plan for disarmament without each government's approval. They also specified that the League could not assign a mandate to a state without its consent. At Wilson's instigation, they omitted from Article 15 the executive council's obligation to recommend measures for implementing its own unanimous decisions, even if a disputing party refused to comply with the proposed settlement. Cecil suggested an amendment, which Sir Robert Borden, prime minister of Canada, had strongly advocated, to remove Article 10's guarantee of territorial integrity and political independence; but he did not press for its acceptance. Wilson, House and Cecil also discussed possible amendments to exempt the Monroe Doctrine and domestic affairs from the League's jurisdiction and to reserve the right of each nation to withdraw from the organization at some future time. Reaching no agreement on these questions, they postponed them for later consideration.

In their determination to control the drafting of the Covenant, British and American leaders refused to consider seriously other statesmen's proposals for revision. With Clemenceau's acquiescence and Wilson's authorization, Cecil and House arranged a meeting between a committee of the League Commission and representatives of twelve neutral countries. At this meeting, delegates of the Allied and Associated Powers gave these representatives the opportunity to suggest amendments to the draft Covenant. But as Cecil clearly stated, the general principles of the proposed League were not subject to reconsideration. The meeting itself was unofficial. Six members of the commission, including Cecil, House, and Bourgeois, merely received various amendments from the neutrals. Although these nations, especially from Europe and Latin America, would be invited to join the League as original members, they lacked any real influence over its inception.

Neither France nor the neutrals succeeded in revising the Covenant. When the League Commission reconvened to consider amendments, only Wilson and Cecil achieved their desired changes. Bourgeois attempted to strengthen the League's jurisdiction over military affairs, again proposing amendments that British and American delegates had previously rejected. Under Article 8 he wanted to empower the executive council or a special commission to investigate and verify the level of military preparedness by the League's members. Wilson objected to this verification as a violation of national sovereignty. Bourgeois also endeavored to establish a "permanent organism" to prepare for military and naval operations so that the executive council could take immediate and effective action in response to aggression. Wilson and Cecil again refused to expand the permanent commission's functions under Article 9. They also declined to broaden the scope of sanctions in Article 16. Opposing Hymans' recommendation to restrict the League's original membership to the Allied and Associated Powers, Wilson explained that he wished "to avoid giving the League the appearance of an alliance." It should instead be "a world league." He defended the neutral nations' right to join the League. He also secured an amendment to Article 15 to exempt domestic affairs from the League's jurisdiction. His final amendment, which would allow any state to withdraw from the League after ten years on one year's notice, encountered French criticism. Larnaude noted that a reference to ten years would give a temporary appearance to the League. To protect a nation's right to withdraw without giving this implication, Italian Premier Orlando suggested a compromise. With Wilson's and Bourgeois' approval, the commission adopted his amendment to permit any member that had fulfilled its obligations under the Covenant to withdraw at any time on two years' notice. The president reserved his right to introduce a Monroe Doctrine amendment at a later time. Cecil and Balfour had attempted to draft such an amendment, but had not obtained either Lloyd George's or Wilson's approval. On other issues, where British and American leaders had agreed, they prevailed in writing their changes into the Covenant.

Their failure to devise an acceptable Monroe Doctrine amendment stemmed from the serious Anglo-American naval rivalry. Lloyd George had decided to force the United States to conclude an agreement on naval policy as a condition for his final approval of the League. Recognizing American sensitivity over the Monroe Doctrine, he selected this issue as the best way to coerce Wilson into accepting a compromise. In this situation the president had refrained from introducing his own Monroe Doctrine amendment in the League Commission. He was fully aware of the seriousness of this impasse. If Wilson expected the Senate to approve American membership in the League, he needed to preserve the Monroe Doctrine. Lodge advised White: "In some form or other the Monroe Doctrine will be protected in any League that is made." Yet Lloyd George refused any amendment for this purpose unless he first achieved a naval agreement.

Lloyd George's tactic of linking the Monroe Doctrine and naval questions was especially powerful because of the Republican position. Congress had refused to pass the naval bill before adjourning on March 4, thereby depriving the president of authority to engage in a naval race with Great Britain. Lodge saw no justification for Anglo-American naval rivalry but insisted upon excluding the Monroe Doctrine from the League's jurisdiction. Politically vulnerable at home on both the Monroe Doctrine and naval policy, Wilson needed to accommodate Lloyd George in order to salvage the League. They delegated the negotiations for a naval agreement to Secretary of the Navy Daniels and Admiral William S. Benson, Chief of Naval Operations, for the United States, and Colonial Secretary Walter Long and Admiral Sir Rossalyn Wemyss, First Sea Lord and Chief of the Naval Staff, for Great Britain. Both sides refused to compromise. Daniels and Benson wanted to expand the American navy as authorized in the Naval Appropriations Act of 1916. They thought the new League's success depended upon a balance between American and British naval strength. The United States, they contended, required a navy equal to the British navy to achieve its goals throughout the world.

This American claim for parity was precisely what Long and Wemyss opposed. Aware of the Republicans' friendly attitude, Long wanted to force the Wilson administration to acquiesce in "the supremacy of the seas" by Great Britain. To him it appeared contradictory for the president to advocate both the League and a larger American navy. Long warned Lloyd George that Wilson was trying "to make England play second fiddle" at the peace conference and that British representatives should do everything possible to prevent him from seizing first place. With the prime minister's approval, Long urged Daniels to reduce the American naval program by three battleships, leaving Great Britain with thirty-three battleships to twenty for the United States. The British navy would also have thirteen battle cruisers to six for the United States. By limiting the American fleet's size to sixty percent of Great Britain's, the British navy could remain equal to the combined naval strength of the United States and France. Lloyd George's argument that new American ships were superior in firepower failed to convince Daniels to accept numerical inferiority. Negotiations remained deadlocked.

Cecil and House regretted that Anglo-American naval rivalry endangered the League's prospects. They hoped to remove this obstacle, but neither of them intended to make any real concession. Cecil protested to Lloyd George that Long and Wemyss, by the confrontational method they were using, were most likely to antagonize Americans without reaching an agreement. He expressed keen disappointment that the prime minister seemed to have abandoned the future League. Rather than pursue this dangerous course, he wanted to separate naval policy from the Monroe Doctrine. Cecil warned Balfour that "the Prime Minister intends to use the League of Nations as a stick to beat the President with until he agrees with him about the Navy. Such a plan may succeed, but I am personally very doubtful of it." By alienating Americans, this tactic might cost Great Britain the political and especially economic assistance the United States might otherwise supply. It might also undermine Lloyd George's government if Parliament learned about its "fantastic" view of the American navy as a threat. Implicit in this assessment was the warning that Cecil himself might resign from the cabinet in protest over Lloyd George's lack of commitment to Anglo-American cooperation in the League. "I feel his policy to be exceedingly hazardous for the whole success of the League," concluded Cecil. ". . . It can only work with the hearty cooperation of the British and Americans."

Lloyd George, by now aware of the dangers of this impasse, authorized Cecil to negotiate a compromise with House. In their exchange of letters on April 8 and 9, which outlined the terms of an Anglo-American naval agreement, these two removed the controversy over naval policy as an obstacle to the League. Cecil reiterated the British contention that American naval expansion was inconsistent with the league idea. To avoid an arms race and promote friendship, he asked the American government to abandon its new naval program after signing the peace treaty. He also wanted assurances that in future years the United States would consult Great Britain about their respective naval programs. With Wilson's approval, House accepted these conditions but carefully excluded from the definition of a new naval program the American fleet as authorized by the Naval appropriations Act of 1916. Lloyd George desired a further promise that the United States would not build under the existing program any new ships that were not already under construction. Without making a commitment, House indicated American willingness to discuss this curtailment and the relative strengths of the two fleets after concluding peace. He especially stressed the president's determination to prevent a naval race with Great Britain. Although Lloyd George preferred a more explicit agreement, he now withdrew his opposition to a Monroe Doctrine amendment to the Covenant. After all, expansion under the current program would still leave the American navy less than two-thirds the size of the British fleet. The naval agreement preserved Anglo-American collaboration in creating the League.

New amendments to the Covenant produced more controversy in the League Commission. Reconvening to review the report of its drafting committee, it readily approved this committee's recommendation to change the name of the body of delegates to "the assembly," and that of the executive council to simply "the council." Problems arose when Bourgeois proposed French as the League's official language, with the French text of the Covenant as the binding version. Wilson ruled this amendment out of order. Both he and Cecil were determined that the English draft should be the Covenant's official text. As an addition to Article 10, the president introduced his amendment that international engagements, such as arbitration treaties or regional understandings like the Monroe Doctrine, would remain valid. This Monroe Doctrine amendment, he argued, would not prevent the League from acting in American affairs, nor would it prevent the United States from participating in European affairs. "The Covenant," he explained, "provided that the members of the League should mutually defend one another in respect of their political and territorial integrity. The Covenant was therefore the highest tribute to the Monroe Doctrine. It adopted the principle of the Monroe Doctrine as a world doctrine." Larnaude and Bourgeois voiced their fear that this amendment might allow the United States to refrain from joining other League members to stop aggression. It might, in effect, divide the League between the Old and New Worlds. Wilson passionately rejected this interpretation. He claimed that the Monroe Doctrine had provided "a successful barrier against the entrance of absolutism into North and South America." Now the United States sought to join other nations in extending "the movement of liberty" throughout the world. To alleviate French fears, Cecil suggested separating the Monroe Doctrine amendment from Article 10. Larnaude and Bourgeois eventually acquiesced in this arrangement, although they still preferred even greater assurances. The Monroe Doctrine amendment was adopted as the president desired.

Walter A. McDougall

Watch on the Rhine

Walter A. McDougall, professor of history at the University of Pennsylvania, treats in the following selection the abortive attempt by the French delegation to supplement what it regarded as the insufficient security guarantees afforded by the League with an independent buffer state in the Rhineland which would serve as a protective shield against German aggression. He summarizes the American and British objections to this unmistakable violation of Germany's right to self-determination and shows how France was compelled to sacrifice its goal of the "Rhine frontier."

When the Paris Peace Conference opened on 18 January 1919 there was no question that Clemenceau intended to fight for a peace of material guarantees against German resurgence. But he was equally intent on saving Allied unity. A balance of power could be restored by weakening the preponderant power, Germany, or by a permanent increase of the forces

From Walter A. McDougall, *France's Rhineland Diplomacy: The Last Bid for a Balance of Power in Europe,* 1987, pp. 57–72. Copyright © 1987 by Princeton University Press. Reprinted by permission of Princeton University Press. Footnotes omitted.

opposing her. This could only be accomplished by an Anglo-American commitment to the Continent. This solution meant heightened tensions, for it involved an escalation of the forces pressing down on the fulcrum of Central Europe, now and in the future. But an Allied commitment to Europe would form a solid base for the very world commitment Wilson would request of all nations through the League. As Wilson himself said, "In the next war there will be no neutrals." Finally, a peace based on Allied unity was a prerequisite for France's financial convalescence and economic recovery. Thus, for Clemenceau, if not for Foch, Poincaré, and the majority of French officials, the Rhine peace was negotiable.

The first weeks of the Peace Conference served to upset the Tiger's more sanguine plans. The League of Nations, it developed, would offer little for France. Though Germany would be excluded from the institution, Wilson refused to permit the League to be used as an anti-German institution for the enforcement of the peace. Clemenceau then argued that if the League was to be an effective deterrent against aggression, it must command armed force. But again he met immovable opposition, this time led by Britain and her Dominions. Given the heady public expectations of a New Jerusalem, perhaps no document could have won approval. But when the League Covenant was made public on 15 February, it was met with universal scorn in the French press and Chamber. Public opinion leaders Jacques Bainville, Léon Bourgeois, and President Poincaré renewed their call for a peace of material guarantees, and a wave of anti-Americanism washed over Paris.

The League could not be a vehicle, then, either for a punitive peace against Germany or for a "constructive" Western alliance. But Clemenceau did not despair of winning Anglo-American approval for French designs. He encouraged the press in the belief of "ralliement," that by steady pressure Wilson could be brought around. Government newspapers recalled that Wilson's political position at home was weak, and that the "people" he thought to serve demanded guarantees against German revenge. If the League was to be ineffective, that very fact strengthened the French case for a Rhenish peace, and Tardieu's staff labored throughout the League debates to marshal the arguments for German dismemberment.

The root justification of Rhenish separation was its value as a security guarantee. Thus, Tardieu was compelled to show the inadequacies of other security plans, particularly that to be embodied in the feeble League. His chief aide, Louis Aubert, attacked defensive alliances as ineffective material guarantees because of the gap between the moment of attack and the arrival of aid from overseas. Without the Rhine barrier to slow up a German "attaque brusque," modern weapons could bring a German army to the Channel in a matter of days, and Britain herself would be threatened. Alliances were a psychological deterrent only. The French military endorsed this analysis. France must never again be simply Britain's buffer on the Continent, she never again must provide the cannon fodder to throw up against an initial German onslaught. Foch's views are known, but in February, as the League Covenant was reaching completion, Émile Fayolle, commander of the two French armies on the Rhine, added his thoughts: "Wilson speaks of the League, but what can this hypothetical society do without a means of action? One promises alliances, but like all human things, alliances are fragile. . . . There will always come a time when Germany will have a free hand. Make all the alliances you like, but the highest necessity for France and Belgium is a material barrier."

Clemenceau did not share this contempt for alliances. It was Clemenceau above all who sought to put teeth into the League; it was Clemenceau who would accept the Anglo-American pact offered in March. But the requirements of European balance, in Eastern as well as Western Europe, meant that an Anglo-American commitment must encompass the Left Bank of the Rhine, the "jumping-off point" of three German invasions in a century, and either guarantee or permit France to guarantee, through access to the Rhine, the stability of the new nations in Eastern Europe. If the Anglo-Americans were intent on leaving Germany intact, they must be willing to commit themselves to her containment. It was not to annex or detach the Rhineland for the cause of French expansion, it was to convince *all* the Allies to remain on the Rhine that Clemenceau pleaded his case. Out of these considerations developed the first French note to the Peace Conference on the fixing of Germany's western border at the Rhine. The carefully reasoned thirty-four page document was based on the Foch program, but was drafted by Tardieu to include all the historical, cultural, economic, and strategic reasons for its adoption. Poincaré termed the famous brief "tout à fait remarquable." On 25 February 1919 Tardieu distributed the text to the Allied delegations, and the battle was joined.

The progression of events in the Rhineland negotiations of the Paris Peace Conference during the months of March and April is well known. Tardieu labeled this "la période héroique" during which he and Clemenceau stubbornly fought for and achieved a double guarantee of French security: military measures including a fifteen-year occupation of the Rhineland and a formal extension of the wartime alliance. But the strength and purpose they showed at the conference table masked a crisis in French strategy. For within the French camp, Clemenceau was the one who placed the highest value on the alliance, and his retreat from a strict Rhineland solution produced a crisis that damaged his prestige and embittered his colleagues and constituents. The reaction of the French Chamber, diplomatic corps, and military to Clemenceau's "surrender" in turn caused grave doubts among the Anglo-Americans as to the requirements of European political stabilization.

The British and Americans were content to listen in the first Rhineland conversations, as Tardieu explained the French position, and the latter came away with the impression that Rhenish independence was acceptable to the Allies. But Lloyd George's policy toward Germany was predicated on a variation of Wilsonian integrationism. Although his reparations policy would turn pro-German only after the 1920 slump clarified Britain's need for rapid German recovery, Lloyd George opposed increases in French power on the continent from the beginning. Grasping for principles to guide him through the era of stabilization, Lloyd George looked to British traditions: opposition to the continental victor of a general war; restoration of balance; control of the seas. France, not Germany, had to be restrained, and the availability of Wilsonian ideals, which implied German unity and economic revival, only made that task easier. Finally, the German revolution was viewed differently in the Foreign Office than in Paris. The Kaiser was gone, the republic must be encouraged, not only to promote peace and recovery, but to forestall Bolshevism.

On 14 March 1919 President Wilson and Lloyd George countered French demands for Rhenish separation with the offer of an Anglo-American guarantee to fight beside France against future German unprovoked aggression. The proffered alliance represented an abrupt break with the traditions of both powers, but in the context of the war just concluded and of Wilson's visions of the postwar world, the logic of the circumstances demanded such a departure. By offering an American alliance, Wilson merely anticipated the commitment America was eventually to make to all nations through the League. To Lloyd George, Rhenish separation would be a constant irritant to peace, a "new Alsace-Lorraine." The alliance would be a balm to French fears and a harness to French ambition.

Whatever the motives, the Anglo-American offer was a solemn pledge. Two days before Clemenceau had been "furious" with Lloyd George. Now he was "très ému." Returning to his office at the Ministry of War, he let Tardieu and Loucheur in on the "great secret," and explained the choice he had been given: stand alone on the Rhine against a vengeful Germany, or rely on distant allies. The following afternoon the three joined Pichon for a fateful interview. The foreign minister was skeptical of alliances. He feared lest France "turn aside from the prey to pursue the shadow," yet he did not see how the offer could be refused. Tardieu felt likewise. He saw the dangers of a permanent French occupation and believed the alliance offer must be accepted, but, he added, this solution did not preclude a return to a Rhineland policy in case of danger. Clemenceau was the most dispirited of all. France's postwar position would be tenuous at best, and the Tiger saw no potential leaders equal to the tasks ahead. In a funk, these four men charged with selecting the grand strategy for European security lacked confidence in either solution—and so they opted for both. Clemenceau instructed Tardieu to draft a new note. France would accept the alliances, but demand supplementary guarantees, including German disarmament, army reduction, demilitarization of the Rhine, and a postwar Allied occupation. Tardieu communicated these added demands to the British and Americans on 17 March. Lloyd George offered Rhenish demilitarization only, Clemenceau refused, and after a bitter exchange the British prime minister left for London with nothing accomplished.

What had become of the once sacred Rhineland separation plans of the French government? They were not entirely abandoned. Clemenceau's team had not made a clear choice between two courses so much as a decision to keep both options open. The dangers inherent in either policy—Western alliance or German dismemberment—were evident. As early as the summer of 1918 Loucheur had foreseen such a dilemma. "If the war ends at Berlin," he wrote, "it is possible the collapse of Germany will remove for a long time the danger of the German army. If, as seems more possible, after the military success of the Entente, we are obliged to make a peace of conditions, leaving Germany the possibility of rebuilding military force, the eventual situation will become grave for France." Though France's peacemakers saw the impossibility of refusing the alliances, they were unwilling to renounce hopes for a Rhenish policy that might ease the task of enforcing in perpetuity the "conditions" placed on Germany. Even as he retreated from the *separatist* plan in his response to the Allies, Tardieu invoked French intelligence of Rhenish *autonomism* and pleaded in the name of self-determination that the Big Three not frustrate the indigenous desire for autonomy from Prussia. A contemporary in-house memorandum declared:

If the idea of fixing the German boundary at the Rhine is abandoned, then the idea of an independent Rhenish state must also be abandoned. But as the idea of a special military regime is retained, the idea of an autonomous *state would best complete the overall conception. This plan, if it takes shape, would have almost all the advantages of an independent state without the inconveniences. . . .We would thus have: a) the supplementary guarantee of our two allies; b) the special military guarantee; c) a chance of attracting toward the French sphere a region that places itself on its own accord on the margin of Germany. The movement for an autonomous Rhenish Republic would appear at first glance to re-enter the general plan of our Rhenish policy.*

Once the dogma of separation had been questioned, iconoclasts appeared in number. Louis Aubert broached the thought that what France required was not so much a strong defensive posture as a means of preventing a war altogether. German dismemberment would make another war inevitable and without the Anglo-Americans France would be left dependent on a river line that military technology would surely find a means to break. A fifteen-year occupation combined with the alliances, however, would guarantee that France would not stand alone and would provide time for her to "cumulate her guarantees [on the Rhine and Eastern Europe, presumably]." The thoughts of the peace-making team were swinging back to the gradualist policy first advocated by the Quai d'Orsay. Berthelot, shut out of the proceedings, now saw the opportunity to press his point. France should be content with the military guarantees contained in Tardieu's note of 17 March. "And to augment the guarantees, one must pursue, *without rupturing German unity*, the separation of the Left Bank from Prussia and Bavaria." In a series of private drafts during the first days of April, Tardieu even considered reopening the whole Rhenish status question. He altered, deleted offensive passages, and in the end decided against a new Rhineland demarche, perhaps at Clemenceau's behest. His note of 4 April only repeated the demand for an occupation and supplementary guarantees. A Rhenish state, independent or autonomous, would not form part of the Versailles settlement. But the renewed interest in a policy of gradual penetration, made possible by an extended occupation, pointed to a policy of revision of the treaty in the future.

The details of France's tentative change of policy did not penetrate the shroud of silence surrounding the Peace Conference, but the fact of a change of strategy did; and it precipitated a second crisis in the French camp. The President of the Republic, the supreme commander, the

Chamber, and the Senate all reacted predictably. They were convinced that Clemenceau was abandoning the Rhine.

Concerned about the delays in peacemaking, Poincaré demanded on 17 March to know: "Where are we going? Are the Allies to fall into military inferiority? What is the progress of the conference; what is the policy of the government?" Under orders from Clemenceau, Pichon revealed nothing. Ten days later, Poincaré asked what had become of the security program outlined in Tardieu's first note. He had heard rumors that it was given up. Poincaré recalled the occupation by Germany of three French *départements* after 1871 as a guarantee of the indemnity. He wanted nothing less for France. The Rhineland must be occupied as long as reparations were due, at least thirty years. In addition, allowance must be made for the "docile" Rhenish population to carry out its desire for autonomy under French protection. When the President met with Clemenceau on 6 April, they came close to a final break. Poincaré fulminated against the Tiger's secrecy and accused him of suppressing the *procès-verbaux.* "I have the right to be informed," he shouted, "and the duty to express my opinion!"

Poincaré's irritation was shared by others in government. "Pichon knows, he understands," mourned Paul Cambon, "*mais quel entourage!* Our policy is in the hands of those petty young men who speak haughtily and turn all against us." By forcing France to give up the Rhine, wrote Cambon, Lloyd George hoped to assuage Germany. Nothing could be more dangerous. "I am ignorant of what has passed at Paris these last weeks," he complained, ". . . but if these hypotheses are exact, it [the British policy] contains the germs of profound misunderstandings between England and the continental allies." He urged that some system of defense on the Rhine be established.

Marshal Foch also moved to the attack when news reached him of a change in French policy. "To renounce the barrier of the Rhine," he bellowed, "would be to admit that unimaginable monstrosity of voluntarily granting Germany, soaked in the blood of her crimes, the possibility of beginning again." On 6 April Foch appealed for an opportunity to address the French delegation. Clemenceau told him to wait until the peace negotiations were over; then he could offer an opinion in his advisory role. Piqued, Foch blasted Allied policy again in an interview with the *Daily Mail,* and again Clemenceau reprimanded him for insubordination.

Foch then appealed to the *Parlement,* where the "war aims bloc" fretted anxiously in its impotence to guide French peacemaking. On 2

December 1918 the Foreign Affairs Commission of the Chamber had adopted a security program: no annexations, but the creation of a "special regime" on the Left Bank of the Rhine and demilitarization of the Right Bank. When Foch's peace plan was made known, a large portion of the French Center and Right accepted it without question. But the deputies had refrained from interpellating the government during the conference on the assumption that the government would accept nothing less. Now there was some doubt. On 14 April a Chamber delegation led by Radical leader René Renoult reminded Clemenceau in person that the Chamber would settle for nothing less than "immediate and material guarantees of French security," including "the organization of a solid frontier." Another deputy, André Lebey, implied in a letter to Clemenceau that the premier no longer enjoyed the full confidence of the Chamber. Lebey advised that the premier abandon his secrecy and appear before the parliament. Clemenceau refused.

Two days later the *Petit Journal,* of which Stephen Pichon himself was a political editor, reported that the British and Americans had agreed to enter an alliance with France. The article went on to quote the *New York Times,* explaining that the American president had no authority to make such a treaty. The French Senate now took initiative. Paul Doumer proposed a resolution insisting that the government "demand instantly the insertion into the treaty of the military guarantees indicated by the Supreme Commander [Foch]." Pichon responded from the tribune on 18 April. Such a resolution would subordinate the civil power to the military and was unthinkable. He threatened to pose the question of confidence, and the senators shied from reversing a government in mid-crisis. Pichon promised that Foch would have a chance to address the Peace Conference. The parliamentary revolt simmered and Clemenceau remained in control of the negotiations. But the premier's exclusivity produced a bitter fruit. The guarantees Clemenceau pursued against determined resistance were condemned by his countrymen before they were even achieved.

French officials on the Rhine were equally disappointed by rumors of Clemenceau's shift on the Rhenish question. The difference in their case was that they had the means to act on their own. When Tirard and Foch repeated their plea for instructions at the beginning of March, Clemenceau's private secretary, Jules Jeanneney, went no further than approval for the obscure "measures" taken in January. Jeanneney enclosed another note from Pichon, remarkable for its obscurity:

> *It is opportune to demonstrate to the populations of the occupied terri-*
> *tories that their prosperity does not necessarily depend on relations with*
> *the German territories of the Right Bank. . . . It remains to profit from*
> *this circumstance. The Rhenish people seem prepared to bow before the*
> *decision of the Allies relative to their fate. It is without doubt the uncer-*
> *tainty of their position that favors in certain circles a current of thought*
> *in the contrary sense.*

The French military authorities could only conclude that once again they had no instructions.

His patience worn thin by the tergiversations of Paris, General Fayolle, commander of the two French armies on the Rhine, acted on his own authority. On 10 March he ordered his army commanders, Generals Augustin Gérard and Charles Mangin, to adopt a new posture vis-à-vis Rhenish politics. Up to the present, Fayolle wrote, occupation policy had not prejudged the future, but the moment had arrived "to go a step farther and prepare the solutions that we deem favorable." He instructed the generals to encourage separatist tendencies by appealing to moral and material interests. Betraying the universal French misunderstanding of Rhenish separatism, he added: "It is necessary to allay all fears of annexation. The countries of the Left Bank will remain free to group themselves according to race, historical laws, and economic advantage, and be free to govern themselves." Plans for a unique West German republic or states encompassing both banks of the Rhine were to be discouraged. Until publication of the peace, Fayolle declared, these were the grand lines of French policy.

Fayolle's orders were in defiance of the principles governing the interallied occupation. He did not inform Paris of his act, but he and General Weygand of Foch's staff did solicit approval for local involvement in Rhenish affairs. They invoked the political immaturity of the Rhenish people and told the Quai d'Orsay that precise directives were needed so that the army might respond to Rhenish "offers of cooperation."

Clemenceau had not given up his hopes for a negotiated separation of the Rhineland only that frustrated generals should foment a revolution. Provocative interference in German internal politics could destroy the compromise being worked out by the Big Three. Besides, the time was not ripe. Colonel Requin, Tardieu's assistant, rebuffed another appeal from Tirard, who felt the Rhenish notables were ready to break with Germany. "No! The moderate parties only desire autonomy. This is already something, but one cannot say they are *acquis à l'idée de sépara-tion.*" Thus, the split in French councils became evident. The military sought separation, as an immediate goal. The government now would be content with autonomy, and as a long-term goal. Despairing of support from Paris, and afraid that Clemenceau was abandoning the Rhine, the generals determined to act.

With Fayolle's blessing, and unbeknownst to Paris, General Gérard in the Palatinate and General Mangin on the middle Rhine began collaboration with the diehard separatists. The months of April to June 1919 witnessed a blind race in which Clemenceau and the generals completed to finish their work before the other. Signature of a peace recognizing German unity would kill the chances of a Rhenish separatist *fait accompli*. But a putsch with French involvement might kill British agreement to the guarantees Clemenceau labored to achieve.

"Very well," muttered Lloyd George, "I accept." On 22 April 1919 he and Woodrow Wilson submitted to the alternate French security formula. They pledged to defend France against future German aggression and granted supplementary guarantees: German disarmament, reduction of the German army to 100,000 men, demilitarization of a zone fifty kilometers east of the Rhine. Finally, they approved a fifteen-year occupation of the Left Bank of the Rhine with four bridgeheads across the river at Cologne, Coblenz, Mainz, and Kehl. If the treaty were fulfilled, evacuation would proceed in three five-year stages. The occupation was not carried as a guarantee of security, but as a pledge of German disarmament, reparations, and adherence to the other clauses of the treaty. The Anglo-American security pacts would guarantee French security. But, sensitive to criticism that alliances were transitory, Clemenceau now drove the final nail into the treaty structure: a guarantee of the guarantee. On the very day of Lloyd George's submission, Tardieu sprung a new demand, approved by the Allies during the last week of deliberation, as Articles 429 and 430 of the treaty with Germany. If, at the end of fifteen years, the guarantees against an unprovoked aggression by Germany were not deemed sufficient by any of the Allied governments, the evacuation of the occupation troops might be delayed.

How far had Clemenceau retreated from the Foch Rhineland scheme of November 1918? He had given up a permanent Rhineland occupation for a temporary one. He had given up Rhenish separation, but he retained in the occupation the means to carry on French penetration and propaganda. Rhenish autonomy was still a possible future goal. He received the Anglo-American guarantees. But the interallied occupation itself was an alliance of sorts, since a hostile action by Germany in the west would necessarily be directed against the flags of all the Allies. What, then, was the value of the pacts? To the French, they were a declaration of permanent Anglo-French-American solidarity, committing the Allies to cooperation in the defense of the treaty, even if force were required. But the Americans and British had a different view of the arrangement. The pacts were meant to restrain France in the use of force, to permit her to be liberal in the application of the treaty. This misunderstanding was the measure of the retreat Clemenceau had made since November 1918, and it rendered ambiguous the system under which European political stabilization was to proceed.

Clemenceau's critics within the government rued this misunderstanding. Paul Cambon feared the erosion of the Anglo-French Entente and Poincaré foresaw the isolation of France. If conflict not only with Germany but with the Anglo-Americans as well was to be avoided, the prerogatives of France and the understanding of the Allies must be clearly defined. Resigned to the alliance-plus-guarantees system, Poincaré made one last effort to secure Allied recognition of French vital interests. It is indispensable, he explained, to cite as *casus foederis* any default by Germany in the execution of the treaty of peace, and Britain must be brought to anticipate the possibility of acts of coercion by France to collect reparations. Above all, the danger would be terrible if France abandoned the territorial guarantee for alliances not yet voted by the American Senate and British Parliament. A limit to the Rhineland occupation must be set only after the pacts were in force.

Poincaré peered into the future with remarkable lucidity. If the occupation did not last as long as reparations, it would encourage Germany to delay execution until the pressure disappeared, while Allied cooperation in case of German default was a dangerous assumption. Finally, the treaty's ratification of Germany unity was another time bomb against Allied unity. If Clemenceau wished to preserve German federalism or Rhenish autonomy as a goal of policy, then recognition of German boundaries destroyed hopes for German political evolution within the Versailles system.

Poincaré seems to have foreseen the diplomatic deadlock of the postwar years. He thought of the treaty not as an abstract system, but as a workable blueprint. He asked how it would survive in practice. He expected Germany to default—precautions were taken. But he expected the British and Americans to "default" as well, if they were not brought to a common interpretation of the alliance. Was this too much to ask in May 1919? The negotiators could hardly be expected to divine the interests of their nations several years in advance, or to sacrifice future freedom of action. There was neither time nor prescience to allow the "resolution of forces, the association of interests" of Clemenceau's vision to operate on the treaty itself. Interpretation and definition of the Allied commitments would be the work of five years of conferences and conflicts. The Treaty of Versailles was only a declaration of intent and it set the powers on a collision course.

The peace satisfied few in the French government, but it was the Tiger's obsession with authority and secrecy that encouraged explanations of failure in which he bore sole responsibility. One of the premier's own peace delegates, Jules Cambon, excoriated his chief for the failure to separate the Rhineland, to "undo the artificial works of the Congress of Vienna without which Prussia would never have been a neighbor." Berthelot despised the practice by which the Big Three decided everything. "As often as possible we prepared notes for Pichon — they rarely left his office." Paul Cambon labeled the Big Three "this trinity, which sees nothing, knows nothing, foresees nothing." Camille Barrère was furious that "French ministers were shut out. Absolute secrecy, a rigorous censorship. The Rhine frontier was abandoned in unknown circumstances. This river which meant so much yesterday is *peu de chose* today. I'm told the Rhine defends nothing." Barrère and Minister of Marine Georges Leygues advocated going over the heads of the Big Three to the British and American people. The justice and simplicity of the French cause could not fail to win out before the jury of peoples. "If [Clemenceau] had wished it," Barrère wrote, "England and America would have ceded on the Rhine frontier." But the Tiger, he surmised, was not up to the effort, being eighty years of age and weakened by the assassin's bullet of 19 February. In March Italian delegate Baron Sonnino found Clemenceau "extremely fatigued, no longer the same man."

Could France have won the Rhine frontier with a different strategy? Or could Clemenceau have won popular acquiescence in abandonment of the Rhine? If the Tiger had included the diplomatic establishment and the *Parlement* in the task of peacemaking, he could have brought them to understand, perhaps, the extent of Allied opposition. But he would not then have been Clemenceau — and a weaker premier might not have been able to stand before the internal opposition to the course he was taking. The irony of the Rhenish question at Paris was that the only man capable of bucking the tide of French opinion and preventing the division of the West before the enemy was incapable of inspiring domestic confidence in his peace. When he left office in January 1920, even after a lengthy exposé before the Chambers, Clemenceau left bourgeois France with the conviction that the Rhine was the French peace, and that it had been abandoned.

"France follows a policy of suicide," declared Barrère. "She marches toward the abyss, and Clemenceau is responsible." With no formula for financial reconstruction, no definitive solution to the Rhenish question, the alliance was a fleshless skeleton, and Germany would be the beneficiary. "For the guarantor powers," Barrère told Berthelot, "the treaty is a piece of paper; for us it is an instrument of servitude. . . . C'était bien la paix boche." [It was the German peace.]

"Oui," Berthelot replied, "c'est la paix boche."

The dangers inherent in the ambiguous alliance became swiftly apparent. French military collaboration with the separatists, begun after Fayolle's orders in March, reached fruition during the nervous period between release of the draft treaty of 7 May and its signature on 28 June. Although the harsh terms caused alarm in Germany and led some Rhenish businessmen to reconsider separatism, the overall response in the Rhineland was relief. The Rhineland was not to be annexed or made a French satellite. Tirard noted a "severe retreat" in separatist ideas. Levy Bruhl was the first to draw the proper conclusion: "Creation of a Rhenish Republic would seem to have been, in the thought of its Centrist partisans, only an artifice to avoid annexation by the enemy."

To the generals in Rhineland, publication of the draft treaty meant that time was running out. General Mangin, patron of Dr. Dorten since April, complained that the treaty would leave the separatists no legal means to proceed. On 17 May he received ten leading separatists, including Kastert and Dorten, and suggested that the only means of action was to confront the Peace Conference with a *fait accompli*. The same day, General Gérard met with twenty-one Palatine "notables," advocates of separation from Bavaria. The Bavarian prefect von Winterstein promptly arrested the dissidents and was himself expelled from occupied territory by Gérard. The *Freie Pfalz* then planned a putsch of its own.

Mangin and Dorten in the north and Gérard and the Palatine leader, Dr. Eberhard Haas, plotted their actions for the end of May. On 29 May Foch ordered all occupying forces to abandon the policy of aloofness, which only benefitted the "Pangermanist Prussian and Bavarian bureaucracies." His orders were "not to become involved in internal politics . . . but to permit no barrier to the liberty of the peoples to dispose of themselves."

Clemenceau took immediate measures upon hearing of possible cabals on the Rhine. He sent Jeanneney on a fact-finding mission to discern the damage done and to forbid military indiscretions. The Weimar Assembly was threatening to reject the treaty; it must be given no encouragement to defy the Allies. Clemenceau granted that "the Rhenish populations are no doubt oppressed by Prussian functionaries," but he reminded Mangin of the limits of military authority. He ordered strict nonintervention in Rhenish affairs. The next day the separatists launched their putsch.

The scenario envisioned by Haas and Dorten, working independently of each other, was farfetched. They believed that the "almost unanimous support" bottled up since Adenauer's "defection" would express itself, once a republic was proclaimed. The Peace Conference must then recognize the Rhenish states on grounds of self-determination. But the putsches were comic in their ineptitude. Haas seized the government palace in Speyer, but before he could deliver his proclamation he was dragged to the street by a crowd. Gérard's cavalry came to the rescue, but the coup was over in fifteen minutes. Dorten fared no better. His posters proclaiming the Rhenish Republic and his own provisional government ignited a general strike in protest. After an abortive effort to seize the government palace in Wiesbaden, the Rhenish Republic evaporated.

The 1 June putsches had ramifications in Paris out of proportion to their importance in the Rhineland. They provided a preview of the conflicts left unresolved between France and Germany, between France and her Allies, and within the French government itself. When Dorten moved on 1 June, Mangin wired Poincaré with the "good news." Poincaré urged Clemenceau to support the putsch. He saw "nothing in it to upset President Wilson," since it was an act of self-determination. There was plenty to upset Clemenceau. His generals had defied him again, apparently in league with Poincaré. And the results he feared arrived quickly. On 2 June the chief of the German delegation in Paris, Ulrich von Brockdorff-Rantzau, protested venomously. France must choose, he said, between the hope of reparations or the fashioning of friendly republics, by which she would sacrifice her treaty rights.

Lloyd George saw his own fears realized before the Germans had even signed the treaty. French occupation of the Rhineland, whether for one year, fifteen, or fifty, meant ceaseless intrigue and efforts at disguised annexation. Already struck by the harsher aspects of the treaty and by fear that the Germans would not sign, Lloyd George redoubled his last-minute efforts to revise the treaty in Germany's favor, including renunciation of the occupation. Clemenceau disowned the putsches, but refused to sacrifice the fifteen-year occupation. On 28 June 1919, when the German delegation signed the Treaty of Versailles, world war and peace were concluded in a spirit of suspicion and foreboding, not reconciliation and new hope.

William R. Keylor; Antony Lentin

The Futile Bid to Create an Atlantic Security System

One of the critical components of the compromise settlement that induced France to abandon its campaign to sever the Rhineland from Germany was the unprecedented commitment by the United States and Great Britain to defend France against unprovoked aggression from Germany. In the follow-ing selections William R. Keylor of Boston University and Antony Lentin of the Open University examine this often-neglected feature of the peace settlement and explain how and why it was never implemented.

The Rise and Demise of the Franco-American Guarantee Pact, 1919–1921

William R. Keylor

Since the opening of the French archives for the post–World War I period in the 1970s, several important studies have appeared on both sides of the Atlantic that trace the deterioration of the Franco-American wartime entente in the years after the armistice of 1918. Most of these

From William R. Keylor, "The Rise and Demise of the Franco-American Guarantee Pact, 1919–1921," *Proceedings of the Annual Meeting of the Western Society for French History*, 15 (1988), 367–373. Reprinted with permission. Footnotes omitted.

From Antony Lentin, "The Treaty That Never Was: Lloyd George and the Abortive Anglo-French Alliance of 1919," Judith Loades, ed., *The Life and Times of David Lloyd George* (Bangor: Headstart History, 1991, pp. 115–128). Reprinted by permission of Antony Lentin. Footnotes omitted.

works have concentrated on the economic side of the relationship, presenting fresh evidence and insights that have forced us to revise long-established assumptions about such familiar sources of transatlantic acrimony as war debts, reparations, trade protectionism, and private American financial policies in postwar France.

Very little scholarly attention, however, has been devoted to the security aspects of the Franco-American partnership as it gradually unravelled during the critical period of transition from war to peace. Apart from a book published thirty years ago, long before the relevant French archives were declassified, the only scholarly treatment of this subject is an article by an American historian who relies entirely on English-language sources and addresses it from a purely American perspective. This retrospective disinterest on the part of historians is all the more remarkable in light of the overwhelming importance that French policymakers at the time had attached to the preservation of the wartime security relationship with the United States that had assured victory in the Great War. This scholarly oversight can be rectified by examining one of the most significant, yet one of the most neglected, episodes in the history of Franco-American relations after the Great War: the controversy surrounding the bilateral security pact that was jointly endorsed by President Woodrow Wilson and Premier Georges Clemenceau at the peace conference of 1919.

The Franco-American security treaty was the outcome of a sharp disagreement among the three principal allied leaders that had surfaced in early spring 1919. As is well known, France's almost paranoid security concerns vis-à-vis Germany had prompted its delegates to propose very early in the peace deliberations what was called a "geographical" solution to its sense of vulnerability. This famous plan, proposed by Marshal Ferdinand Foch and strongly supported by a broad spectrum of French official and public opinion, called for the political separation of the Rhineland from Germany, the establishment of an independent French client state there, and the permanent Allied military occupation of the bridgeheads at the four main river crossings. It soon became evident that this scheme was entirely unacceptable to both the American and British delegations — to the Americans because it undeniably violated the cherished Wilsonian principle of national self-determination, and to the British, because it seemed to ensure perpetual German opposition to the peace settlement by creating, in Lloyd George's memorable phrase, an "Alsace-Lorraine in reverse." The resulting deadlock threatened to block all further progress in the Paris negotiations. Meanwhile, intense apprehension about the domestic consequences of further delays in the restoration of peace-time conditions was evident in all countries concerned, as the heads of government were deluged with insistent calls for speedier demobilization, sweeping social reform, and higher standards of living.

While the British Prime Minister and American President were absent from the conference to attend to these and other pressing problems at home during the second half of February and the first half of March 1919, their two trusted confidants, Philip Kerr and Colonel Edward House, began to explore a novel and quite unprecedented scheme for allaying French security concerns without violating the territorial integrity of defeated Germany. Clemenceau's right-hand-man André Tardieu joined these exploratory conversations early on and became the de facto French spokesman after Clemenceau was incapacitated by an assassin's bullet on 19 February. Whereas Kerr and Tardieu dutifully kept their chiefs fully informed of these exploratory conversations from the very beginning, the headstrong, self-confident House, who fancied himself a master at conciliation, appears to have kept Wilson entirely in the dark.

When Wilson returned to Paris on 14 March, an extraordinarily expeditious resolution of the impasse unfolded: Lloyd George proposed to him the broad outlines of a project for an Anglo-American guarantee for France as a substitute for Foch's Rhineland scheme. Wilson promptly accepted it without reservation and without consulting any members of his delegation, and the two jointly offered it verbally to a surprised Clemenceau later in the day. After a blizzard of memoranda from Tardieu insistently reiterating the case for the Rhine frontier and permanent military occupation of the bridgeheads failed to budge the two "Anglo-Saxon" leaders, the French finally threw in the towel on 14 April, one month to the day after the alternative of the Anglo-American guarantee had been proposed. Though warning he would face a bitter struggle with his military chiefs, Clemenceau accepted as "sufficient" the two bilateral security pacts on the condition that they be reinforced by a set of constraints on German sovereignty in the Rhineland, including a temporary allied military occupation of the region including the bridgeheads on the right bank.

All three parties to this agreement were careful to protect themselves against contingencies that they might regret. Anticipating the possibility of legislative rejection of either or both of these treaties, the French premier obtained Wilson's recognition of France's right to prolong the temporary military occupation of the Rhineland should the guarantees of

French security prove insufficient at the end of the prescribed fifteen-year period. The crafty Lloyd George took the precaution of ensuring that Great Britain would not be left out on a limb as France's lone protector by inserting a clause in the Anglo-French guarantee pact subordinating it to the coming into force of its Franco-American counterpart. Wilson, sensitive to complaints that these two supplementary agreements might be regarded as evidence of the unreliability of the League of Nations and therefore detract from the prestige of his beloved brainchild, secured specific recognition of the League's jurisdictional authority in both the Anglo-French and Franco-American pacts.

What was the broader significance of this remarkable turn of events? From the French perspective, it meant that Clemenceau had abandoned the Rhenish strategy that had been urged on him by Foch and President Poincaré in favor of the Anglo-American guarantees. This policy shift was confirmed when he declined to tender support to the Rhenish separatists who staged an abortive coup d'état in early June with the tacit encouragement of French military officers on the spot. Clemenceau's testimony before the parliamentary commission considering the peace treaties revealed that he considered the security entente with the two English-speaking powers a more effective guarantee for France than the geographical barrier represented by the proposed Rhenish buffer state.

To understand why this was so, it may be instructive to assess France's security dilemma from a more contemporary perspective. What France in effect had obtained from the American president was the pledge of what we would today call "extended deterrence." This now-familiar defense concept represented at that time an unprecedented linkage of American security interests with those of France. Unlike the old prewar alliances and alignments which were shrouded in secrecy and ambiguity, this security agreement was publicly announced and explicitly formulated. It represented an unmistakable warning to Germany that the costs of future unprovoked aggression would include an immediate American intervention on France's behalf. As was to be the case with the North Atlantic Treaty after the Second World War, such a pledge was intended as much to reassure the nervous protégé as to deter the putative aggressor. It would probably have gone a long way toward calming the fears of the war-weary French—obsessed with their demographic inferiority and geographic vulnerability—thereby enhancing the prospects for Franco-German reconciliation and Europe-wide peace.

At first glance it appears that both parties to this compromise solution had forfeited a great deal by acquiescing in it. France seemed to have sacrificed a tangible barrier to aggression from across the Rhine in exchange for an intangible pledge of military assistance from across the Atlantic to repel such aggression. But on closer analysis it becomes evident that, even apart from the prospect of provoking Anglo-American hostility, France's original Rhenish policy would have produced a set of exceedingly costly consequences. Above all, the financial and man-power burdens that France would have had to bear in order to mount a permanent watch on the Rhine from a pro-French buffer state might well have proved overwhelming in an era of budgetary emergency and demographic decline. Contrary to its popular image of belligerence, the postwar French political elite did not exult in the prospect of increased military spending and the maintenance of large standing armies on a wartime footing. Vociferous demands for reductions in government spending and the acceleration of demobilization greeted cabinet ministers at their every appearance before parliamentary commissions. Moreover, a coercive policy on the Rhine would have foreclosed the option of an economic rapprochement with Germany that some French officials were contemplating as early as the opening weeks of the peace conference. Considered within the context of these manifold domestic pressures in France, the unconditional American security guarantee represented a remarkably painless alternative to bigger defense budgets and longer terms of military service, not to speak of the unremitting political and economic warfare with Germany that would most certainly have resulted from the forcible detachment of the Rhineland.

From the French point of view, in other words, multilateral deterrence not only promised to be cheaper and less disruptive than unilateral coercion at a time of grave domestic weakness, but it also had the advantage of preserving at least the principle of the anti-German entente that would have been abruptly shattered if Marshal Foch and his civilian supporters had their way. With the United States committed to the defense of France against unprovoked military aggression—the only nation in the world to which such protection had been promised—it was much more likely that the protector might be persuaded at some future date to reconsider its rejection of earlier French proposals for the preservation of the wartime economic entente through the pooling of raw materials, the establishment of a world reparation fund, the cancellation of interallied war debts, and the like.

But all these real or potential advantages that France stood to gain from the proposed agreement would remain purely academic unless two questions could be answered in the affirmative: would the American guarantee represent an effective deterrent to German aggression; and would it obtain the requisite consent of the United States Senate, despite the radical departure from American tradition that it entailed?

A conclusive answer to the first question is difficult to provide because of the paucity of evidence that the operational aspects of the American guarantee to France were ever explored in detail by military experts in either nation. Wilson and Lloyd George tendered their joint offer to Clemenceau without ever informing, let alone consulting, their respective military advisers. Provisions for joint staff talks, prior coordination of strategy and tactics, and the sharing of intelligence information concerning German military plans were never discussed at any stage of the negotiations. Though some French legislators later raised the logistical problem of transporting American forces to France on short notice in fulfillment of the guarantee, this question seems to have been ignored by the negotiators at the peace conference. The unmistakable signs that the United States was rapidly demobilizing its expeditionary force and replacing its Europe-first strategy of "coalition defense" against Germany with a unilateralist policy combining the aggressive pursuit of American interests in the Caribbean with maritime expansion in the Pacific—though faithfully reported by the French military attaché in Washington—did not cause officials in Paris to wring their hands with doubts about the efficacy of the American guarantee of France's eastern frontier.

The explanation for this equanimity is not difficult to determine: Simply put, the French did not at that time feel that they needed the Americans to protect them from a sudden military offensive from the east—the famous "attaque brusquée" that was later to preoccupy French strategists in the 1930s. The precautionary restrictions on Germany's offensive military capability that had been written into the peace treaty—particularly the provisions concerning disarmament, inspection, and the demilitarization of the Rhineland—had effectively addressed that contingency. Statesmen no less than generals tend to fight the last war, and the last war for France had meant not military collapse in six weeks caused by a "bolt from the blue," but rather gradual economic decline over four years of stalemate and attrition. To avoid a repetition of France's recent pyrrhic victory, what was required—and what the Franco-American security pact seemed to promise—was either that the American pledge to intervene would deter Germany from risking a showdown with France, or that the American intervention in the event of such aggression, albeit delayed because of the geographic and strategic reasons cited above, would eventually bring with it the imposing arsenal of American financial and economic resources that had been accorded gratis to France during the common wartime effort but had been abruptly withdrawn after the armistice.

If we turn from the subject of the *effectiveness* of the American guarantee to the question of its *acceptability* to the American people as reflected in the attitudes of their elected representatives in the Senate, the evidence for optimism is even more compelling. What may have originally seemed a risky, costly commitment of American military power and economic resources to the defense of France came to be recognized as a relatively light burden. Apart from the token and temporary American military contingent that was assigned to show the flag in the inter-Allied occupation force in the Rhineland, the United States was obliged to furnish neither money nor men to reinforce its security pledge. It was the *promise* to tap America's vast *potential* military and technological might to discourage German aggression, not the actual deployment of pre-positioned combat forces to participate in the defense of France, that formed the underpinning of the security pact. In contemporary strategic language, deterrence rather than warfighting was the underlying objective. And in that happy era, when the policy of extended deterrence carried with it no risk whatsoever of retaliation against the American homeland, the security costs to the United States were nonexistent.

It is therefore scarcely surprising that the Franco-American security pact was the least controversial of all of the precedent-shattering agreements that President Wilson brought home with him from Paris. Apart from a handful of "irreconcilables" who opposed any American involvement anywhere in the world, the French pact enjoyed widespread support among Republicans in the Senate. Many of the most vociferous opponents of the League of Nations, who were repelled by the ambiguous, seemingly limitless global undertakings that membership in such a body implied, were prepared to support this precisely defined and geographically circumscribed obligation to defend America's recent wartime associate. Senate Republican leader Henry Cabot Lodge, a staunch supporter of the French security treaty, promised his old friend, French Ambassador Jules Jusserand, that the pact would receive prompt legislative consideration and repeatedly predicted its ratification.

The same optimistic message was conveyed to Paris through other channels by several prominent Democrats, confirming the bipartisan consensus on behalf of the pact. Indeed, this appears to be one of the few matters on which the Wilson and Lodge camps agreed throughout the bitter months of debate over the League. Jusserand remained convinced that Wilson's motivation for inexplicably failing to submit the guarantee treaty to the Senate simultaneously with the League of Nations Covenant—despite a clause in the treaty requiring him to do so—was his fear that the juxtaposition of the two documents might tempt the Senators to endorse the popular French treaty and then defer consideration of the much more controversial League Covenant. When pressure from Republican supporters of the pact finally compelled the president to place it before the Senate nineteen days late, its chances for acceptance seemed excellent. Amid the increasingly vituperative public debate about the constitutionality of article ten of the League Covenant, Jusserand was able to report to Paris that a subcommittee of the Senate Judiciary Committee had unanimously affirmed that the French security pact did not violate the constitution. The British parliament's enthusiastic endorsement of the Anglo-French guarantee with scarcely a word of debate, followed by the formal exchange of ratifications on 20 November, reinforced the sense of momentum.

But as the French embassy in Washington mounted its campaign on behalf of the treaty, a potential complication appeared in the form of article three, inserted at Wilson's behest in Paris, which had established a connection between the guarantee pact and the League of Nations. Lodge and other Republican supporters of the French treaty had long urged that the two issues be considered separately, and there were no obvious legal or constitutional reasons why they should not be. The two references to the new international organization in the security treaty provided for the League Council's registration of the treaty and empowered it to determine when the League's capability of protecting France from aggression was sufficient to permit the special bilateral pact to lapse. But neither of these stipulations required American membership in the projected world body. Indeed, the entire raison d'être of the separate Franco-American agreement was to compensate for the anticipated insufficiency of the League's peacekeeping machinery to alleviate French security concerns.

Politically, however, the matter was exceedingly delicate and complicated. Jusserand confronted the challenging task of retaining Republican support for the French treaty by pressing for the deletion of the offensive (though probably innocuous) reference to the League, while at the same time taking care not to antagonize the president by giving the impression that France was making common cause with his domestic political enemies. He managed this with the skill that one might have expected from the dean of the Washington diplomatic corps who had swum the Potomac with Teddy Roosevelt and crossed the Atlantic with

Woodrow Wilson. Unable to press his case directly with the ailing, incommunicado chief executive, Jusserand cautiously approached—with Lodge's foreknowledge and blessing—a succession of potential intermediaries, including Vice President Marshall, Secretary of State Lansing, Senate Democratic Leader Hitchcock, and Wilson's personal secretary, Joseph Tumulty. All expressed support for the French treaty and promised to do what they could to facilitate its passage by arranging for its separate consideration without the debilitating article three. Some of them, such as Hitchcock and Lansing, had earlier criticized the guarantee treaty as incompatible with the spirit of collective security but had apparently come to recognize the wisdom of trying to salvage at least the French guarantee treaty amid the wreckage of the League Covenant on Capitol Hill. As he orchestrated the bipartisan campaign on behalf of the treaty, shuttling frantically between sympathetic leaders in both camps, the French ambassador received repeated assurances that Wilson would never dare to withhold his signature from a treaty from which article three had been removed, regardless of the fate of the League in the Senate.

As it turned out, Wilson never had to confront the issue of a Franco-American bilateral alliance cut adrift from the League of Nations. Lodge and his fellow opponents of the League were never required to make good their promises to France either. The Franco-American security pact was rejected neither by the American president who had signed it nor by the Republican senators who had endorsed it. Its death was as mysterious as its birth. Just as it seemed to have emerged from nowhere in Paris, without preliminary preparation or discussion, it seemed to have disappeared with hardly a trace in Washington. Not only was it never debated on the floor of the Senate, it was never even discussed in the Foreign Relations Committee. From time to time the French embassy would discreetly inquire after it and some friendly Washington official would offer the customary word of encouragement. As late as January 1921 Jusserand was still entertaining the fantasy that the incoming Harding Administration might be induced to reconsider this bit of unfinished business between the two countries.

In the meantime, John Bull had eagerly grasped the opportunity afforded by Uncle Sam's failure to arrive at the church on time to repudiate his own matrimonial intentions, leaving Marianne insecure, querulous, and alone. As we have seen, this latter flirtation waxed and waned for several years after the end of the Paris Peace Conference. But by that time it had become evident that the memory of Marianne's and Sam's courtship had virtually vanished from the consciousness of both families. In the summer of 1923, when the archival section of the Quai d'Orsay undertook an internal review of the history of this episode, it was discovered that there was no record in the files of the negotiations that had produced the agreement. On the American side, in the year 1935, more than fifteen years after Sam had left Marianne stranded at the altar, some clerk discovered the unfulfilled marriage banns gathering dust in a pigeon hole of the Senate Foreign Relations Committee and thoughtfully returned the papers to the State Department. By that time, of course, many of the apprehensions that had prompted the insecure Marianne to seek solace and safety in the arms of her sturdy but fickle transatlantic swain had been confirmed. But Sam had long since ceased to care.

The Treaty that Never Was: Lloyd George and the Abortive Anglo-French Alliance of 1919

Antony Lentin

I

On the morning of 28 June, 1919, the day of the signing of the Treaty of Versailles, Lloyd George, for Britain, and Clemenceau, for France, set their hands to another international agreement, to all appearances hardly less momentous than the former in the postwar settlement of Europe. This was an Anglo-French alliance, or treaty of guarantee to France, stipulating that "Great Britain agrees to come immediately to her assistance in the event of any unprovoked movement of aggression against her being made by Germany." Ratification by Britain followed in July, when Lloyd George and Curzon successfully steered it through Parliament as the Anglo-French Treaty (Defence of France) Act 1919. In the autumn, Clemenceau likewise secured approval from the National Assembly. Formal ratifications were exchanged between London and Paris in November. A new era of Anglo-French solidarity seemed to have been inaugurated. A month later, the treaty no longer existed, except as a historical memory. Britain's guarantee to France, which Clemenceau described as "nothing less than the ultimate sanction of the Peace Treaty" and "the keystone of European peace," turned out to be a damp squib, a half-forgotten footnote in the annals of the Paris Peace Conference.

Most historians have been content to leave it at that: an unfortunate mishap in Lloyd George's foreign policy, a bold but ill-fated initiative, frustrated by circumstances ultimately beyond his control. The failure of the alliance to become operative, it will be remembered, was occasioned by the failure of the United States Senate to ratify an analogous American treaty of guarantee, which President Wilson had signed on the same day and in the same ceremony as that in which Lloyd George committed Britain to the side of France. Blame for this débâcle tends therefore to fall on Wilson for his political ineptness in failing to secure senatorial approval, rather than on Lloyd George. There were, it is true, critics like Lord Hardinge of the Foreign Office, who singled out the Anglo-French treaty as the most egregious of Lloyd George's attempts to run foreign policy as a "one man band"; and who fulminated against his airy indifference to the professionals, and the ready resort to "stunts" and spur-of-the-moment improvisations which the Permanent Under-Secretary was not alone in seeing as characteristic of Lloyd George's conduct of foreign affairs. "I doubt if any treaty of such vital and far-reaching importance," he wrote, "has ever been negotiated in such a thoughtless and light-hearted manner." Now whether justified or not—and as this essay hopes to demonstrate, Lloyd George's underlying approach to the treaty was neither thoughtless nor light-hearted—such criticisms relate to the Prime Minister's methods, not to his policy as such. They are about means, not ends. While most historians of Lloyd George, including such admirers as Professor Morgan, readily concede his unorthodoxy of method in foreign policy, few have questioned his good intentions in the matter of the Anglo-French alliance. Professor Northedge, indeed, claims that "the revolutionary offer to France . . . was the greatest achievement of the personal diplomacy of the British Prime Minister." Others have had their doubts, but have not followed them up in detail. The current revival of interest in Lloyd George's activities at the Peace Conference, however, invites a closer consideration of the treaty that never was.

II

It is common knowledge that Lloyd George devised the notion of an Anglo-French alliance in order to resolve the grave diplomatic crisis arising from French demands over the Rhineland. The crisis, which emerged in January and February 1919 and came to a head in March, was seemingly unbridgeable. The French insisted that Germany's western frontier be relocated on the Rhine and that all German territory on the left bank be detached from the Reich as a separate buffer-state under French control. They regarded the Rhine as an indispensable strategic frontier and bastion against Germany, the minimum guarantee of French security, without which France would in effect have lost the war. Clemenceau announced that he could sign no treaty which did not include this essential provision. Lloyd George and Wilson, for their part, refused to countenance it. For Wilson, the severance of German territory was a naked violation of the principle of national self-determination. For Lloyd George, it signified the creation of what he called an Alsace-Lorraine in reverse. For both it meant laying up fresh tensions for the future and as such was absolutely inadmissible. There was deadlock between France and the Anglo-Saxons. The Conference came close to a breakdown that threatened the entire work of peacemaking.

Then came Lloyd George's intervention. On the morning of 14 March, President Wilson returned to Paris from the United States, where he had been obliged to attend the opening of Congress. Barely had he reached his residence on the Place des Etats-Unis than he was visited at noon by Lloyd George. Precisely what arguments the Prime Minister used in the private interview with the President that ensued, we do not know. No official record was made of their discussion, nor of that held in the afternoon at the Hôtel Crillon, where the two leaders proceeded for an urgent confidential exchange with Clemenceau. What is known is that Lloyd George made Clemenceau the offer of an immediate military alliance with Britain, undertaking to guarantee France against any future unprovoked aggression on the part of Germany. Wilson for his part volunteered to put a similar proposal to the American Senate. In return they required Clemenceau to give up all thought of detaching the Rhineland. On the strength of these pledges, Clemenceau eventually agreed to abandon his demand for a separate Rhineland, though he insisted that the territory remain a demilitarized zone in perpetuity, with a fifteen-year military occupation by the Allies to protect France in the immediate term. The promise of alliance with Britain and America thus replaced the Rhine frontier as the basis of French foreign policy at the Peace Conference. Lloyd George's initiative enabled the Conference to resume its work, not without difficulties during the next weeks and months over the terms of the treaties of alliance and particularly the length of the Allied occupation. But thanks to Lloyd George, the immediate crisis was over. The peacemakers could proceed to other matters.

The importance of the Prime Minister's personal role in the resolution of the Rhineland crisis cannot be exaggerated. He broached the issue of alliance with France at the highest possible level, with Wilson and Clemenceau direct, and, in Hankey's words, "under very 'hush-hush' conditions . . . without the presence of any official or secretary," not even Hankey himself. He raised it on his own initiative, without prior consultation with any of his colleagues either in the British Empire Delegation or in the Imperial War Cabinet. Not, apparently, until several weeks later did he inform the Foreign Secretary, Balfour, and even then he treated him as a mere drafting amanuensis. The Anglo-French treaty was his own brainchild; and it was his personal offer of a British guarantee to France that made by far the greater impression on Clemenceau. It was, Clemenceau recalled, "an unprecedented historical event. What a stroke of fortune for France! The American agreement was secondary." Lloyd George's démarche was understood as an extraordinary departure in British foreign policy, "an astounding innovation" in the words of Tardieu. Never before had a British Prime Minister in peacetime offered France or any other Great Power a military guarantee of her territorial integrity. When making this sensational offer to Clemenceau on 14 March, Lloyd George also gave the convincing assurance that he would lose no time in authorising the construction of a Channel tunnel, to expedite the transfer of British troops to France, should she ever again be threatened by a German invasion.

To the French, the offer was irresistible. It was meant to be. Clearly, Lloyd George understood that nothing less than a *quid pro quo* on the scale of a full, defensive alliance against Germany could ever induce Clemenceau to abandon his claim to the Rhine. "It was proffered," he admitted, "as an answer to those who claimed that the left bank of the Rhine should be annexed to France." In the succeeding days and weeks, until the treaty was finally concluded, Lloyd George followed up his original offer with further, supplementary assurances. On 27 March, he expressed his readiness, in the event of a German attack on France, "to place all our forces at her disposal." His words suggest the kind of unified Allied command under French leadership that had been entrusted since the spring of 1918 to Marshal Foch. He also hinted at Anglo-French military conversations on the pre-1914 model. Whatever the particular details, Lloyd George also reiterated his overall pledge. On 25 March, he renewed it in his celebrated Fontainebleau Memorandum. On 28 March, attempting to dissuade Clemenceau from his policy of annexing the Saar, Lloyd George cited the inviolability of his own plighted word. Clemenceau must understand, he said, that Britain and America could no more break their word to Germany over self-determination for the Saar than they could go back on their promise to defend France against German aggression. On April 2, he wrote to Clemenceau to remind him of "the pledge I offer on behalf of Britain to come to the support of France if the invader threatens." On 22 April, he formally assented to a written memorandum of agreement with Clemenceau, incorporating the outlines of an Anglo-French convention, offering, two days later, "to publish in full our agreement with France to guarantee her against the risk of invasion." On 6 May, at Clemenceau's urgent request, he and Balfour signed a further protocol of alliance, which Lloyd George formally handed to Clemenceau later the same day after its terms had been publicly announced by Tardieu at a plenary session of the Conference. On 21 May, to Clemenceau's complaints of British bad faith in the Syrian question, Lloyd George indignantly retorted: "I do not think that France has the right to complain of Great Britain's loyalty . . . British opinion freely offers to place the whole of Great Britain's strength at France's disposal if she is in danger." What more could Lloyd George have said or done by way of assurance to Clemenceau before both Prime Ministers put their signatures to the final draft of the Anglo-French treaty on 28 June?

But there was more to Lloyd George's assurances than met the eye. Or rather, as it turned out, there was less. A variety of important qualifications and reservations crept into his original clear undertaking. Not all of them were drawn to Clemenceau's attention, and none of them was communicated to him before 6 May at the earliest, a fortnight after he had formally and definitively committed himself, on 22 April, to giving up the Rhine frontier.

How long, to take an elementary stipulation, was the treaty to remain in force? On 27 March, Lloyd George appeared to intimate to Clemenceau that the guarantee would be of unlimited duration, and the draft agreements of 22 April and 5 May stated that the treaty would remain in force until "the contracting parties" agreed that the League of Nations afforded "sufficient protection" to France. Since by definition there could be no such agreement without France's consent, this gave France the final word in determining the duration of the alliance. Briefing the British Empire Delegation on 5 May, however, Lloyd George gave a different account. The treaty, he informed them, would be "for a period of fifteen years, coterminous with the military occupation of the Rhineland." "Had the Prime Minister intended to deceive?" asks Professor Nelson. "Or had he inadvertently revealed a private misunderstanding, or was he simply confused?" Forgetfulness or confusion seems the most likely explanation, since the plain words of the draft convention were there for all to hear; indeed, Lloyd George read them aloud to the Delegation. Even so, the incident reveals a certain casualness towards a salient term of the alliance.

When Lloyd George pledged Great Britain to come to the defence of France, what did he mean by Britain? On the face of it, there could be no doubt: Britain meant the British Empire; and "the British Empire" is specified in the Fontainebleau Memorandum and indeed in the treaty itself. When Britain went to war in 1914, the Empire automatically marched with her. But the war had brought ideas of a looser relationship with the mother country. Lloyd George informed the Empire Delegation on 5 May that "Clemenceau desired the Dominions to join in his guarantee"; but on hearing the hostile reaction towards the treaty at once expressed by the Prime Ministers of Canada and South Africa, he assured his colleagues there and then that the Dominions would not be bound by it. In the signed protocol which he presented to Clemenceau the next day, a clause was added stating that "the obligation imposed under this treaty shall not be binding on the dominions of the British Empire until the treaty is ratified by the Parliament of the Dominion concerned," Lloyd George explaining to Clemenceau on the eve of final signature that he was not authorized to sign for the Dominions. The implication seems to have been, not that the Dominions would not sign in due course, merely that, as British Prime Minister, Lloyd George could not from a constitutional point of view sign for them. Given his realisation of Dominion feeling against the alliance, this surely suggests some degree of disingenuousness. In any event, South Africa, Canada, Australia and New Zealand, whose men had fought in their tens of thousands on French soil, were exempted by him at a stroke of the pen from his original promise to Clemenceau, express and implied, of aid from a united Empire.

The definition of a *casus foederis* also turned out to be less clear-cut in private than appeared from the Prime Minister's promise to Clemenceau, as engrossed on the face of the treaty. The treaty laid down that British military intervention on France's behalf would be activated "in the event of any unprovoked movement of aggression"; and "movement of aggression" was defined in relation to specific German violations of the demilitarized zone. At the same meeting of the British Empire Delegation, however, chaired by Lloyd George, Bonar Law observed that "the words 'unprovoked aggression' protected us": whether an "aggression was provoked or not" would be for Britain to decide for herself. Bonar Law would never have given such an assurance without the Prime Minister's assent. And indeed in a letter to Botha of 26 June, two days before signing the final treaty, Lloyd George himself confirmed that "we ourselves shall be the sole judge of what constitutes unprovoked aggression."

We have noted Lloyd George's repeated assurances to Clemenceau in March, April, and May, of Britain's absolute commitment to France. However much whittled away in detail, his overall pledge was clear and unambiguous: if Germany attacked France, Britain would go to France's defence. Between 14 March, when he first produced his offer, and 27 June, the eve of the signing, at no time did he suggest that it might be in any way contingent on the American treaty. Writing to Bonar Law on 31 March, Lloyd George stressed the unilateral nature of the British guarantee, adding: "Wilson is inclined to join if he can persuade the Senate." Certainly Wilson never intended any connection between the two pacts. On the contrary, he was particularly anxious to dissociate them. He repeatedly deprecated any link between the British and American guarantees, on the grounds that such an association would be anathema to the isolationist Senate and likely to prove fatal to the American treaty. Wilson's aide, Colonel House, moreover, while doubting that the Senate would ratify Wilson's pledge, believed that "England was resolved to give this guarantee, whether the United States did or not." Lloyd George had told him so on 12 March, two days before approaching the President. Moreover, when revealing to the Empire Delegation on 5 May the existence of the British guarantee, and admitting that he was "apprehensive lest the United States Senate might refuse" to ratify its American counterpart, Lloyd George gave no indication that he regarded the two treaties as in any way connected other than in their subject-matter.

Clemenceau was undoubtedly under this impression. As has been noted, Clemenceau set considerably greater store by Lloyd George's offer than by Wilson's. In an emergency, only British troops could reach France, with or without a Channel tunnel, in time to stem a German invasion. The promise of immediate British aid was therefore absolutely crucial to French security. Clemenceau was clear in his mind that the British and American proposals comprised two distinct offers, of related but unequal importance. "Do not forget," he recalls in *Grandeur and Misery of Victory*, "that it was Mr Lloyd George who had made the original proposal, offering to do all he could to induce the American President to agree to it. Mr Wilson merely came in in the second line as the defender of interests less immediately concerned with us." Lloyd George's guarantee, then, was in Clemenceau's eyes the one that really mattered. Wilson's, if it materialised, would be an additional bonus. Lloyd George confirmed Clemenceau's understanding of the matter. When, on 21 May, Clemenceau pointed out how much France had conceded at the Conference, Lloyd George retorted: "If M. Clemenceau has agreed to sacrifice certain claims, it is because England has promised to come to France's aid if she were attacked." The Prime Minister here acknowledged—and correctly acknowledged—that the overriding consideration, the *sine qua non* for Clemenceau in his reluctant agreement to abandon the Rhine frontier was—the British alliance.

Although drafted in similar terms, therefore, the two treaties, British and American, were quite distinct. How, then, did the British treaty come to be dependent on the American? The link came about at Lloyd George's instigation, by virtue of what eventually became Article 2 of the Anglo-French treaty. The draft convention which Lloyd George signed and presented to Clemenceau on 6 May included a clause stating that the British treaty "will be in similar terms to that entered into by the United States and will come into force when the latter is ratified." An innocent addition on the face of it, signifying no more than that the two treaties, British and American, both having the same purpose, both containing virtually identical provisions, would come into effect simultaneously. It was essential to specify when the British treaty would become operative, and it was not in itself unreasonable to synchronize that date with the ratification of the American treaty. There was no obvious or necessary implication that the one would not come into being without the other. Yet President Wilson dropped a curious remark to one of his delegates. Lloyd George, the President observed, "had slipped a paragraph into the British note about ratification by the United States and . . . he did not think Clemenceau had noticed it." What was there that required notice by Clemenceau?

The answer becomes startlingly clear if we turn to the final draft of the Anglo-French treaty, presented by Lloyd George, be it noted, at one of his very last meetings with Wilson and Clemenceau. It was the late afternoon of 27 June, the day before the Anglo-French treaty and the Treaty of Versailles were to be signed. At 4:30, the three leaders withdrew briefly to a private room. Lloyd George called in Cecil Hurst, legal adviser to the Foreign Office, who, he explained, "had prepared a text" of the alliance. After discussion of some relatively minor amendments, which were duly agreed, Hurst's amended copy of the treaty, according to the official record of the meeting, was "read to and approved by" the three leaders. The final draft, then, of which there was only one authoritative copy—Hurst's—was read aloud, in English only, presumably by Hurst. No translators were present. Into this draft another word had been inserted—the word "only." The operative phrase in Article 2 now read that in relation to the American guarantee, the Anglo-French alliance would come into force "*only* when the latter is ratified" (my italics—A. L.). One word completely altered the sense of the British undertaking, making its fulfilment wholly dependent on the fate of the American treaty. Whether Clemenceau, or his foreign Minister, Pichon, the only Frenchmen present, appreciated or even noticed Lloyd George's surreptitious introduction of the vital qualifying word, is not known. It seems inconceivable that Clemenceau would have assented to the final draft or still less have signed the treaty the following morning, had his attention been drawn to the force of Lloyd George's last-minute interpolation. But Clemenceau never went back on his word—"he was," Lloyd George noted, "a man who kept faith in any bargain he entered into"—and once having signed, he was bound by the treaty whether he had read the small print or not.

III

Lloyd George's manner of negotiating the treaty with France, his repeated assurances to Clemenceau, and the reservations with which he later hedged them once Clemenceau had acted on the strength of those representations, are bound to raise doubts as to his intentions. Tardieu voiced his private suspicions in a conversation in 1920. While acquitting Wilson of any taint of sharp practice, he added; "I am not so sure of the good faith of Lloyd George. Why should he have made the assistance of Britain contingent upon the ratification of the pact by Washington?" Why indeed?

Answers are not far to seek. If the Senate ratified the American treaty, then, in the event of another German attack on France, Britain and France would again have the support of the United States. American intervention would no doubt prove no less decisive in a future conflict than in the late war. But, as Lloyd George suggested to Foch, faced with the certainty of American and British retaliation, it was surely unlikely that Germany would ever again venture to attack France. In all probability, therefore, Britain would never be called upon to fulfil the Prime Minister's promise. If war did come, however, America would automatically and immediately intervene on Britain's side. In this sense, the American commitment was as much a guarantee to Britain as to France. If, on the other hand, the Senate declined to ratify Wilson's guarantee, Britain would not have to act alone. Britain would not be bound to do anything at all. She would be discharged altogether from her treaty obligation to France—paradoxically, by the terms of the treaty itself. Lloyd George would be absolved from what a recent historian rightly calls his "solemn pledge," and the blame could be laid entirely at the door of the United States. As he confirmed in the House of Commons on 18 December: "If there should be such a possibility as the United States not ratifying the compact, undoubtedly we are free to reconsider our decision." Either way, Britain's liability was limited. Either way, Lloyd George was indemnified. Whether the Senate would ratify the American pact remained to be seen. Meanwhile, Lloyd George's promise had served his immediate purpose of resolving the Rhineland crisis, so enabling the work of the Conference to proceed and the Treaty of Versailles to be concluded.

Whatever the outcome in Washington, Clemenceau's formal abnegation of the Rhine frontier on 22 April was irrevocable. Lloyd George knew the man he was dealing with when he made his offer. As he recalled, "Clemenceau had already accepted our proposals and he never went back on an arrangement to which he had assented—however reluctantly." It is tempting indeed to ask whether Lloyd George did not positively hope and intend that the Anglo-French alliance should come to nothing. Viewed in terms of Realpolitik, it might not be wholly to Britain's geopolitical disadvantage to abandon her ally. Major differences between the two countries, especially over reparations and colonial issues, arose at the Conference. Clemenceau recalls that no sooner was the war with Germany over, than Lloyd George began to assume an antagonistic attitude to France and to reassert Britain's traditional hostility. What is certain is that in the event, Lloyd George did leave Clemenceau in the lurch. Clemenceau staked all on the treaty with Britain—and he lost all—the American alliance, the British alliance and the Rhine frontier. In reliance on Lloyd George's promises, Clemenceau had done what his critics feared most: he surrendered the substance for the shadow, the strategic frontier for a scrap of paper. It helped to destroy him politically. More important were the consequences for French foreign policy. More than any other single consideration, it was the evaporation of the Anglo-French alliance, France's principal deterrent against Germany, which intensified French feelings of vulnerability and alarm at the inadequacy of Versailles. Under Poincaré, France clutched desperately at the letter of Versailles because, as a Frenchman put it, "England and America would give France nothing else to stick to."

Let it be assumed in his favour that Lloyd George was sincere in his promise of aid to France in the event of German aggression, however remote such a prospect might seem to him in 1919. Certainly he persuaded the Commons to approve the treaty without a division, using language of passionate moral conviction. Why, then, did he hedge his bet by making Britain's commitment contingent on America's? We are impelled to confront the same insistent question.

Lloyd George was well aware—as were almost all the participants at the Peace Conference, of the real possibility that the Senate might not ratify Wilson's guarantee. The Republicans had won the recent congressional elections. Their opposition to his foreign policy was well known. Republican senators on the Foreign Relations Committee denounced his pledges of overseas commitments as a breach of American neutrality and even of the American constitution. Lloyd George knew that the main object of Wilson's return to America in February 1919 was to arrest this isolationist trend, and he knew that Wilson had failed. It was plain to Lloyd George, as he told the British Empire Delegation on 5 May, that American rejection of a Franco-American treaty was on the cards. Was this perhaps the very reason why he made Britain's commitment conditional on it?

Was Lloyd George a thorough machiavellian, who planned from the start to trick Clemenceau into giving up the Rhineland in return for a worthless promise? Or a casual opportunist, who played the diplomatic game by ear, and adapted his tactics in accordance with shifting circumstances? In support of the latter view, it may be argued that in making his original offer to France, he acted in good faith, hoping that renunciation by Clemenceau of the Rhine frontier would remove that problem permanently from the Conference agenda; but that when Clemenceau insisted on Allied occupation of the Rhineland, and it later emerged that this was the point which aroused most strenuous opposition in the British Empire Delegation as likely to drag Britain into war under the treaty—Lloyd George changed tack and determined to qualify his original commitment.

Even if this interpretation is correct, it follows that Lloyd George represented as an inducement to Clemenceau a set of circumstances which he then found himself constrained, or inclined to abandon. He offered alliance with the British Empire; he subsequently excluded the Dominions. He portrayed the treaty as of unlimited duration; he eventually engineered that it could be terminated by majority decision, unilaterally terminated, that is, by Britain and America. On paper, he promised instant retaliation against German aggression; to his colleagues he confided that it would rest with Britain to define what "aggression" was and when it should be deemed to have taken place. He mentioned military conversations and a Channel tunnel; they never materialised. Above all, he held out the treaty as independent and free-standing; and by what looks suspiciously like a last-minute sleight-of-hand, he made it contingent on the dubious outcome of American domestic politics.

"Had the Prime Minister intended to mislead?" asks Professor Nelson. Whether Lloyd George intended all along that the British guarantee should hinge on Wilson's ability to sway the Senate, or whether this was an inspired afterthought, makes no difference to the outcome for France. Either way, France had reason to complain of *Albion perfide*. For if Lloyd George took seriously his pledge to France, why, when it failed to become legally binding, did he not recommend acceptance of what remained on his own admission a moral obligation? To this it may perhaps be contended that by the end of 1919 political opinion in Britain had turned against the alliance, that circumstances alter cases and that, as Lloyd George observed to his confidant, Sir George Riddell: "if you want to succeed in politics, you must keep your conscience well under control." But was Lloyd George ever serious about the alliance? His original state of mind is of crucial concern to the student of his psychology, strategy and tactics at Paris. At one stage or other, he decided to go back on his word to Clemenceau. Was it before or after he gave it? And was it a question of innocent, or, as Nelson legitimately asks, of fraudulent misrepresentation?

The suspicion of premeditated guile must be strong. Is there evidence to substantiate it? There is the evidence of Lloyd George himself. First, the negative testimony: the absence in *The Truth about the Peace Treaties*, of any attempt to explain, or even to mention the sequel to his promise to Clemenceau. His silence on the point in that lengthy apologia of his conduct of affairs at Paris, is in itself suggestive. But there is also positive evidence of his intentions. It was at a Cabinet meeting on 4 March 1919 that he first mooted the idea of a treaty with France. "If the United States and ourselves would guarantee France against invasion" he declared, "she would be satisfied. This, however," he continued, "was impossible, as the President would not hear of any entangling alliances, as he put his faith in the League of Nations." On 4 March, then, Lloyd George contemplated a solution to the Rhineland crisis in terms of an Anglo-American undertaking to France, but apparently had no belief that America would adhere to one. Nothing suggests that he had changed his mind ten days later, when he put his proposal to Wilson. Indeed by that time he was well aware of the hostility to Wilson's policy in the United States. In other words, when, on 14 March, he approached Wilson about an American guarantee, he was, at the least, open-minded about the prospect of its ever materialising. Why, then, did he bring Wilson into it at all? Why make a point of awaiting the President's return from America and securing his promise of a guarantee on the morning of March 14 before making his own pledge to Clemenceau in the afternoon, unless it was that he intended all along that the two offers should be linked? He admits as much in *The Truth about the Peace Treaties*: "I then conceived the idea of a *joint* military guarantee by America and Britain" (my italics—A. L.). He also indicated at the time that this was his intention. On 23 March, 1919, nine days after making his offer to Clemenceau, in a policy statement marked "secret," he specified a "*joint* guarantee by the British Empire and the United States." (my italics— A. L.) Lloyd George had good reason to believe that Wilson's promise would come to nothing, and that consequently, he would be relieved of his own. The treaty which he devised was a masterpiece of legerdemain, a contradiction in terms: a "joint guarantee" in the sense that it was underwritten by America, but by virtue of Article 2, not severally binding on Britain, so that when the underwriter backed out, the principal guarantor could also default.

If this interpretation is correct, then as far as Lloyd George is concerned the Anglo-French alliance was an illusionist's trick from start to finish; and its disappearance represented not the failure, but the consummation of his real policy. Frances Stevenson once charged him with being "a past master in craft"; Lloyd George did not deny it. Was it not part and parcel of his professional repertoire, his stock-in-trade as a political escapologist? It would not have been the only occasion at the Peace Conference when he fashioned for himself a convenient exclusion-clause behind which to evade the consequences of previous solemn commitments once they had served his purpose. He gloried in such agility as marking "the chief difference between ordinary and extraordinary men. When the extraordinary man is faced by a novel and difficult situation," he told Riddell, "he extricates himself from it by adopting a plan which is at once daring and unexpected. That is the mark of genius in a man of action."

John Maynard Keynes at the time of the writing of *The Economic Consequences of the Peace*. (Charleston Trust, courtesy Tate Gallery London)

The Wreck of Reparations

John Maynard Keynes

The Carthaginian Peace

Our memory of the Versailles settlement bears the indelible imprint of John Maynard Keynes's classic study, *The Economic Consequences of the Peace*. In the following piece, written several months after the publication of his influential book, Keynes summarizes his objections to the reparation section of the treaty and his dire predictions about its deleterious effect on the future of Europe.

About six months have now passed by since I published a book entitled "The Economic Consequences of the Peace." In this period the book has been published in the principal languages of the world, and it has been reviewed in many hundreds of journals. The best and the worst have been said of me. But, at any rate, my facts and arguments have been open to the

From John Maynard Keynes, "The Peace of Versailles," *Everybody's Magazine*, 43 (September 1920), 37–41.

examination of expert critics everywhere; and my conclusions have had to justify themselves before the bar of the educated opinion of the whole world in a manner never required of the half-secret deliberations of Paris.

I am now invited to restate briefly the leading points of my contention and to add a few reflections which the course of events, since I wrote my book, may have suggested. But the space at my disposal is brief, and I must refer to the book itself those readers who are interested in the evidence and arguments in detail.

There are two separate aspects of the peace which we have imposed on the enemy—on the one hand its justice, on the other hand its wisdom and its expediency. I was mainly concerned with the second. But there were certain aspects of the first also with which I thought it my duty to deal carefully.

Its Justice

The nature of the terms which we were entitled *in justice* to impose depends, in part, on the responsibility of the enemy nations for causing so tremendous a calamity as the late war, and in part on the understanding on which the enemy laid down his arms at the time of the armistice. In my own opinion, it is not possible to lay the entire responsibility for the state of affairs out of which the war arose on any single nation; it was engendered, in part at least, by the essential character of international politics and rivalries during the latter part of the nineteenth century, by militarism everywhere (certainly in Russia as well as in Germany and Austria-Hungary), and by the universally practiced policies of economic imperialism; it had its seeds deep in the late history of Europe.

But I believe, nevertheless, that Germany bears a special and peculiar responsibility for the war itself, for its universal and devastating character, and for its final development into a combat without quarter for mastery or defeat. A criminal may be the outcome of his environment, but he is none the less a criminal.

The evidence which has become public in the past year has convinced me that, during the weeks preceding August, 1914, persons in power in Germany deliberately provoked the war and intended that it should commence when it did. If this be so, the accepted standards of international justice entitled us to impose, at Germany's expense, any terms which might be calculated to make good some part of the destruction done, to heal Europe's wounds, to preserve and perpetuate peace, and to terrify future malefactors.

Even so, however, it was our duty to look more to the future than to the past, to distinguish between the late rulers of Germany on the one hand and her common people and unborn posterity on the other, and to be sure that our acts were guided by magnanimity and wisdom more than by revenge or hatred. It was also proper for us to feel and practice some measure of humility at the conclusion of so terrible and extraordinary a struggle, and not to elevate ourselves and our Allies, in boastful and unseemly language, to a level of morality and of international disinterestedness which, whatever the faults of others, we can not claim. But above all, should not the future peace of the world have been our highest and guiding motive? Men of all nations had suffered together, the victims of a curse deep-seated in the past history and present weakness of the European race. The lifting of the curse was a better object in the treaty, if universal justice were our aim, than its relentless execution.

Its Honorableness

But there was another aspect of justice, more earthly than the high topics of which have just occupied us—the question of our promises, in reliance on which the enemy have capitulated. Beginning with the invasion of Belgium, the Allied countries had pronounced the sacredness of engagements and the maintenance of international good faith as among their principal objects. Only thus, in the judgment of the considered wisdom of the world, only by the establishment of the rule of law as between nations, can national egotisms be tempered and the stability of settlements be preserved. It was therefore peculiarly incumbent upon us to practice what we had preached, and even to be so scrupulous as not to take advantage of an ambiguous phrase.

To understand the peace, therefore, and its effect on general confidence in the fairness of the Allies, we have to remember the history of the negotiations which began with the German note of October 5, 1918, and concluded with President Wilson's note of November 5, 1918. . . .

The Armistice Contract

The nature of the contract between Germany and the Allies resulting from this exchange of documents is plain and unequivocal. The terms of the peace are to be in accordance with the addresses of the President, and the purpose of the Peace Conference is "to discuss the details of their application." The circumstances of the contract were of an unusually solemn and binding character; for one of the conditions of it was that Germany should agree to armistice terms which were to be such as would leave her helpless.

What, then, was the substance of this contract to which the Allies had bound themselves? I have examined this in detail in my book. In a word, we were committed to a peace based upon the Fourteen Points and upon the principle that "there shall be no annexations, no contributions, no punitive damages."

It is still maintained by some persons that the enemy surrendered unconditionally and that we are in no way bound by the engagements outlined above. This has been maintained lately, for example, in a lengthy article contributed to the New York *Times* by General Greene. Other advocates of the treaty stand upon the other leg and maintain that, while we are bound by the Fourteen Points, the peace treaty is in substantial conformity with them. This, I understand, is the attitude of President Wilson. I am reckoned a hostile critic of the President because I believe that he holds this attitude sincerely, having been partly deceived and partly self-deceived, his thought and feeling being here cast in what, for lack of a more descriptive phrase, I termed a theological mold. His friends argue, however, that he was well aware of what he was doing in Paris and deliberately sacrificed some part of his professions in the interests of the higher political expediency.

The Enigma of Wilson

The extraordinary story of hopes, ideals, weaknesses, failures and disappointments, of which the President has been the leading figure and eponymous hero, will interest and perplex mankind as long as history is read and the hearts of the great ones are the subject of curious exploration of the multitude. Was Hamlet mad or feigning? Was the President sick or cunning? On what a stage he played, and with what forfeits! Ruling the destinies of nations, now with the words of the philosopher and next with the realities of power; with the voices of heaven at one ear and the party managers at the other; proud and timorous; lofty and small; disinterested and ambitious; soaring to the rarest heights of terrestrial fortune, and there smitten by the blindness of Apollo and the plagues of Egypt.

If the President loves fame, let him be satisfied. Posterity remembers the mixed characters of history who have a star and it fails them. The Emperor William exhibits for us the fluctuations of fate. But he belongs to the satyric drama, a victim of the buffoonery of the gods, whose story may instruct but will not perplex us. For the President a grander niche is waiting, where he and his story will symbolize and illustrate some of the mingled and mysterious strains in our common nature.

Yet I, at any rate, though I have tried to express what I saw, and am not shaken in my opinions by the subsequent passage of events, would shrink from controversy with critics on so doubtful and perplexed an issue as the feelings and the motives of an individual. I have put on record in my analysis of the President the impression produced on a single observer, and I claim no more for it. I wrote in a moment of disappointment, but, to the best of my ability, in a spirit of greater historical objectivity than some of my critics have given me credit for. Events themselves have surely shown that he was not wise, and even that he was deluded. But I do not forget that he, alone among the statesmen of Paris, sought ideal aims, and sincerely pursued throughout the Conference the future peace of the world as his supreme and governing purpose. Even in the futile stubbornness of the past few months an element of nobility has been present. . . .

But there remains the question—greater than that of the actions and motives of individuals—whether in fact we have kept faith with our enemies. I have maintained that on certain matters we have not kept faith, the most important instance within the economic sphere, which was my particular subject-matter, being the inclusion in our reparation claims of huge sums for military pensions and separation allowances, which greatly swell the bill and to which we are not entitled. Our treatment of the Saar Valley, of tariffs, and of Germany's river system afford other examples.

Let me here limit myself to the reparation claims. I venture to assert that my criticism of these claims has not been seriously controverted by any one. It has been stated, since my book appeared, that the President's own advisers in Paris informed him that these claims were illegitimate. Many critics have passed over in silence this particular issue. Yet if it is in fact the case that we have not kept our engagements, is it not a matter of some importance to the national honor of each one of the allied and associated countries, and to the moral government of the world?

Those who have defended the treaty on this issue have done so on the most extraordinary grounds. I select below some of the commoner lines of argument. Some say that Germany, if she had won, would not have kept faith with us, and that this fact absolves us from being overscrupulous with her; the enemy, being themselves unjust—this argument asserts— are not entitled to better treatment in return.

Others say that the information we now have makes it probable that Germany could have been compelled to surrender unconditionally, and that for this reason the President's *pourparlers* before the armistice lose much of their binding character.

Others point out that our engagements were in part vaguely expressed; that they were not cast in legal form; that there is no one to enforce them; and that they can not therefore constitute a "contract." (Imagine, however, with what indignation these same apologists would explode before a similar argument on the lips of a German.)

Others, again, discover that the President was exceeding his powers in his preliminary negotiations as to the basis of the peace, in reliance on which the enemy laid down his arms; and that his promises consequently bound no one.

These are all of them types of man's eternal reasons for not keeping his promises, and their roots are in human nature. But they ill accord with the victorious issue of a crusade for the sanctity of international agreements.

The Treaty's Wisdom

With these brief comments I pass from the justice of the treaty, which can not be ignored even when it is not our central topic, to its wisdom and expediency. Under these heads my criticism of the treaty is double. In the first place, this treaty ignores the economic solidarity of Europe, and by aiming at the destruction of the economic life of Germany it threatens the health and prosperity of the Allies themselves. In the second place, by making demands the execution of which is in the literal sense impossible, it stultifies itself and leaves Europe more unsettled than it found it. The treaty, by overstepping the limits of the possible, has in practice settled nothing. The true settlement still remains to be made out of the ashes of the present and the disillusionment of the future, when the imposture of Paris is recognized for what it is.

For reasons of historical experience, which are easily understood, and with which all men must sympathize (however profoundly we believe that France will deal to herself as well as to her enemy a fatal wound if she yields to them), there were powerful influences in Paris demanding for the future security of France that the peace should complete the destruction of the economic life of Central Europe, which the war had gone far to consummate.

The Shattered Heart of Europe

The German economic system as it existed before the war depended on three main factors:

1. Overseas commerce, as represented by her mercantile marine, her colonies, her foreign investments, her exports, and the overseas connections of her merchants.
2. The exploitation of her coal and iron and the industries built upon them.
3. Her transport and tariff system.

Of these the first, while not the least important, was certainly the most vulnerable. The treaty aims at the systematic destruction of all three, but principally the first two.

Germany has ceded to the Allies all the vessels of her mercantile marine exceeding sixteen hundred tons gross, half the vessels between one thousand tons and sixteen hundred tons, and one-quarter of her trawlers and other fishing boats. The cession is comprehensive, including not only vessels flying the German flag, but also vessels owned by Germans but flying other flags, and all vessels under construction as well as those afloat. Further, Germany undertakes, if required, to build for the Allies such types of ships as they may specify, up to two hundred thousand tons annually for five years, the value of these ships being credited to Germany against what is due from her for reparation. Thus the German mercantile marine is swept from the seas and can not be restored for many years to come on a scale adequate to meet the requirements of her own commerce.

Germany has ceded to the Allies "all her rights and titles over her overseas possessions." This cession not only applies to sovereignty but extends on unfavorable terms to government property, all of which, including railways, must be surrendered without payment. Further, in distinction from the practice ruling in the case of most similar cessions in recent history, the property and persons of private German nationals, as distinct from their Government, are also injuriously affected. Not only are German sovereignty and German influence extirpated from the whole of her former overseas possessions, but the persons and property of her nationals resident or owning property in those parts are deprived of legal status and legal security.

The provisions just outlined in regard to the private property of Germans in the ex-German colonies apply equally to private German property in Alsace-Lorraine, except in so far as the French Government may choose to grant exceptions.

The expropriation of German private property is not limited, however, to the ex-German colonies and Alsace-Lorraine. The cumulative effect of a series of complicated provisions, which I have examined in detail in my book, is to deprive Germany (or rather to empower the Allies so to deprive her at their will—it is not yet accomplished) of everything she possesses outside her own frontiers as laid down in the treaty. Not only are her overseas investments taken and her connections destroyed, but the same process of extirpation is applied in the territories of her former allies and of her immediate neighbors by land.

The above provisions relate to Germany's external wealth. Those relating to coal and iron are more important in respect of their ultimate consequences to Germany's internal industrial economy than for the money value immediately involved. The German Empire has been built more truly on coal and iron than on blood and iron. The skilled exploitation of the great coalfields of the Ruhr, Upper Silesia and the Saar alone made possible the development of the steel, chemical, and electrical industries which established her as the first industrial nation on continental Europe. One-third of Germany's population lives in towns of more than twenty thousand inhabitants, an industrial concentration which is only possible on a foundation of coal and iron. In striking, therefore, at her coal supply, those who sought her economic destruction were not mistaking their target.

Coal

The coal clauses of the treaty are, however, among those which are likely, by reason of the technical impossibility of their execution, to defeat their own object. If the plebiscite results in Germany's losing the coal districts of Upper Silesia, the treaty will have deprived her of territory from which not far short of one-third of her total coal supply was previously derived. Out of the coal that remains to her Germany is required, quite rightly, to make good for ten years the estimated loss which France has incurred by the destruction and damage of war in the coalfields of her northern provinces, such deliveries not to exceed twenty million tons in each of the first five years or eight million tons annually thereafter. She has also, over and above this, for ten years to deliver annually seven million tons to France, eight million tons to Belgium, and from four million five hundred thousand tons to eight million five hundred thousand tons to Italy.

I have estimated that this would leave Germany with about sixty million tons annually against domestic requirements, which, on the prewar basis of industry in her remaining territory, would amount to one hundred and ten million tons. In short, Germany could only execute the coal demands of the treaty by abandoning the bulk of her industries and returning to the status of an agricultural country. In this case many millions of her present population could obtain neither work nor food (nor, indeed, facilities of emigration). Yet it is not to be supposed that the population of any country will submit year after year to an export which dooms many of them to starvation and even to death. The thing is humanly and politically impossible. Men will not die so obediently to the dictates of a document. The coal clauses of the treaty are not being executed and never will be.

But in this event the treaty settles nothing, and the extent of the coal deliveries remains as a source of perpetual friction, uncertainty and inefficiency, which will inhibit the industrial activity of all the European countries alike which are parties to it. The coal will not be delivered; it may not even be mined. No plans which look ahead can be made by anyone. The commodity will be the subject of a perpetual scramble; and even of military occupations and of bloodshed. For, as the result of many various causes, the coal position of all Europe is nearly desperate, and no country will lightly surrender its treaty rights. I affirm, therefore, that the coal clauses are inexpedient and disastrous, and full of danger not only for the economic efficiency but for the political peace of the European continent.

Iron

The provisions relating to iron ore require less detailed attention, though their effects are destructive. They require less attention, because they are in large measure inevitable. Almost exactly seventy-five per cent of the iron ore raised in Germany in 1913 came from Alsace-Lorraine. But while Lorraine contained seventy-five per cent of Germany's iron ore, only twenty-five per cent of her blast-furnaces and of her foundries lay within Lorraine and the Saar basin together, a large proportion of the ore being carried into Germany proper. Thus here, as elsewhere, political considerations cut disastrously across economic.

In a régime of free trade and free economic intercourse it would be of little consequence that iron lay on one side of a political frontier and labor, coal and blast-furnaces on the other. But it seems certain, calculating on the present passions and impulses of European capitalistic society, that the effective iron output of Europe will be diminished by a new political frontier (which sentiment and historic justice require), because nationalism and private interest are thus allowed to impose a new economic frontier along the same lines. These latter considerations are allowed, in the present governance of Europe, to prevail over the intense need of the continent for the most sustained and efficient production to repair the destruction of war and to satisfy the insistence of labor for a larger reward.

Thus in its coal and iron clauses the treaty strikes at organization, and by the destruction of organization impairs yet further the reduced wealth of the whole community.

There remain those treaty provisions which relate to the transport and the tariff systems of Germany. These parts of the treaty have not nearly the importance and significance of those discussed hitherto. They are pin-pricks, interferences and vexations, not so much objectionable for their solid consequences as dishonorable to the Allies in the light of their professions. I can not spare space in this brief article to consider them in the detail they deserve. Taken in their entirety, the economic clauses of the treaty are comprehensive, and little has been overlooked which might impoverish Germany now or obstruct her development in future. So situated, Germany is to make payments of money, on a scale and in a manner about to be examined.

The treaty's claims for an indemnity may be divided into two parts: those which, in accordance with our pre-armistice engagements, we were entitled to make if we judged it expedient to do so, and those which, in my judgment, we had no right to make. The first category includes as its chief items all the direct damages to civilian life and property for which Germany was responsible, more particularly the invaded and occupied areas of France, Belgium, and Serbia, by air-raids, and by warfare of submarines. It includes also compensation for the improper treatment of interned civilians and for the loot of food, raw materials, live stock, machinery, household effects, timber, and the like; and the repayment of fines and requisitions levied on the towns of France and Belgium. I have ventured as a very rough estimate to calculate the total of these items at the following figures:

Belgium	$2,500,000,000
France	4,000,000,000
Great Britain	2,850,000,000
Other Allies	1,250,000,000
	$10,600,000,000

I need not impress on the reader that there is much guesswork in the above, and the figure for France in particular has been criticized on the ground that it is too low.

But I feel some confidence that the general magnitude, as distinct from the precise figures, is not very erroneous; and this may be expressed by the statement that a claim against Germany, based on the interpretation of the pre-armistice engagements of the Allied Powers which is adopted above, would assuredly be found to exceed eight billion and to fall short of fifteen billion.

Indemnity Demands

This is the amount of the claim which we were entitled to present to the enemy. I believe that it would have been a wise and just act to have asked the German Government at the peace negotiations to agree to a sum of ten billion in final settlement, without further examination of particulars. This would have provided an immediate and certain solution, and would have required from Germany a sum which, if she were granted certain indulgences, it might not have proved entirely impossible for her to pay. This sum should have been divided up among the Allies themselves on a basis of need and general equity.

But the question was not settled on its merits, and the above figure is far from representing the whole of our actual claims under the treaty. As a compromise between keeping the letter of our engagements and demanding the entire cost of the war, which French and British politicians had promised to their constituents from the platform, Paris decided to include a claim, which seemed plausible in itself, which recommended itself to sentiment, and which amounted to a large sum; and Germany has been required to discharge in their entirety all military pensions and separation allowances paid or to be paid, which have arisen out of the war. I have estimated that this adds to the bill an aggregate sum of twenty-five billion dollars made up as follows:

France	$12,000,000,000
British Empire	7,000,000,000
Italy	2,500,000,000
Others (including the U.S.)	3,500,000,000
	$25,000,000,000

Adding this figure to my maximum estimate of fifteen billion dollars, we have a total claim against Germany of about forty billion dollars. While the details making up this total have been criticized and much higher figures have been mentioned (as, for example, seventy-five billion dollars by M. Klotz, then finance minister of France), the world has, generally speaking, accepted my figure as representing the facts as nearly as is at present possible, and as supplying a reasonable basis of discussion.

The Blank Check

The reader will observe that this figure is mine, and that no final amount is specified by the treaty itself, which fixes no definite sum as representing Germany's liability. This feature has been the subject of very general criticism, that it is equally inconvenient to Germany and to the Allies themselves that she should not know what she has to pay or they what they are to receive. The method, apparently contemplated by the treaty, of arriving at the final result over a period of many months by an addition of hundreds of thousands of individual claims for damage to land, farm buildings and chickens, is evidently impracticable, and the reasonable course would have been for both parties to compound for a round sum without examination of details. If this round sum had been named in the treaty, the settlement would have been placed on a more businesslike basis.

But this was impossible for two reasons. Two different kinds of false statements had been widely promulgated, one as to Germany's capacity to pay, the other as to the amount of the Allies' just claims in respect of the devastated areas. The fixing of either of these figures presented a dilemma. A figure for Germany's prospective capacity to pay, not too much in excess of the estimates of most candid and well-informed authorities, would have fallen hopelessly far short of popular expectations both in England and in France. On the other hand, a definite figure for damage done which would not disastrously disappoint the expectations that had been raised in France and Belgium might have been incapable of substantiation under challenge.

By far the safest course for the politicians was, therefore, to mention no figure at all; and from this necessity a great deal of the complication of the reparation scheme essentially springs.

According to the letter of the treaty, any part of the sum eventually determined as due which remains unpaid from time to time is to accumulate at interest at five per cent, while the earlier installments of payment are contemplated as follows: Up to May 1, 1921, Germany is to make lump-sum payments, in cash, kind and bearer bonds, so as to bring the net sum available for reparation to fifteen billion dollars. These bearer bonds carry interest at two and one-half per cent per annum from 1921 to 1925, and at five per cent plus one per cent for amortization thereafter. Assuming, therefore, that Germany is not able to provide any appreciable surplus toward reparation before 1921, she will have to find a sum of three hundred and seventy-five million dollars annually from 1921 to 1925, and nine hundred million dollars annually thereafter.

As soon as the Reparation Commission is satisfied that Germany can do better than this, five per cent bearer bonds are to be issued for a further ten billion dollars, the rate of amortization being determined by the commission hereafter. This would bring the annual payment to one billion four hundred million dollars without allowing anything for the discharge of the capital of the last ten billion dollars.

Germany's liability, however, is not limited to twenty-five billion dollars, and the Reparation Commission is to demand further instalments of bearer bonds until the total enemy liability has been provided for. On the basis of my estimate of forty billion dollars for the total liability, this balance will be fifteen billion dollars. Assuming interest at five per cent, this will raise the annual payment to two billion one hundred and fifty million dollars without allowance for amortization.

But even this is not all. There is a further provision of devastating significance. Bonds representing payments in excess of fifteen billion dollars are not to be issued until the commission is satisfied that Germany can meet the interest on them. But this does not mean that interest is remitted in the meantime. As from May 1, 1921, the capital sum of indebtedness is rolling up all the time at compound interest. The effect of this provision toward increasing the burden is enormous, on the assumption that Germany can not pay very large sums at first.

At five percent compound interest a capital sum doubles itself in fifteen years. On the assumption that Germany can not pay more than seven hundred and fifty million dollars annually until 1936 (i.e. five per cent interest on fifteen billion dollars) the twenty-five billion dollars on which interest is deferred will have risen to fifty billion dollars, carrying an annual interest charge of two billion five hundred million dollars.

An Avalanche of Debt

That is to say, even if Germany pays seven hundred and fifty million dollars annually up to 1936, she will nevertheless owe us at that date more than half as much again as she now does (sixty-five billion dollars as compared with forty billion dollars). From 1936 onward she will have to pay to us three billion two hundred and fifty million dollars annually in order to keep pace with the interest alone. At the end of any year in which she pays less than this sum she will owe us more than she did at the beginning of it. And if she is to discharge the capital sum in thirty years from 1936, i.e., in forty-eight years from the armistice, she must pay an additional six hundred and fifty million dollars annually, making three billion nine hundred million dollars in all.

It is, in my judgment, as certain as anything can be, for reasons which I will summarize in a moment, that Germany can not pay anything approaching this sum. Until the treaty is altered, therefore, Germany has in effect engaged herself to hand over to the Allies the whole of her surplus production in perpetuity.

This is not less the case because the Reparation Commission has been given discretionary powers to vary the rate of interest, and to postpone and even to cancel the capital indebtedness. In the first place, some of these powers can only be exercised if the commission or the governments represented on it are *unanimous*. But also, which is perhaps more important, it will be the *duty* of the Reparation Commission, until there has been a unanimous and far-reaching change of the policy which the treaty represents, to extract from Germany year after year the maximum sum obtainable. There is a great difference between fixing a definite sum, which, though large, is within Germany's capacity to pay and yet to retain a little for herself, and fixing a sum far beyond her capacity, which is then to be reduced at the discretion of a foreign commission, acting with the object of obtaining each year the maximum which the circumstances of that year permit. For the first still leaves her with some slight incentive for enterprise, energy, and hope.

Germany's Capacity to Pay

How is Germany placed, in the situation in which the rest of the treaty leaves her, for discharging a vast obligation?

It is evident that Germany's pre-war capacity to pay an annual foreign tribute has not been unaffected by the almost total loss of her colonies, her overseas connections, her mercantile marine, and her foreign properties; by the cession of ten percent of her territory and population, of one-third of her coal and of three-quarters of her iron ore; by two million casualties among men in the prime of life; by the starvation of her people for four years; by the burden of a vast war debt; by the depreciation of her currency to less than one-seventh its former value; by the disruption of her allies and their territories; by revolution at home and Bolshevism on her borders; and by all the unmeasured ruin in strength and hope of four years of all-swallowing war and final defeat.

All this, one would have supposed, is evident. Yet most estimates of a great indemnity from Germany depend on the assumption that she is in a position to conduct in the future a vastly greater trade than ever she has had in the past.

The forms in which Germany can discharge her debt are three and three only:

1. immediately transferable wealth in the form of gold, ships, and foreign securities;
2. the value of property in ceded territory or surrendered under the armistice; and
3. annual payments spread over a term of years, partly in cash and partly in materials such as coal products, potash, and dyes.

There is no other way whatever.

In my book I have analyzed in detail the value of the items under the first two heads. What has occurred since I made my estimate has tended to the conclusion that this estimate is too high rather than too low; nor have my figures been seriously challenged by any one. The general conclusion of this examination of the available data is that a sum of from five hundred million dollars to one billion dollars is the utmost that can be available after payment of the costs of the armies of occupation.

It will perhaps assist the reader to visualize how trifling the tangible and transferable wealth of Germany is, in relation to the fantastic magnitudes mentioned above, if I select one important special item. The total value of the German mercantile marine, which under the treaty the Allies are to obtain for themselves, is probably overstated at six hundred million dollars—six hundred million dollars toward a total liability of forty billion dollars. The vast expenditures of the war, the inflation of prices, and the depreciation of currency, leading up to a complete instability of the unit of value, joined to the fact that what we believed to be the limits of possibility have been so enormously exceeded and those who have founded their expectations on the past have been so often wrong, have made the man in the street lose all sense of number and magnitude in matters of finance. But we must endeavor to regain our sense of proportion.

If the amount of Germany's immediately transferable property is unimportant, it follows that the Reparation Commission must mainly depend on future annual payments. There is literally only one way in which such payments can be made (apart from temporary loans to Germany by foreign countries), namely, by the exports of Germany exceeding her imports. It follows, therefore, that a rational estimate of the possibilities of the case can only be made on the basis of the examination of the trade figures of Germany before the war and of the possible expansion of the export items.

It is not possible within the limits of the space here at my disposal to enter into the details of this examination. But my broad conclusion is that in the actual facts of the case there is no reasonable probability of Germany's being able to make payments in excess of five hundred million dollars annually. This figure has not been challenged in detail by any one, and has been supported, as being in the neighborhood of the best estimate, by many distinguished authorities.

Her Export Powers

A few leading facts may be summarized. The staple exports of Germany are:

(1) Iron and steel goods; (2) machinery; (3) coal, coke and briquettes; (4) woolen goods; (5) cotton goods; these five classes between them accounting before the war for nearly forty percent of the total exports. As regards two of the categories, namely, cotton and woolen goods, the increase of an export trade is dependent upon an increase of the import of the raw material, since Germany produces no cotton and practically no wool. These trades are therefore incapable of great expansion unless Germany is given facilities for securing these raw materials (which can only be at the expense of the Allies) in excess of the pre-war standard of consumption, and even then the effective increase is not the gross value of the exports, but only the difference between the value of the manufactured exports and of the imported raw material.

As regards the other three categories—namely, machinery, iron goods, and coal—Germany's capacity to increase her exports will have been taken from her by the cessions of territory in Poland, Upper Silesia, and Alsace-Lorraine. As has been pointed out already, these districts accounted for nearly one-third of Germany's production of coal. But they also supplied no less than three-quarters of her iron-ore production and thirty-eight percent of her blast-furnaces. Unless, therefore, Alsace-Lorraine and Upper Silesia send their iron ore to Germany proper, to be worked up—which will involve an increase in the imports for which she will have to find payment—so far from any increase in export trade being possible, a decrease is inevitable.

Yet an enormously increased export is necessary. For, so far from Germany's exports exceeding her imports before the war, her imports exceeded her exports on the average of the five years ending 1913 by about three hundred and seventy million dollars. On the assumptions, therefore, (1) that we do not specially favor Germany over ourselves in supplies of such raw materials as cotton and wool (the world's supply of which is limited); (2) that France, having secured the iron-ore deposits, makes a serious attempt to secure the blast-furnaces and the steel trade also; (3) that Germany is not encouraged and assisted to undercut the iron and other trades of the Allies in overseas markets; and (4) that a substantial preference is not given to German goods in the British Empire and other Allied countries, it becomes evident by examination of the specific items that not much is practicable.

I reach, therefore, the final conclusion that, including all methods of payment—immediately transferable wealth, ceded property, and an annual tribute—ten billion dollars is a safe maximum figure of Germany's capacity to pay. In all the actual circumstances, I do not believe that she can pay as much.

A capacity of forty billion dollars or even of twenty-five billion dollars is, therefore, not within the limits of reasonable possibility. It is for those who believe that Germany can make an annual payment amounting to thousands of millions of dollars to say *in what specific commodities* they intend this payment to be made, and *in what markets* the goods are to be sold. Until they proceed to some degree of detail, and are able to produce some tangible argument in favor of their conclusions, they do not deserve to be believed.

A Dead Treaty

Such, in brief, are the economic provisions of the Treaty of Versailles, which the United States has refused to ratify and most of Europe would now unwrite if it could. A year has passed since it came into existence, and authority has already passed from it—not, in my judgment, because there has been much softening of sentiment toward Germany, but because the treaty is no treaty, because it is now generally recognized that in truth it settles nothing. After what has passed, Europe requires above all a *settlement*, and this the treaty has not given it. If you pledge a man to perform the impossible, you are no nearer a decision as to what in fact he is to do; for his pledge is, necessarily, a dead letter. The reparation and coal clauses of the treaty are its most important economic features. But being composed of foolish, idle words, having no relation to the real facts, they are without practical effect, and they leave the prospects of the future undetermined.

What, then, are we to do? Before I venture an answer, there is one element in the attitude of the United States to the treaty which deserves attention. The United States has refused to ratify the treaty; the United States gets nothing out of the treaty; the ideals of the vast majority of the inhabitants of the United States are probably at variance with the treaty; even at Paris it was the representatives of the United States who fought most sincerely and resolutely for the modification of the treaty—yet it is in the United States that the treaty now finds its most whole-hearted defenders.

The Situation Here

The explanation of the paradox is to be found, I think, in this: in England the treaty was swallowed in the first instance without much criticism or comment; it has never become in any intense degree a party question; Mr. Lloyd George himself now appears among those most willing to modify it; and consequently there is no vested interest in defending it. But in the United States the treaty has become a bitter party question. The President, in a spirit, as I believe, of sincere delusion, or, as his friends maintain, of calculated wisdom, has maneuvered himself or been maneuvered into the position of defending the integral acceptance of the document. The personal adherents of the President must follow his single track. An American professor or an American lawyer back from the Conference writes about the treaty in newspapers articles of hot eulogy, such as are not common in Europe. My own American colleagues from Paris, whose views I so much shared and whose labors against the treaty I so much admired, now, alas! find themselves committed by loyalty to an honored chief to representing the treaty, what no one in Europe now thinks it, as an instrument of substantial wisdom. Truly the President carries his own cross, doomed by a perverse fate to support a settlement which has at the same time shattered his prestige and defeated his ideals.

It will therefore be difficult, I fear—though I speak at a distance and without knowledge—so long as the treaty remains a party issue, for the United States to approach its great problems in the impartial and disinterested spirit which their special position makes possible and will, I believe, eventually make actual.

Remedies

From this necessary digression I return to the question of the policy of the immediate future. For my own part I hold with increasing conviction that the revision of the treaty is the necessary and inevitable first step forward. In the book which I wrote nearly a year ago I proposed various other remedies, including an international loan and the cancellation of war debt between Allies. I believe that these, perhaps utopian, plans were of value a year ago; they may be of value again a year or two hence, though by that time the circumstances of the day may demand a different solution in detail if not in spirit. But I concede that at this moment of time the attitude of the United States and the actual condition of Europe have combined to render them impracticable. Until by the revision of the treaty we are furnished with a sound foundation on which to build, the best laid schemes will fail.

Let me add that I differ profoundly from those who, admitting the imperfections of the treaty, look for succor to the provisions contained in it for its progressive modification in practice by the unanimous consent of the leading Allies. The difference between revising the treaty at once and progressively modifying it under the force of circumstances is the difference between building a firm foundation and underpinning day by day a tottering structure.

The Future

This revision is bound, as matters now are, to be primarily the affair of Europe. But it will be a disaster for the world if America isolates herself. I do not regret that the Congress of the United States has repudiated the treaty of Paris. But I pray that out of the ashes of this treaty and out of the embryonic shapes of the present League of Nations a new settlement and a new League may even now arise which will command the allegiance of all men.

The current of time seems to move slowly sometimes to the passengers upon its surface. In the interval, perhaps a short one, which must now elapse, I hope that we, the various peoples of the world, may abstain from vulgar and unmerciful words. It has been said that individuals everywhere are lovable and all nations detestable. There are very few nations at this time against which an accuser could not draw a just and injurious indictment. But Burke spoke deeply when he declared that he did not know the method of drawing up an indictment against a whole people. "I really think," he added, "that for wise men this is not judicious, for sober men not decent, for minds tinctured with humanity not mild and merciful."

Marc Trachtenberg

The Evidence of French Moderation

In the following selection Marc Trachtenberg, professor of history at the University of Pennsylvania, disputes Keynes's characterization of French reparation policy as intransigent and vindictive. Relying on archives unavailable to earlier commentators on the topic, he presents a much more balanced assessment of the financial settlement after the Great War and highlights several "lost opportunities" after the First World War that would become realities after the Second World War (such as American government aid for European reconstruction and Franco-German economic cooperation).

In his article "Ten Years of Peace Conference History," which appeared in this journal in 1929, Robert Binkley attacked as simplistic those accounts which depicted the conference as a struggle between "heroes and villains." Binkley was convinced, however, that with time the moralistic tinge would fade from the historiography of the peace settlement and a more sophisticated understanding of the period would take shape. Over half a century has now passed since the Treaty of Versailles was signed, but in essentials the original picture that Binkley condemned remains intact: The conference is still almost universally portrayed as a struggle between forces of light and forces of darkness or, to put the interpretation in the new form given it by Arno Mayer, between

From Marc Trachtenberg, "Reparation at the Paris Peace Conference," *Journal of Modern History*, 51 (March 1979), pp. 24–44. Reprinted by permission of the University of Chicago.

the forces of movement and the forces of order. In terms of national policies, the struggle is usually represented as a conflict between America, moderate and conciliatory, and France, anxious for a crushing "Carthaginian" peace.

In the standard accounts of the peace conference, the interpretation of the reparation issue plays a key role. A harsh, even "vengeful" France is commonly portrayed as the driving force behind the demand for reparation. The French government, it is frequently assumed, sought to use reparation as a means of crippling Germany economically. At the very least, the French are blamed for counting too heavily on German reparation payments for a solution to their economic and financial problems: Clemenceau's Minister of Finance, L.-L. Klotz, is frequently ridiculed in the textbooks for basing his policy on a blind faith that "Germany would pay"—the slogan "L'Allemagne paiera" is said to typify French policy at the time. American policy was much more moderate and more attuned to economic realities. The British delegates were somewhere in between; Lloyd George's heart was with the Americans, but he was forced by political conditions at home to press for a harsher settlement than he himself would have liked.

This general picture of the reparation issue in 1919 is an important element in the accepted interpretation of the peace conference as a whole. What I want to do here is test the common picture of reparation against the documentary evidence. I believe the analysis will show that the traditional view in this limited area simply cannot stand up. Because of the importance of reparation in the standard accounts, a conclusion of this sort implies that the Manichaean interpretation of the peace conference period needs to be fundamentally reconsidered. If traditional views are so off the mark on reparation, how valid are they for other issues? And on broader questions as well—for example, the basic aims of the different governments—there is a real need to reexamine how well established accepted ideas are. The case of reparation suggests in particular that the traditional identification of the Wilsonian left with a peace of reconciliation is too pat—the punitive overtones of the moralism of the moderate left have to be taken seriously. On the other hand, the "realism" of the right cannot be automatically identified with harsh policy: Clemenceau's realism was the basis of what will be shown to be his moderation on reparation.

Beyond such historiographical considerations, this study—and this, I think, is its real justification—has its own importance in terms of the analysis of international politics between the wars. It was preeminently in the struggle over reparation that the structure of power in Europe was worked out in the early 1920s; the outcome of this struggle sealed the fate of the system of constraints on German power embodied in the Treaty of Versailles and thus paved the way for the resurgence of Germany as the dominant force in Europe. To understand this struggle, it is obviously necessary to start at the beginning with an analysis of how the reparation question developed in the first place.

What then will this analysis demonstrate? First that the emergence of reparation as an important issue—as in fact the dominant issue in postwar international politics—was by no means inevitable, at least from the standpoint of French policy. The French government hoped during the war and even into the armistice period to solve French economic problems through what it called Allied cooperation, above all through the continuation of the inter-Allied economic system that had taken shape essentially in the last year of the war. Reparation played a very secondary role in French wartime schemes for post-war reconstruction; it was only America's unwillingness to go along with these plans that led the French to turn to reparation. At first the idea was to use enormous reparation claims as a means of manipulating the United States: If the Americans wanted to avoid a harsh peace, they had better be generous with France. But the American delegation refused to give in, and the French soon gave up the game and presented their real reparation demands, which were in fact rather modest. Thereupon French and American reparation policies more or less converged. It was Britain that proved the stumbling block to a relatively moderate settlement. British figures consistently remained higher than those the Americans and the French were willing to accept.

There is only one way to prove these things, and that is through the close analysis of figures. It is regrettable that this is the case, because it is hard to sustain interest in a detailed analysis of this sort. Nevertheless in the past a large part of the failure of historiography to understand reparation was due to an inability or an unwillingness to examine this side of the issue with even minimal skill. Figures representing present value (the principal of the debt) are mentioned in the same breath as figures derived from adding up annuities (principal and interest), as though the two were comparable; figures are cited which do not appear in any of the documentary sources; sometimes the problem is virtually dismissed, as in Stephen Schuker's reference to the "astronomical figures bandied about at the peace conference"—this kind of phrase tends to obviate the need for close analysis. But here the negotiations for a fixed sum will be taken seriously, and the examination of figures will be at the center of the study.

I

During the war French officials had elaborated grandiose plans for the permanent reorganization of the world economy. Etienne Clémentel, minister of commerce for most of the war, was the principal architect of these plans. Clémentel wanted above all to institute a permanent inter-Allied control of raw materials: The Allied governments, acting together, would directly ration out at set prices the vast supplies of raw materials they controlled. Such an arrangement would be the heart of an Allied-led economic bloc that he hoped would emerge in some form from the war. The control of raw materials would be supplemented by other forms of cooperation—for example, preferential tariffs within the bloc and accords on financial and currency questions.

An Allied economic system, similar in scope and structure to the kind of system to which Clémentel aspired, was brought into being in the last year of the war to deal with the critical economic problems then confronting the Alliance. In 1918 inter-Allied bodies—the "programme committees" and "executives"—set the aggregate supply programs of the European Allies; American credits were automatically extended to cover these purchases. Clémentel hoped that a permanent Allied bloc would evolve naturally out of the wartime regime; it was taken for granted in official French circles that the wartime system would at the very least be retained to solve the problems of reconstruction.

On the eve of the armistice, Clémentel outlined his views in an important letter to Prime Minister Georges Clemenceau. It is clear from this document that Clémentel pinned his hopes for economic resurgence on Allied "cooperation"—that is, on the continuation of the wartime system of economic controls—and not on reparation. To be sure, French officials wanted certain things from Germany—liquid assets like foreign securities and vital raw materials, especially coal—but they were aware that their real demands on the German economy were relatively modest. In this letter of September 19, 1918, moreover, Clémentel noted "the material impossibility for Germany to rebuild" the devastated areas and warned that to hold Germany financially liable for all war damages "would completely crush her and reduce her to a state of economic bondage which would strip away from humanity all hope of a lasting peace." Instead he called for a "world fund for the reparation of war damages."

On September 28, 1918, Clemenceau formally accepted the ideas outlined in this letter as the basis of French policy. He perhaps viewed Clémentel's sweeping plan to create a permanent economic bloc with some skepticism, but the idea of an Allied solution to the economic problems of the immediate postwar period was both viable and attractive. In general, Clemenceau hoped to base the peace on the effective continuation of the wartime Alliance, rather than on the destruction of Germany, and the kind of program his Minister of Commerce advocated for the period of reconstruction was well within the orbit of Clemenceau's fundamental ideas.

The Americans, however, refused to cooperate with any of these plans. A few days before the armistice Herbert Hoover, then President Wilson's chief adviser on economic matters, cabled his representative in London that the American government would "not agree to any programme that even looks like inter-Allied control of our resources after peace." The next month, during the negotiations on the organization of relief, Clémentel again pressed for continued economic "cooperation." But the Americans resisted, and for the moment, Hoover wrote, Clémentel abandoned the idea of a "complete economic Council controlling all raw material, finance, transportation and food."

At the end of the year, Clémentel outlined a strategy designed to overcome American resistance. At the peace conference the French should stress that the kind of settlement "imposed" on Germany would be a function of the arrangements the Allies made among themselves. If the Allies and the Americans abandoned the wartime policy of mutual assistance and economic solidarity, then France would insist on a harsh peace. The "associated states" gathered at Paris to make peace would then be presented with a choice: "They must decide if they will institute, by means of measures based on common agreement, an economic organization designed to assure the world a secure recovery in the aftermath of the upheaval, or if the only guarantee of this security that they envisage is a peace of reprisals and punishments." The document attached to this letter left little doubt that an enormous demand for reparation would figure prominently in the bargaining. The French claim would initially be huge. If it were admitted at the peace conference that such reparation was beyond Germany's capacity to pay, then "it will be up to the Allied and Associated governments to study alternative schemes to assure the nations who have suffered most from the war the full reparation of their losses."

When the peace conference convened in January, the French delegation sought to apply this strategy and supported the British position that war costs should be included in the bill. The Americans rejected this idea: The Allies, they argued, had no legal right to demand war costs. The "pre-armistice agreement"—that is, the set of conditions under which the Germans had agreed to lay down their arms—bound the Allies as well as Germany. Under the terms of this agreement, the German government had only promised to make compensation for damages done to the civilian population; the Allies, the Americans argued, were not entitled to ask for anything more. Nevertheless, the French initially supported the British on war costs.

At the same time, however, French officials hinted strongly that their support of a moderate peace settlement would depend on American willingness to "cooperate." A Clémentel memorandum of February 5 explicitly stated that French approval of a moderate peace was contingent on the continuation of Allied "cooperation"; if the Allies refused to accept this, the French would insist on a harsh peace. Minister of Finance Klotz insisted on February 20 in the conference's Financial Commission on the link between reparation and the settlement of inter-Allied financial questions. "The attitude of the Minister of Finance," he said, "will depend to a certain extent on the way inter-Allied questions are solved." If French reparation claims were not adequately satisfied, "it will then be necessary for my friends to come to my assistance."

French representatives were more specific in private conversations. They made it clear to the Americans that they wanted to pool war costs and reapportion the inter-Allied debt, each nation paying according to its ability. President Wilson and his advisers were extremely hostile to these plans and would not even discuss them. Norman Davis, Wilson's principal financial counseler in Paris, wrote the President on February 2 to inform him of the "concerted movement, which is on foot, to obtain an interlocking of the United States with the continental governments in the whole financial situation." Wilson assured Davis on February 5 that he was already aware of it and "on my guard against it."

The American position was starkly laid down in early March. In a letter of March 8, Albert Rathbone, an Assistant Secretary of the Treasury, declared his displeasure at reports that Klotz favored the reapportionment of war debts. "I have, however, to state most emphatically," he wrote, "that the Treasury . . . will not assent to any discussion at the peace conference, or elsewhere, of any plan or arrangement for the release,

consolidation or reapportionment of the obligations of foreign governments held by the United States." The Treasury would discontinue
advances to any government that supported such schemes. And on
March 9, Davis "very frankly" stated to Klotz

> that his efforts to bring pressure to bear from one direction for the in-
> crease of American advances to France, and from other direction to bring
> up the matter of reapportioning war debts, etc., was very ill advised, be-
> cause no one can do anything or give any consideration to the latter, but
> should there be any further attempt to bring it up for discussion, it would
> have to be insisted by us that the discussion be had with the Secretary of
> the Treasury and that we would feel obliged, pending such discussion, to
> make the suggestion to the Secretary of the Treasury that it would not be
> advisable to continue to accept further obligations.

From the American point of view, this harsh medicine brought the
French back to their senses. His declarations to Klotz, Davis wrote, "apparently had the desired effect and it was stated by Klotz that he would
not again bring the matter forward." A few days later, Davis expressed
satisfaction that the French were "not difficult to do business with now
that the intrigue had been rounded out of the situation."

As for Clémentel's hope of perpetuating the wartime system of economic controls, this too foundered on the rock of American resistance.
At first the Americans seemed to favor a limited system of controls designed to facilitate the reconstruction of the devastated areas, but soon
the American delegation came to oppose all economic controls on principle. To be sure, the Supreme Economic Council (SEC) was created
in early February to deal with such questions as "finance, food, blockade control, shipping and raw materials" during the period prior to the
signing of the peace treaty. The creation of an institutional framework
for cooperation, however, meant little in itself. Inside the SEC the
Americans continued to resist sweeping plans for inter-Allied control of
raw material, shipping, and finance. As a result, the SEC handled only
problems of relief and blockade; the problem of French reconstruction
was hardly even touched. Clémentel himself was keenly aware that the
American attitude was responsible for the final frustration of his
schemes. "The very sharp opposition of the American delegation," he
wrote in November 1919, "prevented the S.E.C. from carrying out . . .
the task that had been vested in it."

Thus the French effort to manipulate the United States had ended
in utter failure. That the effort was made at all is in itself remarkable,
for it was based on a profound and surprising misunderstanding of

American attitudes and policy. By the beginning of March, there was no use in playing the game any longer, and from then on the French delegation pursued an essentially moderate reparation policy.

II

It was Louis Loucheur, Minister of Industrial Reconstitution and Clemenceau's chief adviser on economic matters, who was to carry out this policy. Loucheur represented France in the really decisive negotiations on reparation; in these meetings he demonstrated the French government's willingness to agree to modest figures and accept a reasonable reparation settlement. It was the intransigent attitude of the British government that consistently prevented agreement on a relatively moderate fixed sum.

The domestic political situation is commonly blamed for the tough reparation policy pursued by the British government at the time. The documents, however, do not support the view that the Lloyd George government pressed its reparation demands reluctantly, solely in response to inescapable political pressure. Indeed, at times Lloyd George seemed eager for a punitive peace. "Germany had committed a great crime," he told the Imperial War Cabinet in August 1918, "and it was necessary to make it impossible that anyone should be tempted to repeat that offence. The Terms of Peace must be tantamount to some penalty for the offence." As the armistice approached, he seemed furious that hostilities would end before the war touched Germany: "The Prime Minister said that industrial France had been devastated and Germany had escaped. At the first moment when we were in a position to put the lash on Germany's back she said, 'I give up.' The question arose whether we ought not to continue lashing her as she had lashed France. Mr. Chamberlain said that vengeance was too expensive these days. The Prime Minister said it was not vengeance but justice."

When the peace conference opened, Lloyd George appointed consistent advocates of a heavy indemnity to key positions on the commission set up by the peace conference to deal with reparation. Two of these men—William Morris Hughes, prime minister of Australia, and Lord Cunliffe, former governor of the Bank of England—had signed the December 1918 report of the Cabinet Committee on Indemnity. This report had asserted that Germany could pay the entire cost of the war—a view later condemned by Lloyd George in his memoirs as a "wild and fantastic chimera."

Cunliffe in fact was chairman of the subcommission charged with examining Germany's capacity to pay. It was in this body that the French, obliquely at first and then more directly, began to break away from the British and side more with the Americans on the key issue of a relatively moderate fixed sum.

On February 21 in the subcommission Cunliffe asserted without any real evidence that Germany could pay a bill including war costs, which he estimated at 480 milliard gold marks ($120,000,000,000). Loucheur began an indirect attack on Cunliffe's position. First he stated that if war costs were included, the bill would come to about 800 milliard gold marks, but for the sake of argument he would take the British figure of 480 milliard. He estimated that Germany could make an immediate payment of about 20 milliards, principally in gold, ships, and foreign assets and securities. The balance had to be amortized at 5 percent over a fifty-year period. This amounted to an annual payment of about 24-28 milliard gold marks. Reparation in kind—coal, wood, and potash, principally—could account for 3 or 4 milliards annually. The balance of the annuity amounted to 22 milliards. "Is this an impossible figure?" Loucheur asked. "I do not think so." But far from being an expression of support for Cunliffe's position, this statement was merely the first step in a *reductio ad absurdum* argument designed to demolish the idea that such a large figure was within reason.

Loucheur surveyed some possible means of payment. A tax on German exports? "That is one way" that the Germans might be made to pay. "But I fear," he said, "that the use of this means of payment might hurt us more than it would help us, for it threatens to put Germany in such a state of inferiority in export markets that she will no longer export at all." He concluded that for the balance of the annuity beyond what Germany could pay in kind, "I declare myself unable to indicate the means of payment. I would be very happy if any of our colleagues can bring up any new ideas which might open up horizons that I am presently unable to see."

The next day he took the argument to its conclusion that enormous payments were impossible. The American delegate on the subcommission, Thomas Lamont, had suggested a bill of 120 milliard gold marks. This was equivalent to an annuity of about 6.4 milliards. But was even this relatively modest figure within Germany's capacity? "I have listened with great care to all that has been said here," Loucheur declared, "and I am obliged to state that all the means of payment that we have succeeded at finding can only cover an annuity of 4 to 5 milliards [of francs, equivalent to about 3 to 4 milliard gold marks]. If the commission adopts the figure of 1000 milliards [800 milliard gold marks— equivalent to an annuity of over 40 milliard gold marks], what new means of payment will we propose? I see only one, seizing the fortune of the enemy countries in the enemy countries themselves. I am not suggesting that we adopt this method. Only if we demand that much this is what we will have to do."

He then posed the question more sharply. Should the Allies become the owners of German forests, mines, houses, and factories? Perhaps ownership of the forests was possible. But as for the mines, "I confess that I would not want them at any price, because the mine without the miners, and the miners without political control is impossible." Should the Allies seize Germany's industrial fortune, say half of her corporate wealth? Loucheur doubted whether the Allies were willing to take this kind of measure. If this was out of the question, he said, "our labors are just about over. We have only to sum up and conclude first, that we can get an immediate payment of 25 milliards [20 milliard gold marks], and second, that they will pay us an annuity of 8 milliards [6.4 milliard gold marks, corresponding to Lamont's 120 milliard figure for the debt], or 33 milliards [26.4 milliard gold marks, corresponding to Cunliffe's 480 milliard figure], that we can just about see how the payment of the 8 milliards can be made, but as for the payment of the 33 milliards, *we leave to the poets of the future the task of finding solutions.*"

By this analysis, Loucheur completely discredited Cunliffe's baseless estimates. He was thereby laying the groundwork for a relatively modest settlement. At this meeting of February 22, Loucheur, Cunliffe, and Lamont were appointed to a special committee to draft the subcommission's report. These three delegates used the occasion to negotiate privately on the size of the German liability. "To Lamont, Loucheur appeared very conciliatory, for he agreed rapidly to make a great concession, to come down to 160 milliard marks. After this, Cunliffe promised to consider a figure of 190 milliard marks. As Lamont has said, 'This was progress'; but then Cunliffe and Sumner 'put their heads together, went off the deep end, and refused to compromise at all.' According to Lamont, Loucheur had been brought substantially to accepting the American view, but Cunliffe proved the chief obstacle to complete agreement."

This evidence of French moderation disturbed both the British and the American delegation. Cunliffe suspected foul play. He wrote Lloyd George on March 2 that the American and French delegates on his subcommission had "come to some arrangement" whereby the latter had reduced his reparation figure from 600 down to 160 milliard gold marks. "I cannot say what the bargain is," Cunliffe added, "but the result is that we shall be practically left out in the cold." He urged Lloyd George to "settle" the matter directly with Colonel House.

House himself was concerned about the situation. According to his intimate, Sir William Wiseman, he informally indicated to the British that he was "very anxious to avoid an open collision of view between the British and the Americans with the French supporting the Americans against us." In outlining the situation to the Cabinet on March 4, Lloyd George did not take an accommodating tone; he merely noted that since the British "had been the chief financiers of the war, it was intelligible that the French and the Italians would not be so greatly concerned about the size of the indemnity as ourselves." Nevertheless, he did cooperate with a new effort initiated by House to reach agreement on a figure: "after some hesitation and largely on my advice," according to House, Lloyd George appointed Edwin Montagu, the Secretary of State for India, to a three-man committee charged with working out a fixed sum. Loucheur represented France on the committee, and Norman Davis was the American delegate.

The Committee of Three reported to the heads of government on March 15. It recommended a reparation debt of 120 milliard gold marks, payable half in gold and half in German currency. According to Davis, Lloyd George at first protested this figure but then was persuaded by Davis's argument to agree to its inclusion. Loucheur recorded that at this meeting Lloyd George "cried out against the smallness of this figure" but does not record his eventual agreement. Loucheur, incidentally, noted that Clemenceau had approved the concessions he had made.

Three days later, on March 18, Sumner had replaced Montagu as the British representative on the Committee of Three, and Lloyd George denied that any figure had been accepted. The pretext for Montagu's replacement was that he had to return to Britain because of his mother's death. But he was able to return to Paris shortly, and the substitution of Sumner, who took a much harsher line, must be seen as a political move.

At the end of March, Lloyd George, afraid that harsh peace terms might drive Germany to Bolshevism, is widely supposed to have pressed for a moderate peace settlement. In particular, Arno Mayer claims without evidence that he "opted" for a reasonable reparation settlement at this time. Although he set out the argument for a mild peace in the famous Fontainebleau memorandum, the noble rhetoric of this document cannot be taken at face value. There was no opting for a moderate figure, and in reality the Fontainebleau memorandum marked no change in actual British reparation policy, which in its essentials remained as unbending as ever.

The memorandum was circulated to Lloyd George's colleagues on the Council of Four on March 25. In it he declared that "we ought to endeavour to draw up a peace settlement as if we were impartial arbiters, forgetful of the passions of the war." It seems, however, that Lloyd George was talking mainly about the territorial settlement, not the reparation clauses. When the Council of Four discussed the memorandum on March 27, he rhetorically asked: "What did France resent more, the loss of Alsace-Lorraine or the obligation to pay an indemnity of five milliards? I know your answer in advance. What impressed me the first time I went to Paris most was the statue of Strasbourg in mourning." Germans must not be placed under Polish rule. Anything else, he declared, the Germans would accept, *"including a very large indemnity."*

A just peace was an attractive ideal, but what did it amount to insofar as reparation was concerned? Here the Fontainebleau memorandum was unclear. It even seemed to continue the call for a heavy burden: "Our terms may be severe, they may be stern and even ruthless, but at the same time they can be so just that the country on which they are imposed will feel in its heart it has no right to complain." Lloyd George evidently supposed that the German people would share his conception of justice, that they would feel "in their hearts" Germany's guilt and their consequent obligation to pay an indemnity. The treaty, declared the Fontainebleau memorandum, must take "into account Germany's responsibility for the origin of the war, and for the way in which it was fought."

The more explicit references to reparation were remarkably vague. "If possible," he hedged, the reparation burden should disappear "with the generation that made the war"—a statement no one would disagree with. In the attached "Outline of Peace Terms," the section on reparation began with the statement that Germany was "to undertake to pay full reparation to the allies." But since this was greatly in excess of Germany's capacity, "it is therefore suggested that Germany should pay an annual sum for a stated number of years." But this in effect was what the American and French delegates had already agreed to in the negotiations on a fixed sum, only to be blocked by British intransigence in holding out for higher figures. And the Fontainebleau memorandum marked absolutely no change in the British position on this question, as will be demonstrated presently.

Finally, without even explicitly endorsing it himself, he declared that "it has been suggested" that a commission be set up to allow postponement of payments and cancellation of interest on these payments, but only "during the first few years." The one precise suggestion he made referred to the allotment of German payments. He proposed that they be distributed according to the formula 50:30:20—50 percent for France, 30 percent for the British Empire, 20 percent for everyone else. In view of the fact that the British Empire had not been directly touched by the war in its home territories, this suggestion was neither very generous nor very enlightened. It contradicted Lloyd George's principle that the Allies should limit their claims to those the Germans would regard as just, for an indemnity to Britain would be viewed by the Germans as a clear violation of the prearmistice agreement.

It is important to note, however, that the Fontainebleau memorandum and even Lloyd George's harsh criticism of a proposed reparation scheme in the Council of Four led to no change in the substance of British policy. On March 22, Lloyd George had told Davis and Lamont that 100 milliard marks would be "quite acceptable to him" if they could get Sumner and Cunliffe to agree, "which he would like to have for his own protection and justification." Lloyd George, that is, had given a veto over a reparation figure to a man who he realized was very far removed from the spirit of the Fontainebleau memorandum: On March 26, the day after the memorandum was circulated, Lloyd George told his colleagues on the Council of Four, "when I spoke to Lord Sumner . . . of the danger of Bolshevism in Germany if we went too far in our demands, he answered, 'in that case the Germans would be cutting their own throats, I could not hope for anything better.'"

Indeed, the same day that the memorandum was circulated, the reparation figure proposed by Sumner was considerably higher than those proposed by the French and American representatives. The British suggested 220 milliard marks, the French a minimum of 124 and a maximum of 188, and the Americans a minimum of 100 and a maximum of 140 (in the French and American schemes, a commission would each year fix the annuity between the minimum and maximum levels). Thus the noble generalities of the Fontainebleau memorandum had little to do with actual British reparation policy. Whether or not Lloyd George in his heart desired a moderate reparation settlement is beside the point. For whatever reason, the reparation policy of the British delegation was markedly more unyielding than that of any other Allied delegation.

It was British policy, especially British intransigence on figures, that was ultimately responsible for the failure of the treaty to include a fixed sum. The French and American delegates evidently wanted a figure. The latter repeatedly argued that the uncertain atmosphere that would prevail if the treaty failed to name a fixed sum would be disastrous to all concerned, to Germany as well as the West. In particular, a restoration of the international credit system was dependent on a fixed sum. No one would lend Germany anything, it was argued, if the amount due for reparation were not limited, for the money which would otherwise be used to repay such loans might have to go into paying reparation. But unable to borrow, Germany would be unable to procure "working capital," and the reparation annuities could not begin to be paid, let alone "mobilized" through the sale of reparation bonds abroad.

The French delegates could not fail to be impressed by these arguments. They needed the money immediately, and besides, "mobilization" would relieve them of the worry of enforcing payment. This would become the problem of the bondholders. The French insisted, however, that their share of the reparation receipts cover the direct material damages they had suffered in the war: The French share of Loucheur's "minimum" figure of 124 milliard gold marks would "just about cover," he told the Council of Four on March 26, "the reparation of material damages."

At this meeting, Clemenceau supported the plan outlined by Loucheur: The treaty would set minimum and maximum figures, and within these limits a commission would each year set the German annuity, taking account of German capacity. The American and French delegates had agreed on the principle of the plan, differing somewhat (by about 25 percent) on the figures. Clemenceau further declared that the government could reserve the right to make further cuts in these figures and could "even suppress the minimum" if it became clear this was more than Germany could pay; he even was willing to discuss the question with the Germans themselves, a point later reiterated by Loucheur: "there remains the possibility of not definitively setting our figure before discussing it with the Germans at Versailles." It is remarkable that in the discussion that followed, and in spite of the conciliatory language of the Fontainebleau memorandum circulated the previous day, Lloyd George completely ignored this French suggestion; as for Wilson, he also paid no attention to the idea.

In early April, Clemenceau continued to favor some kind of fixed sum. He told Loucheur that it was "necessary to put a figure in the treaty." How moderate a figure would Clemenceau and Loucheur accept? They were willing to go quite far—indeed, all the way back to the Fourteen Points and the prearmistice agreement. In the afternoon meeting of the Council of Four on March 26, Loucheur presented the French claim for material damages—80 milliard gold francs, or approximately 64 milliard gold marks. Lloyd George vehemently attacked these figures as exaggerated and then demanded that British pensions be reimbursed at the higher British rate—he opposed Loucheur's proposal for a uniform scale based on the lower French scale.

To avoid these unseemly battles over what amounted to apportionment, Norman Davis proposed the setting of percentages through direct negotiation. Loucheur and Lloyd George agreed; the heads of government left and the experts began to negotiate. Loucheur gave a history of the previous bargaining on apportionment. By accepting direct bargaining on percentages at all, he said, France was abandoning the principle of an absolute priority for direct material damages and so was making a great concession. He had at first proposed a proportion of 72:18, while the British suggested 50:33. "In a conversation with Mr. Montagu," he continued "I went down to 58:25. Mr. Montagu suggested 56:28, which would have given England half of what France was to receive. I did not accept this suggestion, which in addition was not a firm proposition; from this Mr. Montagu concluded that no accord was possible."

John Maynard Keynes, representing the British treasury, asked Loucheur if he still proposed 58:25. Although Clemenceau had not authorized him to go that far, he replied, he was willing to endorse this proposition; "as a proof of good faith," he would even recommend the proportion 55:25. Since the negotiations with Montagu in early March, however, the British had hardened their position. While Montagu had been willing to accept 56:28, Lloyd George and now Sumner insisted on 50:30, considerably less from the French point of view than the Montagu ratio. Loucheur declared this unacceptable.

He then made an extraordinary declaration. He was willing, he said, to accept the literal definition of the word "reparation," "even if it excludes pensions." "I would prefer," he said, "the pure and simple application of the Fourteen Points to what is proposed." Limiting reparation to direct material damages would mean allotting France 70 percent of the payments. (Since he had estimated French direct material damages at 64 milliard gold marks, a strict application of the Fourteen Points would have meant a total German liability of only 91 milliard gold marks.) But France had "made a concession to England taking into account her political situation." The French government, however, could go no further.

Davis's response was equally remarkable. "If we Americans had followed our instincts," he said, "we would have kept to a strict interpretation of the Fourteen Points, which could not have yielded more than 25 milliard dollars [100 milliard gold marks]. We do what we can to interpret this definition in a broad sense, in order to find what is necessary to cover the pensions." The French were now more "Wilsonian" than the Americans! Davis refused the opportunity to form a common front with the French on a really moderate reparation settlement, firmly based on the prearmistice agreement, and this at a time when the arguments of the Fontainebleau memorandum might have been used most effectively to overcome British obstruction.

Instead, Davis urged the French to compromise more. He proposed a ratio of 56:28, which was supported by Sumner. Loucheur would not go beyond 55:25 (so in a sense he was primarily defending the interests of third parties like Italy and Belgium), in spite of continued American pressure. "I hope M. Loucheur will show the same spirit of conciliation" as Sumner had shown, Davis declared; "we have nothing further to propose." This was too much for Loucheur. "Les Américains nous lâchent plutôt," he wrote in his diary, and to his fellow experts he declared: "In my mind and in my soul, I cannot recommend what is not just. I made a great step forward; I regret that it has not been appreciated more, particularly by our American friends, and I regret to appear intransigent when I have gone beyond my instructions and beyond what I consider as strictly in conformity with justice."

III

The most striking evidence of relative French moderation on reparation in 1919 comes from an unexpected source, the German archives themselves. In March the French began to talk to the Germans about these problems. First through Haguenin, the Berlin representative of the French Foreign Ministry, and then in May through Haguenin's assistant René Massigli, the French government made repeated overtures to the Germans. It held out the possibility of substantial revision to be worked out through direct negotiation; final agreement would be reached only after the treaty was signed. Both Haguenin and Massigli indicated French willingness to talk about the peace settlement in general—even about the territorial clauses—but they stressed especially the French government's intention to discuss financial and economic questions, such as reparation, reconstruction, and industrial collaboration. Massigli, who did not hesitate to use the phrase "collaboration franco-allemand," pressed in these talks for "practical, verbal discussions" between experts on the basis of German proposals; toward the end of May he even went so far as to suggest the lines along which such negotiations should proceed.

It is clear from the substance and even more from the tone of these talks that what the French government had in mind went far beyond a mere business arrangement with Germany. It was in fact aiming at a political arrangement. French willingness to contemplate such a prospect was a consequence of disillusionment with their allies, and in these talks Massigli's remarks bristled with hostility toward the "Anglo-Saxon Powers." The impression in Germany that France was Germany's only real enemy, he said, was "entirely mistaken." Massigli instead stressed the common interest of the two countries in opposing "Anglo-Saxon" domination, declaring that the "deepening of the opposition" between France and Germany "would lead to the ruin of both countries, to the advantage of the Anglo-Saxon Powers." On reparation, Massigli admitted that Germany's capacity to pay had been overestimated, but he felt that Germany and France could cooperate on reconstruction within the context of the Reparation Commission system.

The problem of bringing about such a rapprochement was politically difficult, and both Haguenin and Massigli urged the Germans not to make matters worse by taking a defiant and intransigent position on the peace terms. But the German leaders, with barely an exception, were not at first particularly interested in these French overtures or even in the idea of a policy of accommodation with France. These French initiatives were suspect in German eyes. It was possible that France was deliberately raising false hopes just to get the Germans to sign the treaty "as is." Or perhaps France was trying to divide Germany from America, the ex-enemy power most likely to take up the German cause. The German foreign minister, Brockdorff-Rantzau, was so committed to this policy of aligning Germany with American policy—or at least with Wilson's policy as it was understood in Germany—that as a matter of principle he refused to engage in direct negotiations with any individual Allied power, and in particular, by and large refrained from making the kind of concrete proposals that could test French sincerity. One German diplomat even argued that Germany had no interest in encouraging French moderation, since France's excesses simply alienated her from her allies. Rantzau himself ignored French pleas not to be overly concerned with the exact text of the treaty and to work out arrangements which would in fact amount to a revision of the treaty after it was signed.

How seriously in fact are these overtures to be taken? Unfortunately there is apparently no record of these talks from the French side. But it is hard to believe that Haguenin and Massigli were acting without official sanction; Haguenin was in close contact with the highest officials at the Quai d'Orsay at this time. It is equally difficult to argue that the French government was not serious in this affair, that it was just trying to trick the Germans into signing. The moderation of its policy in the inter-Allied negotiations demonstrates clearly enough its willingness to work out a relatively modest settlement. Even more significant in this connection is the fact that it tried, beginning in August 1919, to work out a kind of economic entente with Germany; this effort was taken very seriously by moderate elements within the German government itself but was effectively blocked by the leaders of German heavy industry. Nor was this the end: In 1920 especially, but also even into 1922, the French sought repeatedly but unsuccessfully to work out mutually acceptable arrangements with the Germans on economic questions. When seen in this context the overtures of the spring of 1919 take on their real significance: They were no flash in the pan, without deep roots, but rather an initial stage in what was to be an important strain—in some respects the dominant strain—in France's postwar foreign policy.

Sally Marks

The Myths of Reparations

Sally Marks, author of the useful synthesis of international relations in the 1920s, *The Illusion of Peace*, considers in the following passage the actual operation of the reparation provisions of the Versailles treaty after the breakup of the peace conference. She disputes the conventional wisdom that the reparation obligation eventually imposed on Germany was beyond that country's capacity to pay and discusses how the Weimar Republic succeeded in avoiding payment during the 1920s.

From Sally Marks, "The Myths of Reparations," *Central European History*, 18, No. 3 (1978), pp. 231–249, 254–255. Reprinted by permission of the author and the publisher. Footnotes omitted.

Reparations after World War I can be divided into two categories: non-German reparations, which remain largely *terra incognita* to the historian, and German reparations, an excruciatingly tangled thicket into which only a few intrepid explorers have ventured. Understandably, most students of twentieth-century history have preferred to sidestep the perils of travel on territory of extreme financial complexity and, as a consequence, a number of misconceptions about the history of German reparations remain in circulation. This brief summary is not addressed to those few brave trailblazers, whose work it indeed salutes, but rather to those many who have assiduously avoided the subject and to the myths about reparations which still adorn studies of the Weimar Republic and interwar history.

The myths about German reparations begin with the Versailles Treaty. The much-criticized "war guilt clause," Article 231, which was designed to lay a legal basis for reparations, in fact makes no mention of war guilt. It does specify "the responsibility of Germany and her Allies for causing all the loss and damage to which the Allied and Associated Governments and their nationals have been subjected as a consequence of the war imposed upon them by the aggression of Germany and her allies." That Germany committed an act of aggression on Belgium is beyond dispute. Further, upon the theory of collective responsibility, the victors incorporated the same clause, *mutatis mutandis*, in the treaties with Austria and Hungary, neither of whom interpreted it as a declaration of war guilt. In later years, however, German politicians and propagandists fulminated endlessly about "unilateral war guilt," convincing many who had not read the treaties of their injustice on this point.

While Article 231 of the Versailles Treaty established an unlimited theoretical liability, Article 232 in fact narrowed German responsibility to civilian damages as defined in an annex. Much ink has been wasted on the fact that civilian damages were stretched to cover war widows' pensions and allowances for military dependents. In reality, since the German reparations bill was established in 1921 on the basis of an Allied assessment of German capacity to pay, not on the basis of Allied claims, these items did not affect German liability but merely altered distribution of the receipts. In brief, inclusion of pensions and allowances increased the British share of the pie but did not enlarge the pie. The chief effects of the expanded British claim were to increase vastly the difficulties of inter-Allied agreement on a reparations settlement and to heighten German resentment as German opinion reacted to the misleading appearance of enlarged liability. In this matter, as in so many other aspects of reparations, appearance and reality diverged, giving rise to one of the many myths of reparations.

Much has also been made of the fact that the treaty did not specify the total German reparations liability. While some financial uncertainty was thus engendered in both Germany and the victor states, and Germany was able to propagandize effectively about the iniquity of having to sign a "blank check," delay was actually in Germany's interest. Because of inflated popular expectations in the victor countries, the reparations totals discussed at the peace conference were astronomic, ranging to sixteen times the amount finally set. The British experts, Lords Sumner and Cunliffe, were so unrealistic that they were nicknamed "the heavenly twins." As time passed, the proposed figures were progressively reduced and by 1921 a substantial degree of realism had set in.

Finally, the Versailles Treaty specified that Germany make an interim payment of 20 billion gold marks before May 1, 1921, by which time the Reparation Commission was to set the total liability. In fact, 20 billion marks is approximately what Germany paid during the entire history of reparations. During the interim period, she paid less than 8 billion marks, mostly as credit for transferred state properties. Technically, none of this was considered reparations, as it was fully consumed by prior charges, notably occupation costs and the expense of provisioning Germany. In time, however, there developed a certain tacit recognition of the 8 billion as reparations.

Reparations were to be paid in several categories. There were to be periodic cash payments and deliveries in kind, that is, continuing shipments of certain commodities. For Germany, "kind" meant coal, timber, chemical dyes, and pharmaceutical drugs. The gold value of the shipments was to be credited as payment against Germany's total reparations bill. With two exceptions, reparations credit was also given for state properties in territories transferred to the victors, such as the Saar coal mines and German state railways in districts awarded to Poland. Except in the case of Alsace-Lorraine, countries receiving German territory assumed part of the German imperial and state debts as of August 1, 1914. Finally, reparations included certain one-time requirements. Return of art treasures did not receive reparations credit but materials to replace the destroyed Library of Louvain did. Similarly, supplies of livestock, agricultural implements, factory machinery, and construction materials in compensation for wholesale removals during the German retreat were credited to the reparations account.

The reparations provisions of the treaties with Austria and Hungary were similar in broad outline to those imposed upon Germany. Again, the total figure was left unspecified, and the costs of carrying out the peace treaties were to be prior charges against payments made, not credited to reparations accounts. However, credit was to be given for payment in cash, deliveries in kind, and transfer of state properties, while the successor states also were to assume substantial portions of the prewar Austro-Hungarian state debt. The Bulgarian treaty set a fixed sum, which was soon revised downward. In the unratified Treaty of Sèvres, Turkish reparation liability was sharply limited in view of the magnitude of Turkish territorial losses, and in the Treaty of Lausanne it was eliminated altogether. Austria became so impoverished that she paid no reparations beyond credits for transferred property, while Hungary paid little. As it became clear that Germany was the only defeated power able to pay appreciably, the battle was joined over German reparations.

Some controversy arose over credits for transferred state properties and one-time restitution shipments, but there was constant dispute over all varieties of continuing German payments in cash and kind. While shipments of dyes occasioned much difficulty, most of the problems were not of Germany's making. In this connection, it should be noted that, contrary to common belief, the United States had claims upon Germany amounting to almost $1½ billion (or nearly 6 billion gold marks) and that the United States received regular shipments of dyes until late in 1922, when she renounced her right to reparations dyes. Counting mixed claims of private individuals, Rhineland occupation costs, and governmental reparations claims, the United States eventually received over 400 million gold marks.

Dyes were a peripheral issue, however, and the United States government was a peripheral power in the reparations question. Attention focused upon cash, coal, and timber, while the actively concerned Allied powers were France, Britain, Italy, and Belgium, who were to receive the lion's share. Coal shipments were below quotas almost from the outset. At the Spa Conference in July 1920, the victors agreed to pay Germany a five-mark premium for each ton of coal, officially to provide better nourishment for the miners, and advanced Germany sizeable loans to facilitate coal shipments. Still the quotas were not met. An Allied occupation of the Ruhr to force Germany to meet her obligations was first discussed at the London Conference of March 1920, and was seriously considered at Spa. Thereafter the question arose frequently, as defaults continued under the permanent plan which replaced the interim scheme in 1921.

As required by the Versailles Treaty, the Reparation Commission announced on April 27, 1921, a total German liability of 132 billion gold marks. This figure was a Belgian compromise between higher French and Italian totals and a lower British figure. It represented an assessment of the lowest amount that public opinion in continental receiver states would tolerate. The British pressure for a lower total and the continuing British effort thereafter to reduce German reparations derived from an assumption that restoration of British economic prosperity depended upon a rapid return to prewar patterns of trade which in turn required an immediate German economic revival. As British leaders assumed that sizeable German reparations payments would delay this sequence of events or overstimulate German exports to the detriment of British producers, they opposed enforcement of substantial reparations requirements upon Germany.

Historians have focused upon the figure of 132 billion without examining the nature of its implementation. The London Schedule of Payments of May 5, 1921, both enshrined the sum and demolished it. The full liability of all Central Powers combined, not just Germany alone, was set at 132 billion gold marks, subject to certain arithmetic adjustments. The German debt, however, was to be organized in three series of bonds, labeled A, B, and C. Of these, the C bonds, which contained the bulk of the German obligation, were deliberately designed to be chimerical. They were entirely unreal, and their primary function was to mislead public opinion in the receiver countries into believing that the 132-billion-mark figure was being maintained. Allied experts knew that Germany could not pay 132 billion marks and that the other Central Powers could pay little. Thus the A and B Bonds, which were genuine, represented the actual Allied assessment of German capacity to pay. The A Bonds, amounting to 12 billion gold marks, constituted the unpaid balance of the interim 20 billion, while the B Bonds amounted to 38 billion. Therefore the A and B Bonds represented the total German reparations liability to a face (or nominal) value of 50 billion gold marks or $12½ billion, an amount smaller than what Germany had recently offered to pay. The London Schedule also established modalities of payment toward redemption of the A and B Bonds, including two schedules of quarterly deadlines for fixed and variable annuities.

In the summer of 1921, Germany met her first cash payment of one billion gold marks in full. She did so because west German customs posts and an area around Düsseldorf were under Allied occupation. These measures had been taken in March 1921, primarily in an effort to induce a satisfactory German offer, and were continued to force German acceptance of the London Schedule. After the 1921 cash payment, the Allies relinquished the customs posts but remained at Düsseldorf. Thereafter, Germany paid a tiny portion of the variable annuity due in November 1921 and small amounts on annuities due in early 1922, but made no further payments in cash until after the Dawes Plan went into effect late in 1924. Through 1922, payments in kind continued, although never in full, while a variety of expedients papered over the absence of cash payments. However, these stopgap measures would expire at the end of 1922 when either a new reparations plan had to be imposed or the London Schedule would revert to full force.

By the summer of 1922, it was clearly impossible to restore the London Schedule, which was in virtual abeyance, but there was no agreement on what to do. By this time, Germany's currency depreciation had become acute. This depreciation had begun during World War I and had continued at an erratic pace. A conjunction had developed between reparations deadlines and dramatic inflationary lurches of the mark. Germans argued that reparations were destroying their currency while British and French experts agreed that Germany was deliberately ruining the mark, partly to avoid budgetary and currency reform, but primarily to escape reparations. In this, the Entente experts were correct. Those historians who have accepted the German claim that reparations were the cause of the inflation have overlooked the fact that the inflation long predated reparations. They have similarly overlooked the fact that the inflation mushroomed in the period from the summer of 1921 to the end of 1922 when Germany was actually paying very little in reparations. They have also failed to explain why the period of least inflation coincided with the period of largest reparations payments in the late 1920s or why Germans claimed after 1930 that reparations were causing deflation. There is no doubt that British and French suspicions late in 1922 were sound. The Reich Chancellery archives indicate that in 1922 and 1923 German leaders chose to postpone tax reform and currency stabilization measures in hopes of obtaining substantial reductions in reparations.

However, the Entente agreement on the facts yielded no solutions, as Britain and France drew opposite policy conclusions from the same assessment. The British maintained that, since Germany had succeeded in destroying her currency, she should be granted a full four-year moratorium on all reparations payments to facilitate financial reconstruction, while the French objected to awarding a long moratorium as a bad conduct prize and insisted upon Allied seizure of something—mines, state forests, customs posts, or whatever—as a revenue-yielding guarantee that payment would eventually resume. The British opposed the seizure of "productive guarantees," arguing that any compulsion would damage German recovery, while the French maintained that a moratorium without them would mean the end of reparations. Through the latter part of 1922, neither the Reparation Commission nor Allied conferences achieved any compromise.

The tension heightened on December 26, 1922, when the Reparation Commission by a three to one vote, with Britain dissenting, formally declared Germany in default on timber deliveries. There was no disagreement about the fact of the default nor its size. Contrary to historical myth, the timber default was massive even though 1922 timber quotas had been based upon (in most categories derived downward from) a German offer. Nor was there any Allied dispute about the causes of the default, which implied German governmental bad faith. But Britain opposed declaring the default for fear that declaration would lead to action. The only feasible Entente action of consequence was an occupation of the Ruhr Basin, which Britain opposed with mounting vigor as the prospect came closer. While no action was taken on the timber default, its declaration raised the spectre of a formal declaration of coal default in January, as French patience was exhausted and French leaders became determined to use the technicality of repeated coal defaults to force execution of the Versailles Treaty in general. Coal quotas were monthly; Germany had fulfilled them in January and October of 1920, but otherwise had defaulted regularly in varying amounts, despite several downward quota revisions, especially after Germany lost the Silesian coal fields. Thus in January 1923 there occurred the thirty-fourth coal default in thirty-six months.

On January 2, 1923, the Entente powers and Germany met at Paris. Each country except Belgium brought a plan and published it at once, thus inflaming public opinion everywhere. The German plan, offering a Rhineland pact and thus foreshadowing Locarno, was an unsuccessful attempt at distraction from reparations default. The French and Italian plans called for limited economic sanctions and Entente unity, although France declared that, in the absence of full unity, she would take more drastic steps. The British brushed both plans aside and insisted that theirs was the only basis for discussion. The new British prime minister, Andrew Bonar Law, ailing, inexperienced in reparations, and distracted by domestic politics and the Turkish crisis, had accepted the plan of

Sir John Bradbury, British delegate to the Reparation Commission. This scheme was merely a variation of one already rejected by France, and it had been termed "impossible of execution" by Germany. It was so excruciatingly complex that Carl Bergmann, the leading German expert, grumbled that he would rather pay reparations than master the Bradbury Plan. Amongst its other unpalatable features, the British scheme would have destroyed all Belgian benefits from reparations, granted Germany a four-year moratorium (twice what she had requested in December) on payments in cash and kind without any productive guarantees, required open cancellation of C Bonds (a politically difficult act), reduced and reconstructed the Reparation Commission to end French preponderance therein, provided a British veto on any punitive measures against future defaults, and accorded Britain full dictation of Entente policy on non-German reparations. As this plan would have meant the practical end of reparations, no continental politician could accept it and expect to remain in office. None did, and the conference failed.

On January 9, 1923, the Reparation Commission declared the coal default by a vote of three to one and, by the same vote, decided to occupy the Ruhr. On January 11, French, Belgian, and Italian engineers entered the Ruhr to procure the coal, accompanied by small contingents of French and Belgian troops. Britain stood aloof, denouncing the occupation as immoral and illegal, but rendered it feasible by permitting France to mount it on British-controlled railways in the Rhineland. While the question of morality perhaps depends upon viewpoint, the British legal opinion was based more upon what British leaders wished the Versailles Treaty had said than upon what it actually did say. Although no definitive ruling was ever made, since a unanimous opinion of the Reparation Commission was impossible, a close reading of the text of the Versailles Treaty indicates that the majority view had much legal substance.

As German passive resistance escalated the Ruhr occupation into a major military operation, Britain refused to take sides and thus both prolonged and exacerbated the crisis. Bonar Law dreaded breach with France and refused to recognize that it had arrived. As he wished above all to keep the breach from becoming irreparable, he took no decisive action in either direction. He also failed to understand the French premier, Raymond Poincaré. In the weeks before the occupation, Bonar Law ignored evidence that Poincaré was seeking to avoid such a drastic step, and he never realized that, in combination with the French right, notably Alexandre Millerand, he had forced Poincaré into the Ruhr by rejecting more moderate options. Once the step had been taken, Poincaré recognized that France had played her last trump and must win on this card or go down to permanent defeat. She was inherently weaker than Germany and had already failed to enforce delivery of alleged war criminals, to obtain German compliance with the military clauses of the treaty, or to gain any effective German participation in the costly French reconstruction of the devastated provinces. If Germany did not pay reparations and remove some of the burden from France, her innate economic superiority, together with further progressive crumbling of the peace treaty, would soon tip the balance altogether. In applying the ultimate sanction of the Ruhr occupation, Poincaré was above all making a final effort to force Germany to acknowledge her defeat in World War I and to accept the Versailles Treaty. He well knew that the fundamental issues were not coal and timber but rather survival of the treaty and of France's victory in the war. The British never realized that they were watching an extension of World War I and, comprehending neither the basic issues nor France's genuine need for coal and money, could not understand why Poincaré hung grimly on when Italy and Belgium lost heart.

The British, who clearly won the propaganda battle, also claimed that the Ruhr occupation was unprofitable. Misleadingly, they compared the Ruhr receipts to the London Schedule of Payments, ignoring the fact that the London Schedule was dead beyond recall and that the choice, at their own insistence, had been between the Ruhr receipts and nothing. In fact, the Ruhr occupation was profitable, modestly so at first and then very considerably after the end of passive resistance. After all expenses and Rhineland occupation costs, the net Ruhr receipts to the three powers involved and ultimately to the United States amounted to nearly 900 million gold marks.

Others benefited as well. As the German government financed passive resistance from an empty exchequer, the mark reached utter ruination. The astronomic inflation which ensued was a result of German policy, not of the occupation itself. The inflation enabled the German government to pay off its domestic debts, including the war debt, and those of the state enterprises in worthless marks. Certain industrialists close to the German cabinet profited greatly as well. The ailing British economy also benefited considerably from the disruption of German exports, but British officials would never acknowledge this fact, even to themselves. Convinced that their economic data bore no relation to the evil event, they never ceased to urge resolution of the crisis.

Their urgings became more imperative after a new German government under Gustav Stresemann abandoned passive resistance in September 1923 and quickly terminated the inflation. A new reparations plan was necessary, along with German financial reconstruction and a scheme to extract France and Belgium from the Ruhr. Other powers quickly combined to minimize the damage to Germany, and France found herself increasingly isolated. A decline of the franc further weakened her diplomatic position. When President Calvin Coolidge indicated that American experts could participate as private citizens in drawing up a new reparations plan, thus facilitating the essential involvement of American bankers, a certain degree of inevitability set in. Poincaré could and did delay, but he could not prevent altogether. Thus the Dawes Committee began work in January 1924. Its labors signified that while Poincaré had won the war, he had lost the peace.

The Dawes Plan of April 9, 1924, operated at two levels. Its precise technical details owed much to the Belgian *Études* of June 11, 1923, concerning potential sources of reparations revenues, while the deliberately ambiguous political settlement was chiefly the work of the American expert, Owen D. Young. Although the Dawes Committee indicated that the problem of the Ruhr occupation was outside its frame of reference, it tacitly assumed an immediate end to the economic occupation and reduction of the military occupation to a skeleton force (to save French face). The plan called for complete reorganization of German finances with foreign supervision, a large international loan to Germany, and an Agent-General for Reparations in Berlin to oversee a complex supervisory structure. To raise revenues toward reparations, the plan demanded mortgages on German industry and the state railways, reassumption of domestic indebtedness by the German government, and sweeping tax reform to end the anomaly (and Versailles Treaty violation) of much lower tax rates in Germany than in the victor powers. While some accounts indicate otherwise, in fact the incorporation of occupation costs, commission costs, and all other previously prior charges into the global amount of annual German reparations payments effectively reduced the total reparations bill, although the size of the reduction was unclear, as the duration of the plan was not specified. Germany would pay one billion marks the first year, chiefly out of the international loan, increasing amounts for three years, and 2½ billion gold marks for one year. Thereafter she would pay 2½ billion marks plus a percentage based upon a complex index of German prosperity.

The call for commensurate taxation in the Dawes Plan was political window-dressing on the order of the C Bonds of the London Schedule. Tax rates equivalent to those in the victor powers were not imposed because the leading British expert, Sir Josiah Stamp, estimated that such rates would yield a surplus applicable to reparations of 4½ billion marks a year, far more, he thought, than could be transferred. The transfer problem (that is, the difficulties involved in transferring real resources from one country to another or, in effect, in converting German wealth into foreign currencies for reparation payments without depreciating the mark) plagued the history of reparations and provided a convenient impediment to payment. Those who for political reasons stressed the impediments to transferring reparations generally remained silent about the vast investment of foreign capital into Germany before and after the Ruhr débâcle, which constituted transfers of real wealth lost to the foreign investors through hyperinflation or debt repudiation and which provided Germany with foreign exchange for reparations payments. As to the German payments themselves, such transfer difficulties as arose with payment of the first billion in 1921, which constituted the only payment of substance before the Dawes Plan went into effect, were largely induced by Germany in an effort to escape reparations. In the later history of reparations, with the reduced payments of the Young Plan, transfers caused no problem. Under the Dawes Plan itself, protection against potential transfer difficulties was provided by specifying that Germany pay reparations into the new German *Reichsbank* and empowering an Allied Transfer Committee under the American Agent-General for Reparations to decide when transfers could safely be made.

When the Dawes Plan was issued in April 1924, the countries concerned were uniformly unenthusiastic for widely varying reasons, but each accepted it for lack of an alternative. There remained the mechanics of its implementation, reconstruction of the Reparation Commission, and arrangements to remove France from the Ruhr. These were devised at the London Conference of July and August 1924, which was a personal triumph for the British prime minister, Ramsay MacDonald. He deserves considerable credit for jollying his reluctant colleagues toward compromise, although the inexperience of the new French premier, Édouard Herriot, eased his task. Behind the scenes, however, decisive pressure was exerted by representatives of J. P. Morgan and Company, whose imprimatur was essential to raise the large loan to Germany upon which the Dawes Plan depended. Further, the French franc had continued to decline, and France urgently needed loans from American bankers, again dependent upon Morgan approval. Thus France had to accept the final scheme, even though Morgan agents required provisions making future sanctions against default virtually impossible, since the American loans would extend for twenty-five years, whatever happened to reparations. Financial crisis and diplomatic isolation equally obliged France to swallow other unattractive terms. As a perceptive British observer remarked, "The London Conference was for the French 'man in the street' one long Calvary . . . as he saw M. Herriot abandoning one by one the cherished possessions of French preponderance on the Reparation Commission, the right of sanctions in the event of German default, the economic occupation of the Ruhr, the French-Belgian railway Régie, and finally, the military occupation of the Ruhr within a year. . . ."

The ultimate effect of German failure to pay reparations in substantial quantity was transfer of the burden to the victors. Reconstruction of the devastated regions still had to be paid for. Pensions for disabled veterans and war widows still remained. So did Allied war debts. In the end, the victors paid the bills. It is evident that the net effect of World War I and the peace settlement was the effective enhancement of Germany's relative strength in Europe, particularly in regard to her immediate neighbors. As Gerhard Weinberg has remarked, "The shifting of the burden of reparations from her shoulders to those of her enemies served to accentuate this disparity."

In addition to reinforcing German economic superiority, the history of reparations generated a vast bureaucracy, a mountain of arcane documents, much bitterness, endless propaganda, more than its share of historical myths, and just over 20 billion gold marks or $5 billion, which was predominantly financed by foreign loans, many of which were eventually repudiated by Hitler. It is evident that Germany could have paid a good deal more if she had chosen to do so, particularly since she paid little out of her own considerable resources. But Germany saw no reason to pay and from start to finish deemed reparations a gratuitous insult. Whether it was wise to seek reparations from Germany is arguable, although the consequences of not seeking them would have been far-reaching, as the failure to obtain them proved in time to be. Certainly it was unwise to inflict the insult without rigorous enforcement. In the last analysis, however, despite the fact that reparations claims were intended to transfer real economic wealth from Germany to the battered victors and despite the financial complexity of the problem, the reparations question was at heart a political issue, a struggle for dominance of the European continent and to maintain or reverse the military verdict of 1918.

Historians, distracted by the intricacies of the reparations question, have either avoided the problem altogether or have tended to focus upon German capacity to pay, often on the basis of dubious assumptions, instead of addressing the more relevant question of German will to pay or, to be precise, determination not to pay. German leaders clearly recognized the political implications of the reparations issue and, from beginning to end, devoted their inexhaustible energies to avoiding or reducing payments. As the international climate became increasingly hostile to the use of force during the twenties, Germany had her way in the end at great cost to herself and to others. Since Germany would not pay and the other Central Powers could not, reparations dwindled and died. The tangled history of reparations remains to confound the historian and also to demonstrate the futility of imposing large payments on nations which are either destitute or resentful and sufficiently powerful to translate that resentment into effective resistance.

Emir Faisal (front) with his British interpreter and advisor T. E. Lawrence ("Lawrence of Arabia") (second row, second from right) outside the peace conference. (Corbis-Bettmann)

The Colonial Settlement

Alan Sharp

The Mandate System in the Colonial World

The following selection by Alan Sharp, professor of history at the University of Ulster and author of a recent study of the Paris Peace Conference, traces the decision-making process whereby the victorious Allies disposed of the German and Ottoman territories in Africa, Asia, and the Middle East. Sharp shows that the trusteeship arrangement under the League of Nations, which paid lip service to the principle of self-determination, gave the victors effective control of these lands and the peoples that inhabited them.

From Alan Sharp, *The Versailles Settlement: Peacemaking in Paris, 1919,* pp. 159–168, 175–184. Copyright © 1991. Reprinted with permission of St. Martin's Press, Inc.

The statesmen in Paris faced problems beyond the confines of Europe. The liquidation of the German empire in Africa and Asia, with over 1,000,000 square miles and approximately 14,000,000 people, and the collapse of Ottoman power in the Balkans, Asia Minor and the Middle East meant that their task was much greater than that of any previous peace conference. It was of little consolation to them that a fair measure of their difficulties were the self-inflicted results of their own wartime policies, or that their conflicting promises would now return to dog their footsteps. The loss and gain of imperial territories had been a familiar part of most European settlements in the previous two centuries, but once again, the Paris conference had set itself a higher moral standard than its predecessors and this too would complicate the resolution of an already complex situation. Too often the newly-discovered device of mandates served only to act as a figleaf for the desire of the great powers, and in the British case, of her own empire, to annex territories formerly owned by the defeated powers.

The Mandate System

The German empire overseas was destroyed by the end of 1916, although in East Africa her forces continued to fight even after the armistice in Europe. Elsewhere British, French, Belgian, Japanese, Australian, New Zealand and South African troops defeated the German forces left isolated by the failure of their expensive navy. The fate of these colonies posed a problem, since the victors, with the exception of Great Britain, made it plain that they intended to annex the territories that they had conquered. Wilson did not object to Germany losing her colonies—indeed that matter was promptly settled in Paris with practically no discussion on 24 January, at the first Council of Ten meeting on the subject—but he was not prepared to accept an old-fashioned colonial readjustment. Instead he pressed for a system of international trusteeship which would apply the principle of self-determination under the auspices of the League of Nations in "A free, open-minded, and absolutely impartial adjustment of all colonial claims." His anti-annexationist doctrine, proclaimed also by the Bolsheviks, found a receptive audience amongst radical and socialist circles in Britain who were pressing for international control in the colonial field. This clashed with the perceived needs of the Dominions, particularly Australia, New Zealand and South Africa, whose leaders left the British government in little doubt as to their demand for the outright ownership of neighbouring German colonies which they felt menaced their security. They were supported by a powerful imperial lobby in London which hoped to consolidate the empire into an international organisation with more cohesion and practical value than Wilson's idealistic League. Anxious to avoid the accusation that the war had been fought in the British eighteenth-century tradition of imperial expansion, conscious of the importance of cooperation with the United States, but also aware of the need to ensure imperial security, a concept which apparently had no finite boundaries, the British government found itself under intense pressure.

In typical fashion, admired by some as pragmatic realism and condemned by others as hypocrisy, the British resolved their problem by arguing that it did not exist, and that they could achieve all their major objectives within a framework which would appear to be, nay would be, Wilsonian. Indeed Wilson was merely institutionalising the current good practice of the British empire, therefore by accepting his principles, they might, at little practical cost to themselves, obtain valuable American support in the colonial field. The Americans might even accept a share of "the white man's burden" by becoming a mandatory power in some difficult area such as Armenia or Constantinople. For these insights they had to thank the astute and flexible minds of Lloyd George and Smuts, the man who conceived the mandate system, though not originally in the context of the German colonies. The potential minefield of self-determination could be avoided if the wishes of the traditional tribal rulers were assumed to be those of their peoples—a formula the British were confident would work in their favour. The Germans were unfit colonial rulers, a concept not in strong evidence before the war but now conveniently discovered, and therefore must lose their possessions, not because they had been defeated but on moral grounds. It was not clear, however, whether the Dominion leaders could be persuaded to substitute this policy of international trusteeship for simple annexation.

Smuts had proposed, in *The League of Nations: A Practical Suggestion*, the idea that the League should act as the trustee for "territories formerly belonging to Russia, Austria-Hungary and Turkey." He excluded the German colonies because they were inhabited by "barbarians" incapable of attaining self-government in the conceivable future. These territories should be annexed outright and for this idea he had the firm backing of the French, the Japanese and the Dominions, with the exception of Canada, acutely aware of a need for good relations with her neighbour. In Paris, where the colonial question was the first major item of discussion, references to Austria-Hungary and Russia were dropped, but a battle-royal ensued over the inclusion of the German colonies. Wilson was insistent that there must be international control, his opponents adamant that there should not. Premier Hughes of Australia, who was especially dismissive of Wilson and his League "toy," revealed the weakness of the Wilsonian appeal to world opinion and moral justice. Taxed by Wilson as to whether Australia would refuse to accept any German colonies under mandate despite the appeal "of the whole of the civilised world," Hughes replied, "That's about the size of it, President Wilson." Hankey commented, "Hughes and Massey [the New Zealand prime minister] . . . are our principal difficulty, but President Wilson . . . is even more obstinate."

It was again Smuts and Lloyd George who found a way out of the impasse. Although still anxious to exclude the Pacific islands and South-West Africa from any mandate system, Smuts, supported by Robert Cecil, his colleague on the League commission, proposed to the British delegation on 27 January that the victorious powers should accept responsibility for the government of these territories under three classes of mandate: "A," where the peoples concerned were near to self-government but needed minimal assistance along that path; "B," where the mandatory power would be responsible for the administration of the territory, subject to League conditions prohibiting trade in slaves, arms and liquor, and forbidding militarisation; and "C," which amounted to annexation, subject only to the same safeguards as the "B" mandates. All mandatories would submit annual reports to the League on their stewardships. Smuts thought that the "A" mandates would arise in the new states formed from the Turkish empire, the "B" mandates would occur in the ex-German colonies of Central Africa and the "C" mandates would apply to ex-German colonies with a neighbouring British Dominion. On 29 January Lloyd George bullied and persuaded his colleagues from Australia, New Zealand and South Africa that the "C" mandate scheme should apply also to the Pacific islands and South-West Africa. Hughes continued to fight "like a weasel—which he somewhat resembles—for annexation in the Pacific," until Lloyd George lost his temper and told him that he had no intention of quarrelling with the United States over the Solomon Islands. Hughes finally acquiesced on receiving assurances that, in contrast to the "B" mandates, he would retain full control over immigration—a matter of great significance to the Pacific powers, which were anxious to exclude the Japanese—and trade. He commented that the terms of the "C" mandate—the wording of which was drafted by an Australian—achieved his major objectives and differed only "from full sovereign control as a nine hundred and ninety nine years' lease differs from a fee simple."

Wilson reacted favourably on first seeing the proposal, but when the Ten discussed it on 30 January he was piqued by a newspaper article Hughes had written, accusing the president of impractical idealism, and this produced unforeseen difficulties. Wilson now argued that the Smuts plan was helpful, but that there could be no final decisions yet as to which states would obtain which mandates; Australia, for example, might not be the mandated power for New Guinea. Hughes was furious, but a dignified intervention by Louis Botha, the South African premier, restored calm and assured the acceptance of the principle. The final text became Article 22 of the Covenant. Although Wilson was anxious to postpone the distribution of mandates as long as possible to avoid the charge "that the Great Powers first portioned out the helpless parts of the world, and then formed a League of Nations," there was an implicit understanding that, for example, South-West Africa would go to South Africa, and that the Australian and New Zealand wishes would be met. Orlando declared that Italy agreed to the principle and, somewhat anxiously, assured the Council that she would accept responsibilities in this field. Clemenceau was prepared to accept mandates provided that he could use their human resources to defend France in the event of another war. He assured Lloyd George that he had no intention of training "big nigger armies for the purpose of aggression," but more privately he told Poincaré that the League would have no real authority: "I can accept the League as a guarantor of peace but not as a colonial power."

Germany's Colonies in Africa and Asia

The conference decided that since the League was not yet in existence, Germany's colonies, together with all her property in those colonies, should be surrendered, without compensation, to the five victorious great powers. The treaty did not specify how the responsibility for governing the colonies would be divided, this being a matter for decision between the powers themselves. On 6 May, conveniently in the absence of the Italians who had not yet returned to the conference, Wilson bowed to the strong pressure of the British Dominions, the French and Japanese, and agreed to allocate mandates amongst the victors. The outcome was predictable, despite Wilson's earlier reservations; in general it was the power which had occupied the territory which gained the mandate, though, as the Belgians discovered, this was not always the case.

Wilson would not accept any African or Asian mandates for the United States, though he still toyed with the idea of a mandate for Armenia.

Lloyd George's proposals for the allocation of mandates were accepted by a brief meeting of the Four as they left the ceremony at the Trianon to present the draft treaty to the German delegation on 7 May. In Africa, all the mandates fell into the "B" category. The Togoland and the Cameroons mandates would be divided between Britain and France (who were to return to the conference with a joint proposal) whilst that for German East Africa went to Britain. South Africa gained the mandate for South-West Africa. Italian interests were nominally safeguarded, but as Milner commented, "Ultimately, I presume, Italy will have to be satisfied with what France and Great Britain are prepared to give up." This amounted only to the cession of the Juba valley by Britain and some Saharan oases by the French. The Belgians, who had occupied much of German East Africa, were incensed at their exclusion from the settlement, and the Portuguese also had claims. In August the conference approved an Anglo-Belgian compromise which granted the Ruanda-Urundi mandate to Belgium. Portugal was consoled with a morsel of territory, the Kionga triangle in northern Mozambique, which she gained in full sovereignty. Britain and France agreed the division of Togoland and the Cameroons in July 1919, the larger share of each going to France, but the final conditions were only settled in December 1920.

In the Pacific, Australia received New Guinea, the islands of the Bismarck Archipelago and islands south of the equator, New Zealand received Samoa whilst Japan gained the islands north of the equator. The island of Nauru, which was an important source of phosphates, became the responsibility of the British empire, to allow time for the Australians, British and New Zealanders to work out an acceptable arrangement between themselves. This they did on 2 July, much to the annoyance of Smuts, who argued, unsuccessfully, that the three states could not assume that they were, for this issue, the entire British empire. These territories, apart from the "B" mandate for Samoa, were all allocated under "C" mandates and, despite their earlier objections, the two Dominions came to see great advantages in the system in their dealings with the Japanese, of whom they were increasingly distrustful. It enabled them to prevent Japanese immigration into their mandates and, in theory, stopped the Japanese fortifying their mandated territory.

The fate of the German concessions of Kiaochow, Tsingtao and Shantung in China had also to be settled by the conference. The Japanese (with minimal British assistance) had occupied these areas in

1914, and in May 1915 had forced China to accept their "Twenty-one demands," which included recognition of their hold over Shantung and the granting of extensive economic rights within China. In 1917 Britain sought extra naval assistance from her Japanese allies, in return offering her support for Japanese claims in Shantung and the German islands north of the equator. This represented a mixture of cynicism and wishful thinking. Britain felt the Japanese demands were inevitable and irresistible and hence that she should try to sell her support for the best attainable price. Further, the agreement might make the equator the limit of Japanese expansion. China declared war on Germany in August 1917, but her claim that the former German concessions should return to her was ignored. At the conference Britain, not without misgivings, felt obliged to second the Japanese demands, and she was supported by France. Wilson, who was increasingly suspicious of Japanese ambitions in the Pacific, found himself isolated. When the question came before the conference in April 1919 his position was weakened further by the Italian boycott over Fiume. He could not afford a Japanese walk-out at the same time; hence, reluctantly, on 30 April he accepted the outright transfer of Germany's concessions to Japan. Lloyd George had failed to persuade the Japanese to accept the areas under a "C" mandate, but they did agree to promise the eventual return of Kiaochow to Chinese sovereignty, although the date was unspecified. Bitterly disappointed, the Chinese refused to sign the treaty.

Not unnaturally, when they arrived in Paris in May 1919, the Germans protested that these decisions were incompatible with Wilson's idea of a free and fair colonial adjustment, but their efforts achieved nothing. The contemporary *History of the Paris Peace Conference* argued that the Allied refusal to contemplate the return of any of the German colonies was justified because of her poor reputation as a colonial power and because "the burden of miscalculation would fall well-nigh exclusively upon the helpless natives." This was not a convincing argument. Germany's colonial record had differed little from that of the other imperial powers, and was certainly better than that of Leopold of the Belgians in the Congo, though not, in fairness, of that of the Belgian government once it replaced the king as the responsible party. The fairness of the colonial settlement was, like reparations, an issue which came to trouble commentators and politicians in Britain, and a proposed revision of its terms often formed part of later attempts to appease Hitler, although it is doubtful whether either he, or the Weimar leaders, rated the question as highly as their British counterparts hoped or feared.

The Collapse of Ottoman Power

The collapse of the Ottoman empire posed similar problems to the collapse of the Russian, Austro-Hungarian and German empires in eastern Europe and had parallel consequences. What new authority would replace the old regime at the centre, and who would inherit the legacy of the empire in its outlying regions? The confusion of contending candidates seeking to fill the vacuum, and the manner in which their expectations had been raised by contradictory promises from one or more of the great powers, seeking a temporary advantage at times of pressing urgency during the war, were shared experiences. The Middle East had the added refinement that three of the Big Four had direct interests in the region, though the Americans, who were not at war with the Ottomans, tried to act as a restraining force. The Italians had ambitions, which had indeed been recognised and encouraged by the Treaty of London in 1915, but it was the rivalry between France and Britain which assumed a particular importance in the negotiations. As in eastern Europe, the problems of this region were never entirely ignored by the peacemakers, but they did tend to have a lower priority than the German settlement, and thus their resolution took a long time. There was a vital difference, however, in that the presence of over 1 million British troops gave the conference a real authority in the Middle East, at least at the outset. The gradual dissipation of that authority, the tragic over-ambition of the Greeks in the Near East and the re-emergence of a revived nationalist force under Mustapha Kemal in Turkey, forced a revision of the first attempt by the conference to establish a new order.

The outbreak of war between the *Entente* and the Turks in November 1914 caused a revolution in British (and, to a lesser extent, in French) attitudes towards the future of the Ottoman empire. Throughout the nineteenth century Britain had a particular interest in Constantinople and the control of the Straits since the implications for her naval supremacy were enormous if the Russians had free access to the Mediterranean from bases in the Black Sea. Thus she tried to limit the erosion of Turkish power in Asia and to preserve, as far as possible, the authority of the Ottomans, particularly *vis-à-vis* the Russians, despite the misgivings which the Turkish treatment of their subject peoples sometimes caused. This seemed to her the best way of safeguarding the approaches to India without herself assuming enormous burdens in Arabia, Afghanistan and Persia. That policy was less clearcut in the twentieth century than it had been in the nineteenth, and certainly less successful: the Ottoman empire lost 32.7 per cent of its population and a fifth of its territory within a generation, whilst its foreign debts were so huge that, by 1914, a quarter of its state revenue was controlled by the Ottoman Public Debt Administration, a body imposed upon the empire by the powers in 1881. Nonetheless the British and French acceptances of Russia's demand for Constantinople and the Straits, on 12 March and 18 April 1915 respectively, signalled a remarkable transformation. This carried important consequences for Britain, which had already annexed Cyprus outright and declared a protectorate over Egypt, abandoning any pretence of a Turkish role. It implied also a reversal of her traditional policy of keeping the Straits closed, and after the Russian collapse created a new dilemma about the future status of Constantinople. In their January 1918 speeches both Lloyd George and Wilson promised the Turks secure sovereignty in the lands "which are predominantly Turkish in race." For Lloyd George these lands included Constantinople, provided that the Straits were opened and internationalised, but Wilson was less clear. Elsewhere it seemed unlikely that the Ottoman empire would survive an Allied victory.

That victory was a long time in the making. The Gallipoli and Kut campaigns were failures, which exacted a high toll of men, money and, perhaps most importantly, prestige. Faced with the unexpectedly vigorous opposition of an empire that was supposed to have been ailing throughout the nineteenth century, and with the proof of new Turkish atrocities, most notably of their massacre of over a million Armenians in 1915–16, a consensus hostile to the Turks emerged from the previous divisions within the British political spectrum. Gladstone's policy, that the Turk must be ejected from Europe, "bag and baggage," was now adopted even by Conservatives erstwhile sympathetic to the empire. The collapse of Russia in 1917, and Ottoman success against the resulting fledgling Transcaucasian republics of Georgia, Armenia and Azerbaijan in 1918, freed the Turks from danger in that quarter. The British, with their Arab allies, gained great victories in the Middle East in 1917 and 1918 but could not hope to menace the Turkish heartlands until 1919. It was only with the long-delayed break-out of the Allied forces at Salonika in September 1918, and their rapid defeat of Bulgaria, that Constantinople was in real and imminent danger. When the collapse came, however, it was sudden and complete. The new Turkish government, which replaced the previous Committee of Union and Progress government, sought an armistice in mid-October, and to British surprise accepted their full list of twenty-four conditions without question. The

British negotiator had been instructed that only the first four, including the opening of the Straits, were vital and that the rest were negotiable, or even dispensable. The armistice, signed at Mudros on 30 October 1918, marked a complete Allied, largely British, triumph. As Nicolson boasted, "The Ottoman Empire lay at our feet dismembered and impotent, its capital and Caliph at the mercy of our guns." It is thus ironic that the Turkish treaty proved to be the longest and most difficult to finalise, and that, despite this abject surrender, it would be the only negotiated treaty of the entire settlement.

Wartime Developments in the Middle East

Just as it is possible to recognise the current shape of eastern Europe in the Versailles Settlement, so there is a clear correlation between the current pattern of states in the Middle East and the map redrawn in 1919 and immediately afterwards. Some of the names have changed: Mesopotamia (Iraq), Trans-Jordan (Jordan), the Hijaz (Saudi Arabia); some, like Syria and Lebanon, have remained the same. Palestine (Israel) has changed its name but we remain familiar with the original because it continues to reflect one of the long-term problems created by the war and its consequences. Nor are the borders exactly as they were in 1919, but the broad outline of the Middle East of today may be discerned. The parallel with eastern Europe was not sustained in one vital respect, however, for only Arabia emerged as an independent state from the conference. The other parts all fell into the ambit, in varying degrees, of the great powers, whose empires, nominally at least, were vastly expanded by the conference.

The probability that the Ottoman empire would become part of the spoils of war encouraged Britain to decide what her aims were, to reconcile her wishes with those of her allies, particularly the French, and to ensure that the war was won. It was the conflicting demands of these pressures which drove the British into a series of complex deals with a variety of partners, a process aptly described as selling "the same horse, or at least parts of the same horse, twice." The Constantinople agreement was followed by the Treaty of London, 26 April 1915, which promised Italy a share in any partition of the German and Turkish empires. The Sykes–Picot agreement, 16 May 1916, divided the Ottoman empire between the Russians, the British and the French, with provision for an independent Arabian state, or confederation of states. This was amended by the abortive Treaty of St Jean de Maurienne, 19–21 April

1917, which gave the Italians a stake in Asia Minor. The Russians dropped out of the war without ratifying this treaty, which was substantially amended, to Italy's detriment and the advantage of Greece, in 1919. The Russian claims lapsed, thus leaving the field open for Anglo-French domination. These arrangements between the great powers were supplemented in Britain's case by a series of bargains struck with other forces either in the region or felt to be influential in world opinion.

It is interesting to note that, whereas in eastern Europe, the British were initially reluctant to employ revolutionary tactics against the traditional rulers, they had no such inhibitions when it came to the Turks. In October 1914 Lord Cromer suggested that "a few officers who could speak Arabic, if sent into Arabia, could raise the whole country against the Turks." Others had the same idea, and from this, particularly after the failure of the Gallipoli expedition, sprang the negotiations between the British and the Arab leaders which precipitated the great revolt in the desert, inextricably linked with the name of T. E. Lawrence, Lawrence of Arabia. In 1915 and 1916 Sir Henry McMahon, the British High Commissioner in Egypt, agreed in principle to the demands of the Sherif of Mecca, Hussein, that as the price of a revolt, Britain would recognise a large and independent Arab Kingdom, subject to certain reservations in territories of direct interest to Britain and France. These were the districts of Mersina and Alexandretta and portions of Syria, together with Baghdad and Basra, where "special administrative arrangements" would be required to protect Britain's established political and economic interests. The key letter in their correspondence was that of 24 October 1915, later described as "hopelessly muddle-headed" in its drafting. In particular it disguised the probable extent of French influence within Syria, and it left ambiguous the destiny of Palestine, since the letter referred to areas of Syria "west of the *vilayets* of Damascus, Homs, Hama and Aleppo." Since *vilayet* can mean either "district" or "province" this loose drafting was to lead to complications, although it seems likely that McMahon meant "district," and hence did not exclude Palestine from the Arab area. On the other hand, the letter was not a precise agreement, merely a declaration of intent in a continuing correspondence about the possibility of an Arab revolt, though that was not how Hussein perceived it.

Later the British also sought to invoke worldwide Jewish assistance for their cause (not least in revolutionary Russia) by issuing the Balfour Declaration of 2 November 1917. This stated that "His Majesty's Government view with favour the establishment in Palestine of a National home for the Jewish people." Was Palestine now the "twice-promised land"? Yet, despite all their previous arrangements and agreements, some of which embarrassingly had been published by the Bolsheviks, Britain and France sought to reassure the Arabs with their declaration of 7 November 1918 that they were fighting for "the complete and definite emancipation of the peoples so long oppressed by the Turks and the establishment of national governments and administrations deriving their authority from the initiative and free choice of the indigenous populations." To what extent were these undertakings contradictory and mutually incompatible? Further, would they stand the test of the conference and the changes in international circumstances since their creation, most notably the collapse of Russia as a great power and the larger-than-anticipated British share in the victory?

Part of the answer lies in what Britain meant by Arab "independence" and here Milner's definition during the conference is revealing, "what we mean by it is that Arabia while being independent herself should be kept out of the sphere of European political intrigue and within the British sphere of influence: in other words that her independent native rulers should have no foreign treaties except with us." This concept of an area which would continue to need European assistance and protection echoed that of wartime officials and advisers. This deliberately ambiguous approach to the Arabs may help to explain the thinking behind the Sykes–Picot agreement. It would be sensible, from an Anglo-French standpoint, to clarify their mutual spheres of influence in the region, and to exclude ambiguity in their relationship, which was always of much greater mutual importance than any arrangement with the Arabs, which few British or French advisers believed would amount to much. Hence the Sykes–Picot agreement divided the region into sections, with varying degrees of Anglo-French or Allied control. Between Cilicia, coastal Syria and Lebanon, which were to be French, and Baghdad and Basra, which were to be British, they were prepared to recognise an independent Arab state or states, with the proviso that the area was divided into two portions, "A" (blue) and "B" (red): "In the blue area France, and in the red area Great Britain, shall be allowed to establish such direct or indirect control as they may desire and as they may think fit to arrange with the Arab State or Confederation of Arab States." Palestine was reserved to an international administration, the form of which was to be decided after consultation with Russia, then the other allies, and Hussein.

Although the Italians were cut in on this deal in 1917 by the treaty of St Jean de Maurienne, the key developments in the Middle East were the collapse of Russia (which left the St Jean treaty unratified) and the striking successes of the British forces in the region. In 1917 Allenby captured Baghdad and Jerusalem, in 1918, Damascus and Syria. The Russian collapse removed an important player and rival from the game and altered significantly the British perception of the role of France in the region. Whereas before Britain had been anxious to interpose the French between her spheres of influence and the Russians, this no longer seemed so important, and France now appeared more as a rival than as a useful buffer. Further, the fact that the vast majority of Allied forces in the area were British encouraged them to believe that the wartime agreements should be adjusted in their favour, particularly in oil-rich Mosul and in Palestine. Clemenceau, whose main priorities were European and whose interest in, and knowledge of, the Middle East were minimal, was not averse to a readjustment. It is unlikely, however, that his generosity in London in December 1918 was entirely due to emotion at his reception from the cheering crowds. According to Lloyd George, Clemenceau "asked me what it was I specially wanted from the French. I instantly replied that I wanted Mosul attached to Irak, and Palestine from Dan to Beersheba under British control. Without hesitation he agreed." Clemenceau clearly believed that this gesture would be reciprocated, probably by British support for France on the Rhine, a share in the oil of Mosul, and the honouring of the remainder of the Sykes–Picot agreement. If so, he was to be disappointed, particularly during the Rhineland debates, whilst there was already a powerful lobby in Britain questioning the wisdom of French control in Syria. The bitterness resulting from this Anglo-French misunderstanding was unfortunate and persistent.

The Middle East at the Conference

The conference did not reach its final decisions on the Middle East until April 1920, by which time many of the conditions prevailing at its outset had dramatically altered. The peacemakers were faced with a complex web of interconnecting problems and aspirations, which led to a series of clashes: between the great powers, most notably Britain and France; between the powers and the representatives of the indigenous populations; between the powers and Zionists; and between Arabs and Zionists. As in eastern Europe, the powers found themselves trying to come to terms with their earlier encouragement of the ideals of self-determination and nationalism, with the added complication of their own aspirations in the area. The principle of mandates helped to present the ambitions of the European powers in a form acceptable to Wilson, but the question of their allocation remained thorny and unresolved. The withdrawal of the Americans, the re-emergence of a Russian threat, in the shape of bolshevism, and the revival of Turkish fortunes under Mustapha Kemal also posed additional problems as time passed, although in the event, the renegotiation of the Sèvres settlement at Lausanne did not greatly affect the arrangements for the non-Turkish parts of the Ottoman empire.

Syria

The single most difficult question which arose in Paris was the future of Syria. The Arab delegation was led by Emir Feisal, Hussein's son. There is no doubt that they added an air of romance to the proceedings, even Robert Lansing was moved to poetic prose when describing Feisal: "his manner of address and the tones of voice seemed to breathe the perfume of frankincense and to suggest the presence of richly colored divans, green turbans, and the glitter of gold and jewels." Yet they were also an embarrassing reminder of the difficulties ahead, indeed it was only upon British insistence that the French were moved to grant the delegation official status at the conference. On 6 February Feisal presented his case to the Ten. He argued for the independence, and eventual unification, of the Arab peoples in Asia, and condemned the Sykes–Picot agreement. He did not oppose the idea of assistance from a mandatory power, but he pressed for the right of the population to choose its own mandatory. Arab nationalism now threatened European calculations. The French knew that Feisal had already suggested that whereas Mesopotamia might need a mandatory power, Syria did not. Even if forced to accept a mandatory power, the population would not choose France, yet the French regarded Syria as theirs, whether or not it was mandated to them. Lloyd George's advisers warned him of the importance of Anglo-French cooperation, but he was determined to exploit the Syrian issue to Britain's advantage both in the Middle East and in forcing the French to accept British solutions in Europe, and this led to some acerbic exchanges with the French during a series of unofficial negotiations outside the conference in February and March.

In an attempt to reconcile Arab and French aspirations, the British had proposed various deals to the French which fell far short of the Sykes–Picot arrangements and which weakened French control in

Syria to the point of non-existence. In return they offered Lebanon and Alexandretta to France. Clemenceau was outraged: "Lloyd George is a cheat. He has managed to turn me into a 'Syrian'." When the Middle East was discussed at the Council of Four on 20 March Pichon insisted on a French mandate for Syria, whereas Lloyd George, claiming to be the Arab champion, resisted this. Wilson proposed a commission to test opinion in Syria which Clemenceau accepted, provided its terms were to encompass Mesopotamia and the other areas of interest to Britain. Clemenceau believed he had done well, and that his support of Wilson's proposal would, at one stroke, embarrass the British and bring Wilson round to his policy in the Rhineland, but his advisers were appalled. They knew that the commission would reveal the weakness of support for France in Syria, and saw Clemenceau's actions as bordering on the insane. "They must be drunk the way they are surrendering . . . a total capitulation, a mess, an unimaginable shambles," Paul Cambon expostulated, whilst the Quai d'Orsay took the highly unusual step of organising a press campaign against its own government's Middle Eastern policy, the success of which put Clemenceau under pressure from French public opinion.

Other issues dominated the conference throughout much of April and May and, in the event, the commission never really materialised. It was sabotaged, by accident or design, by the continuing Anglo-French confrontation. The European states refused to send representatives on the commission, which became an entirely American affair. The findings, in August, of the King–Crane commission were not officially made known to the conference, but everyone knew they confirmed that the Syrians did not want the French as mandatories, preferring the Americans, or the British. "A report hardly likely to improve Anglo-French relations," commented one British official, and indeed the Middle East did bring relations between the two states to a very low ebb. The British refusal to evacuate Syria to allow French troops to replace them; the cancellation of the Long–Berenger agreement on the apportioning of oil supplies from Mosul and elsewhere; and what he saw as British avarice and Lloyd George's ill-faith, drove Clemenceau to the point of apparently offering to fight a duel with Lloyd George. The Syrian question continued to drift as the Four finalised the German settlement in May and June, though it became clear that the Americans would not accept a mandate, and that the only possible candidates were the French. Balfour remarked that the inhabitants could indeed "freely choose; but it is Hobson's choice after all."

Palestine

The future of Palestine was an added complication, inextricably linked to the Syrian issue, not least because the Arabs claimed Palestine as part of Syria. Lloyd George and Balfour were deeply committed to the Zionist cause and to the idea of a British mandate in Palestine. Quite why is not clear; there were certain strategic advantages to Britain, but British control in Palestine was not dependent upon the success of the Zionist cause. British and French observers shared the view that if the Jews were given a special position, the Palestinian mandate would become a poisoned chalice, with the mandatory merely acting to keep Jews and Arabs from killing each other. Sir Mark Sykes discovered, in a two-month visit to Palestine and Syria in late 1918 and early 1919, that there was strong local opposition both to the Zionists and to the Sykes–Picot agreement, but he died of influenza shortly after his return to Paris, before he could convince others of the need for a reappraisal of policy. Nonetheless Balfour knew that Britain was in a difficult position since she was supporting Arab self-determination in Syria against French interests, but had to argue for its suspension in Palestine, where "If the present inhabitants were consulted they would unquestionably give an anti-Jewish verdict," a judgement which the King–Crane commission confirmed.

The Ten heard the Zionist case on 27 February when Dr Chaim Weizmann, a Jewish scientist who enjoyed a very close relationship with Lloyd George and Balfour, argued that the empty spaces of Palestine could accommodate at least 4 to 5 million Jews "without encroaching on the legitimate interests of the people already there." Eventually, after some years of immigration, when they "formed the large majority, they would be ripe to establish such a Government as would answer to the state of development of the country and to their ideals." Although Weizmann and Feisal enjoyed amicable relations in Paris, there was no doubt that Arab and Jewish aspirations were incompatible, and that Britain's association with the Zionist cause must affect her relationship with the Arabs. Curzon, who was not noted for his willingness to give up British influence, feared that British support of the Zionist claim to a homeland would develop into support for a Jewish state, and looked to Wilson's Middle East commission to extricate Britain from this situation. This did not happen, and Britain became entangled in a labyrinth from which she has still not entirely escaped.

From Versailles to San Remo

The Four proved unable to reach a settlement in the former Ottoman territories and it was left to their successors to complete the task. The broader consequences of the continuing Anglo-French acrimony, particularly in dealings with Turkey, aided by the pressure on Britain's military and financial resources imposed by her worldwide commitments, convinced Lloyd George that an accommodation must be reached with France in the Middle East. At Deauville on 15 September Lloyd George accepted that British forces would evacuate Syria and Cilicia and be replaced by the French. By November this had occurred, whilst in October Feisal was told to reach the best deal he could with France. Trapped between the powers and the rising tide of Arab nationalism, Feisal felt betrayed by the British, but there was little doubt that Britain's relationship with France was of paramount importance. If forced to choose between French demands for control in Syria and Arab aspirations, particularly at a time when Hussein and Feisal were being eclipsed as Arab leaders by the formidable Ibn Saud, Britain would have no option but to support France. This policy was dictated by the need for French assistance in the enforcement of the wider settlement, and by an underlying community of interests in the Middle East, despite their bitter quarrels. Balfour was quite candid: "Neither of us wants much less than supreme economic and political control, to be exercised no doubt (at least in our case) in friendly and unostentatious cooperation with the Arabs—but nevertheless, in the last resort, to be exercised."

This control was threatened in late 1919 by the possibility of links between increasing Arab unrest and the Kemalist movement in Turkey, creating the danger of a great anti-European crusade. Feisal, reluctantly, tried to make terms with the French, but since their aim was little short of total control, he found this very difficult. His attempts to enlist the support of Syrian nationalism merely left him squeezed between two implacable forces. Feisal was offered the throne of an independent Greater Syria, including Lebanon and Palestine, by an assembly in Damascus on 8 March 1920. Simultaneously, a group of Iraqi officers present in Damascus proclaimed the independence of Iraq, with Feisal's brother Abdullah as king, and announced their common cause with the Syrians. Neither Britain nor France was prepared to make concessions to this movement, and at an inter-Allied conference at San Remo in April 1920, they finalised the details of the Middle Eastern settlement, largely ignoring the Arabs, despite Curzon's complaints of harassment: "Syrians,

Zionists, Armenians. . . . They take rooms in the same hotels as we are in and they dog our footsteps wherever we go." Feisal's Syrian subjects refused to accept the reality of French control, even after their forces were defeated and Damascus occupied in late July. Feisal abandoned his hopeless task and left Syria on 1 August. In 1921 the British made him king of Mesopotamia.

The British and French had already reached agreement, at the London conference in February 1920, on the frontier between Palestine and Syria, which gave Lloyd George his line from Dan to Beersheba, and on the French proposal for the frontier between Syria and Turkey. A new oil agreement, which was very similar to the Long–Berenger agreement dropped the previous year, was concluded at San Remo on 26 April. The mandates for Syria and Lebanon went to France, those for Palestine and Mesopotamia to Britain, under terms which they themselves proposed. The boundaries between the British and French mandates were not finalised until December 1920, and the whole arrangement was only sanctioned by the League on 24 July 1922.

The American withdrawal, and the Italian role as ineffective spectators, reduced the question of the future of the Middle East to an Anglo-French affair. It is generally agreed that their response to the challenge was in the worst traditions of pre-war imperialism, despite their wartime promises. Yet, ironically, this part of the overall settlement contributed little to Anglo-French goodwill, with Lloyd George and Clemenceau exchanging artillery barrages throughout the negotiations, and reaching agreement only grudgingly and under pressure. The settlement paid little attention to the needs of the native populations, but was determined by the requirements of the two powers. Their actions, and their disregard for Arab nationalism, did damage both to the region, and to their own relations with its peoples. Britain managed to keep most of Arabia free from the influence of other powers, but this was about the limit of her success. Her attempts to retain control through client rulers fell apart as they fell out, and she found herself subsidising several sides in a Middle Eastern muddle. France gained control of Syria and Lebanon, but her quarrel with Britain and her bad relations with her new subjects made her grasp insecure and her position always difficult. Curzon had predicted, accurately, that the French "do not realize what they are in for." Serious uprisings in Syria, Palestine and Iraq during 1920 revealed the depth of Arab resentment at this imposed settlement, a resentment which has continued to play a part in the troubled history of the region since the end of the Great War.

Julian W. Mack et al. and Faisal I

Zionism and Arab Nationalism in the Middle East

The following two selections reveal the conflicting aspirations of Zionism and Arab nationalism in the portion of the Middle East that was detached from the defeated Ottoman Empire. The first is a letter from American Jewish leaders soliciting President Wilson's support for a Jewish "home" in Palestine that had been promised by the British government in the Balfour Declaration. The second is a selection from the minutes of a meeting of the Council of Ten at which Prince Faisal, son of the Arab leader who had been promised British support for an Arab state, appears in the company of the British liaison officer T. E. Lawrence to issue a fervent appeal on behalf of self-determination for his people.

The President.   March 1, 1919.

As representatives of the delegates elected at the American Jewish Congress, held in Philadelphia December 18, 1918, we respectfully ask that the Peace Conference recognize the aspirations and historic claims of the Jewish people in regard to Palestine; that such action be taken by the Conference as shall vest the sovereign possession of Palestine in such League of Nations as may be formed and that the Government thereof be entrusted to Great Britain as the mandatory or trustee of the League.

Under the mandate or trusteeship, Palestine should be placed under such political, administrative and economic conditions as will secure

Letter from Julian W. Mack, Louis Marshall, and Stephen S. Wise, "Enclosure II [March 1, 1919]," *The Papers of Woodrow Wilson*, Vol. 55 (1986), pp. 381–385. Copyright © 1986 by Princeton University Press. Reprinted by permission of Princeton University Press. Footnotes omitted.

From Secretary's notes of a meeting of the Council of Ten, February 6, 1919, *Papers Relating to the Foreign Relations of the United States: The Paris Peace Conference, 1919* (Washington, D.C.: U.S. Government Printing Office, 1943) (hereafter *FRUS*) v. 3, 889–894.

the establishment there of a Jewish National Home, and will ultimately render possible the creation of an autonomous Commonwealth, it being clearly understood that nothing shall be done which might prejudice the civil and religious rights of existing non-Jewish communities in Palestine, or the rights and political status enjoyed by Jews in any other country. That there shall be forever the fullest freedom of religious worship for all creeds in Palestine, and that there shall be no discrimination among the inhabitants with regard to citizenship and civil rights on the ground of religion or of race.

The Historic Basis for these Claims

Palestine is the historic home of the Jews. There they achieved their greatest development. From that center, through their agency, there emanated spiritual and moral influences of supreme value to mankind. By violence they were driven from Palestine, and through the ages large numbers of them never ceased to cherish the longing and hope of return.

Palestine is not large enough to contain more than a part of the Jews of the world. The greater portion of the fourteen millions or more scattered through all countries must remain where they now abide, and it will doubtless be one of the cares of the Peace Conference, as we have already urged upon you, to ensure for them wherever they have been oppressed, as for all peoples, equal rights. Such a Palestine would be of value to the world at large, whose happiness is in large measure derived from the healthy diversities of its civilizations.

The land itself needs rehabilitation. Its present condition is a standing reproach. Two things are necessary for its reconstruction, a stable and enlightened Government, and an addition to the present population of energetic and intelligent men and women, devoted to the country, and supported by such resources as are indispensable to development. Such a population the Jews alone, it is believed, could supply. Inspired by these convictions, Jewish activities during the last thirty years have operated in Palestine to the extent permitted by the Turkish administrative system. Large sums have been expended in the establishment of Jewish agricultural settlements, which have for the most part proven highly successful. With commendable enterprise the Jews have adopted modern scientific methods and have proven themselves to be capable agriculturalists. Hebrew has been revived as a living language. It is the medium of instruction in the schools, and is in daily use. A Jewish university has been founded at Jerusalem, and funds have been pledged for its creation and support. For the further development of the country, large sums will be required for drainage, irrigation, the building of highways, railways, harbors, and public works of all kinds.

The Action of the British and Other Governments

The historic title of the Jews to Palestine was recognized by the British Government in its Declaration of November 2, 1917, addressed by the British Secretary of State for Foreign Affairs to Lord Rothschild and reading, as follows:

> "His Majesty's Government view with favor the establishment in Palestine of a National Home for the Jewish people, and will use their best endeavours to facilitate the achievement of this object, it being clearly understood that nothing shall be done which may prejudice the civil and religious rights of existing non-Jewish communities in Palestine, or the rights and political status enjoyed by Jews in any other country."
>
> The Governments of France and Italy have declared their approval of this Declaration. You, Mr. President, have expressed your sympathy with the spirit of the British Declaration, and among others, the Governments of Japan, Greece, Serbia and China have added their approval.

Great Britain as Trustee

The resolutions of the American Jewish Congress have asked that Great Britain act as mandatary or trustee of the League of Nations for Palestine. Its selection as such mandatary or trustee is urged on the ground of the desire of the Jews, due to the peculiar relationship of England to the Jewish Palestinian problem. The return of the Jews to Zion has not only been a remarkable feature in English literature, but in the domain of statecraft it has played its part, beginning with the readmission of the Jews under Cromwell. It manifested itself particularly in the 19th century in the instructions given to British consular representatives in the Orient after the Damascus incident; in the various Jewish Palestinian projects suggested by English non-Jews prior to 1881; in the letters of endorsement and support given by members of the Royal Family and Officers of the Government of Lawrence Oliphant; and finally, in the three consecutive acts which definitely associated Great Britain with Zionism in the minds of the Jews, viz,—The El Arish offer in 1901;

the East African offer in 1903, and lastly the British Declaration in favor of a Jewish National Home in Palestine in 1917. Moreover, the Jews who have gained political experience in many lands under a great variety of governmental systems, whole-heartedly appreciate the advanced and liberal policies adopted by Great Britain in her modern colonial administration.

The Terms of Trusteeship

In connection with the Government to be established by the mandatary or trustee of the League of Nations until such time as the people of Palestine shall be prepared to undertake the establishment of representative and responsible Government, the following terms are deemed important.

1. In any instrument establishing the constitution of Palestine, the declarations of the Peace Conference shall be recited as forming an integral part of such constitution.
2. The Jewish people shall be entitled to fair representation in the executive and legislative bodies and in the selection of public and civil servants.
3. In encouraging the self-government of localities, the mandatary or trustee shall secure the maintenance of local communities of proper standards of administration in matters of education and communal or regional activities. In granting or enlarging autonomy, regard shall be had to the readiness and ability of the community to attain such standards. Local autonomous communities shall be empowered and encouraged to combine and cooperate for common purposes.
4. Assistance shall be rendered from the public funds for the education of the inhabitants, without distinction of race or creed. Hebrew shall be one of the official languages and shall be employed in all documents, decrees and announcements issued by the Government.
5. The Jewish Sabbath and Holy Days shall be recognized as legal days of rest.
6. The established rights of the present population shall be equitably safeguarded.
7. All inhabitants of Palestine who, on a date to be specified, shall have their domicile therein, except those who, within a period to be stated, shall in writing elect to retain their citizenship in any other

country, shall be citizens of Palestine, and they and all persons born in Palestine or naturalized under its laws after the day named, shall be citizens thereof and entitled to the protection of the mandatary or trustee.

We are confident, Mr. President, that in common with the representatives of the Allied Governments, you will lend to these aspirations the powerful support which through you the American people is ready to exert at this historic moment.

Respectfully submitted, Julian W. Mack

Louis Marshall

Stephen S. Wise

Bernard G. Richards   Secretary

Secretary's Notes of a Conversation Held in M. Pichon's Room at the Quai d'Orsay, Paris, on Thursday, 6 February, 1919, at 3 p.m.

(The Delegates for the Hedjaz and their technical advisers entered the room.)

EMIR FEISAL said that

In his memorandum of January 29th to the Peace Conference, he had asked for the independence of all the Arabic speaking peoples in Asia, from the line Alexandretta-Diarbekir southward.

He based his request on the following points:—

i. This area was once the home of important civilisations, and its people still have the capacity to play their part in the world.

ii. All its inhabitants speak one language—Arabic.

iii. The area has natural frontiers which ensure its unity and its future.

iv. Its inhabitants are of one stock—the Semitic. Foreigners do not number 1% among them.

v. Socially and economically it forms a unit. With each improvement of the means of communication its unity becomes more evident. There are few nations in the world as homogeneous as this.

vi. The Arabic speaking peoples fought on the side of the Allies in their time of greatest stress, and fulfilled their promises.

vii. At the end of the war the Allies promised them independence. The Allies had now won the war, and the Arabic speaking peoples thought themselves entitled to independence and worthy of it. It was in accord with the principles laid down by President Wilson and accepted by all the Allies.

viii. The Arab army fought to win its freedom. It lost heavily: some 20,000 men were killed. Allenby acknowledged its services in his despatches. The army was representative of Arab ideals and was composed of young Syrians, Lebanese, Hejazis, Mesopotamians, Palestinians, and Yemenis.

ix. The blood of Arab soldiers, the massacres among the civil populations, the economic ruin of the country in the war, deserved recognition.

x. In Damascus, Beyrout, Tripoli, Aleppo, Latakia, and the other districts of Syria, the civil population declared their independence and hoisted the Arab flag before the Allied troops arrived. The Allied Commander in Chief afterwards insisted that the flag be lowered to install temporary Military Governors. This he explained to the Arabs was provisional, till the Peace Conference settled the future of the country. Had the Arabs known it was in compliance with a secret treaty they would not have permitted it.

xi. The Syrians who joined the Northern Army were recognised by the Allies as Belligerents. They demand through this delegation their independence.

His Father did not risk his life and his Kingdom by joining in the war at its most critical time to further any personal ambitions. He was not looking for an Empire. He rose up to free all the Arabic provinces from their Turkish Masters. He did not wish to extend the boundaries of the Hedjaz Kingdom a single inch.

His ideal was the ideal of all Arabic patriots. He could not believe that the Allies would run counter to their wishes. If they did so the consequences would be grave. The Arabs were most grateful to England and France for the help given them to free their country. The Arabs now asked them to fulfil their promises of November 1918. It was a momentous decision the Conference had to take, since on it depended the life of a nation inhabiting a country of great strategic importance between Europe and Asia.

The greatest difficulty would be over Syria. Syria claimed her unity and her independence, and the rest of the Arabic liberated areas wished Syria to take her natural place in the future confederation of liberated Arabic speaking Asia, the object of all Arab hopes and fears.

Some of the people of the present province of Lebanon were asking for French guarantees. Some of them did not wish to sever their connection with Syria. He was willing to admit their independence, but thought it essential to maintain some form of economic union in the interest of mutual development. He hoped nothing would be done now to render the admission of the Lebanon to the future confederation impossible, if it desired admission.

For the moment also the inhabitants of the rest of Syria hoped that the Lebanon people would of their own accord decide for federal union with themselves in Syria.

The Arabs realised how much their country lacked development. They wanted it to be the link between the East and West, to hand on Western civilisation to Asia. They did not wish to close their doors to civilised people; on the contrary, as rulers of their own country, in their zeal for their country's betterment, they wanted to seek help from everyone who wished them well; but they could not sacrifice for this help any of the independence for which they had fought, since they regard it as a necessary basis of future prosperity. They must also guard their economic interests, as part of their duty as Governors. He hoped no Power imagined that it had the right to limit the independence of a people because it had material interests in their country.

Arab religious differences were being exploited. These had been triumphed over in the Hedjaz army, in which all creeds co-operated to free their country. The first efforts of the Arab Government would be to maintain this welding of the faiths, in their common service of the principle of nationality.

Palestine, for its universal character, he left on one side for the mutual consideration of all parties interested. With this exception he asked for the independence of the Arabic areas enumerated in his memorandum.

When this principle was admitted, he asked that the various Provinces, on the principle of self-determination, should be allowed to indicate to the League of Nations the nature of the assistance they required. If the indications before the Conference in any one case were not conclusive as to their wishes for their complete independence or for their mandatory power, he suggested that an international inquiry, made in the area concerned, might be a quick, easy, sure and just way of determining their wishes.

MR. LLOYD GEORGE asked how many troops the Hedjaz had put into the field.

EMIR FEISAL replied that it was impossible to give the exact figure; but, including the Hedjaz Army, the Arabs had put about 100,000 men into the field. There was, in addition, a considerable number of Irregulars who were not on his registers. He thought he could assert that every man of fighting age in possession of a rifle between Mecca and Aleppo had joined the Arab standards. How many that might have been it was difficult to say, as he had no figures of the population. There remained four Divisions of Regulars as the standing army: the Irregulars had dispersed to their own homes.

He wished to explain that the Arab Government had been organised, as it were, in the firing line. It had been born after the outbreak of war and was not yet regularly constituted. Hence the difficulty of producing exact figures. Medina had only surrendered a few days ago.

MR. LLOYD GEORGE asked whether the Arab troops had taken any part on the Mesopotamian front.

EMIR FEISAL replied that all their operations outside the Hedjaz had been in Syria. In Mesopotamia there had been no need for an independent Arab movement and no scope for one in that region. Five of his Commanding Officers, however, and many of his men came from Mesopotamia. They had fought in his army to vindicate their rights to self-government.

PRESIDENT WILSON asked the Emir whether, seeing that the plan of mandatories on behalf of the League of Nations had been adopted, he would prefer for his people a single mandatory, or several.

EMIR FEISAL said that he would not like to assume towards his people the responsibility of giving an answer to this question. It must be for the Arab people to declare their wishes in respect to a mandatory authority. Neither he, nor his father, nor, he thought, any person now living, would be ready to assume the responsibility of deciding this question on behalf of the people. He was here to ask for the independence of his people and for their right to choose their own mandatory.

PRESIDENT WILSON said that he understood this perfectly, but would like to know the Emir's personal opinion.

EMIR FEISAL said that personally he was afraid of partition. His principle was Arab unity. It was for this that the Arabs had fought. Any other solution would be regarded by the Arabs in the light of a division of spoils after a battle. The Arabs had fought a hard fight to achieve unity. He hoped the Conference would regard them as an oppressed nation which had risen against its masters. The Arabs asked for freedom only and would take nothing less. He thought the Conference would be of the opinion that the Arab revolt had been as well conducted as any rebellion of an oppressed people in recent memory. The Arabs were an ancient people, civilised and organised at a time when the nations represented in this room were unformed. They had suffered centuries of slavery and had now seized the chance of emancipation. He hoped that the Conference would not thrust them back into the condition from which they had now emerged. The Arabs had tasted slavery: none of the nations gathered in the room knew what that meant. For 400 years the Arabs had suffered under a violent military oppression, and as long as life remained in them, they meant never to return to it.

MR. LLOYD GEORGE said that he would like the Emir to give a short account of the services rendered by the Arab forces in the defeat of the Turkish Armies.

EMIR FEISAL said, when his father rebelled against the Turks, he was hereditary Governor of Mecca—a position held by the family for 800 years. He had no arms, machine-guns, guns, ammunition or supplies, and only took Mecca with difficulty. He was unable to take Medina. The Turks then sent 35,000 men to retake Mecca. God helped the Arabs, and the English also sent them material assistance. Officers and volunteers from the old Turkish army joined them and formed the nucleus of a regular force. In 14 months the Arab forces advanced 800 miles to the North and cut the Hedjaz railway South of Maan. This was an important military achievement as the Turkish army at Medina threatened the rear of the Arab forces. He had then attacked Maan by a frontal attack without any hope of success, in order to cover General Allenby's preparations and to prevent a Turkish concentration. He had placed his army voluntarily under General Allenby's command and did this to co-operate with him. General Allenby then asked the Arab forces to attack the three railways at Derat. The Arab army did its duty and cut these lines two days before General Allenby's attack which eventually led him to Damascus. The Arab army entered Damascus together with General Allenby's forces. From that point the Arab revolt spread like a flame and in one bound reached Latakia, which was entered by the Arabs the day before the French entered Beyrout. His forces were the first to enter Aleppo. Throughout these operations the Arab plan had been subordinated to General Allenby's. They had abandoned all ambition to shine by themselves, or to do anything spectacular. They took 40,000 prisoners, who were delivered to the Allies. He need add nothing to the praise bestowed on the Arab troops in General Allenby's despatches.

M. PICHON asked whether the French had taken any part in the Arab operations on this front, and asked Emir Feisal to describe it.

EMIR FEISAL said that with him there had been a French contingent with four 65 mm. guns and two 85 mm. guns. This contingent had done wonderful work, and the help rendered by the French detachment placed upon the Arabs a debt of perpetual gratitude. There had also been with him a British detachment to whom he was equally grateful. He did not wish to praise them as their actions were beyond praise, as were those of his own troops which he had also abstained from praising.

Besides the military effort made by the Arabs, he wished to draw attention to the civil losses incurred. The Allied Officers who had witnessed the destroyed villages of Tafaz and Ahwali, could testify to the extent of the massacres perpetrated on the Arab population.

MR. LLOYD GEORGE asked whether the Emir could say whether there was any Arab population in Turkey outside Arabia and Syria: for instance in Anatolia.

EMIR FEISAL replied that there were a few in the Adana district; a few in the Tarsus and Mersina area; but none in Anatolia. In all these regions they were a small minority and the Arabs were not claiming minority rights anywhere. Part of the population in the Diarbekir area spoke Arabic. There were also Arabs living across the Persian border. But no other considerable portions of the Arab population lived in isolated enclaves at a distance from the bulk of the race.

MR. LLOYD GEORGE asked whether there was any affinity between the Arabs and the Kurds.

EMIR FEISAL said that he would be delighted to claim all the Kurds as Arabs; but he felt he would ruin his case if he made even one questionable statement.

Finally he begged that he should not be penalised because he only spoke Arabic, an ancient and honourable tongue and the language of an ancient and honourable people.

(The Emir Feisal then retired and the meeting adjourned.)

Arthur Walworth and V. K. Wellington Koo

The Blow to Chinese Nationalism

The following discussion of China's unsuccessful claim to self-determination at the peace conference comprises three selections. In the first selection Arthur Walworth provides the context of the conflicting claims of the Japanese Empire and the Chinese Republic and assesses the consequences of this dispute for the future of Asia. The second and third selections are taken from the transcript of the testimony of the Chinese representative, V. K. Wellington Koo, who fails to persuade the Big Four to support his country's claim to regain control of its coastal province of Shantung that had been seized by Japan.

Under agreements that had been made in 1917 with the Allies, Japan, in addition to receiving title to the German islands that lay in the Pacific north of the equator, also was to take over the rights that Germany had held in China's Shantung Province under a ninety-nine-year lease. The Japanese delegates were disappointed when they learned in January of 1919 that they would receive the Pacific islands not outright, as they had expected, but under the qualifications of a League mandate. Moreover, their forebearance was taxed when their demand for an acknowledgment of racial equality in the League Covenant was rejected. Now, in April, they were still without any recognition of their claim to the preferred status that Germans had enjoyed in territory in Shantung that Japanese armed forces had seized. The Chinese government at Peking had declared war on Germany on August 14, 1917, thus terminating the German rights.

The claims of Japan touched vital interests of the United States: not only the security of its Pacific frontier and the Philippines, but its future

From *Wilson and His Peacemakers: American Diplomacy at the Paris Peace Conference, 1919,* by Arthur Walworth, pp. 359–361, 362–364, 369–375. Copyright © 1986 by W. W. Norton & Company, Inc. Reprinted by permission of W. W. Norton & Company, Inc.

"Hankey's Notes of a Meeting of the Council of Ten," V. K. Wellington Koo from *The Papers of Woodrow Wilson,* Vol. 54, pp. 316–318, 505–509, and Vol. 57, pp. 615–626. Copyright © 1986, 1987 by Princeton University Press. Reprinted by permission of Princeton University Press.

relations with China as well. The Department of State was committed to a policy of long-standing that had grown out of American impulses to befriend the Chinese people and to trade with them. The United States had stood apart from the infringement upon China's territorial integrity by colonial powers, while at the same time benefiting from the security that was provided by this infringement. The American government had sought no special concessions of its own, and for two decades it had advocated the preservation of an "open door" for the educational and commercial enterprise of all nations. At the same time American citizens had contributed generously to improve the conditions of life in China.

Japan, a late entrant in the quest for outlets overseas, had been asserting political influence in many parts of China so effectively that Americans wondered whether the Chinese people would be able to absorb the Japanese intruders as they had absorbed earlier invaders. In 1915 Japan, following the example of colonial powers of Europe, had given Peking a forty-eight-hour ultimatum presenting twenty-one demands. It required the transfer of all German rights in Shantung to Japan and also asked for special privileges in other provinces of China. The ultimatum had provoked a public warning from the United States government that it could not recognize any agreement or undertaking which had been entered into or any which might be entered into between the governments of Japan and China, impairing the treaty rights of the United States and its citizens in China, the political or territorial integrity of the Republic of China, or the international policy relative to China commonly known as the open door policy.

As early as September of 1917, Colonel House had perceived the difficulty of reconciling the immediate pressure of Japanese expansion with the traditional policy of the open door and the friendly impulses of the American people toward China. He warned Wilson that, inasmuch as Japanese immigration to the United States had been restricted, some concession should be made in the Far East to relieve the overpopulation of the island empire. Shortly after this, Secretary Lansing and Viscount Ishii had worked out a formula of understanding. They were able to agree that Japan would respect the open door and the independence and territorial integrity of China. At the same time the United States would recognize that since "territorial propinquity creates special relations between countries," Japan had "special interests in China, particularly in the part to which her possessions are contiguous." The ambiguity of the Lansing-Ishii agreement left it subject to diverse interpretations.

At the end of the war Secretary Lansing abandoned the policy that had failed to produce anything more substantial than this vague accommodation. He told Ishii on November 16, 1918, that Japan's operations in north China were "certainly opposed" to American views. Encouraged by the installation of a moderate ministry in Tokyo, Lansing went to the Peace Conference convinced that resolute opposition to Japanese plans in Shantung would help the moderates in Japan to overcome the militants decisively.

The question of American policy toward the aspirations of the coalition delegation that China sent to Paris came before the State Department very soon after the armistice. V. K. Wellington Koo, third in rank among the five plenipotentiaries and China's minister at Washington since 1914, talked for fifteen minutes with the president on November 26. Charmed by the diction of the young man ("he talks English the way Macaulay wrote it," Wilson said), the president gave general assurance that China would have the support of the Americans at the Peace Conference. However, he alluded vaguely to "many secret agreements between the subjects of China and other powers" and said that the Far East was one part of the world where there might be "trouble" in the future. He went so far as to invite Koo to travel to France with him on the *George Washington*. Soon thereafter it was generally understood in China that with the support of Wilson that country could achieve what Koo had envisioned—namely, the vindication of the principles of territorial integrity, preservation of sovereign rights, and economic and fiscal independence.

Officials of the State Department, however, doubted both the wisdom and the propriety of interference in the politics of China. They wondered to what length they might safely go in giving comfort and advice to spokesmen of a people that had no reliable central government. When the question was brought to the president by Lansing, Wilson gave the opinion that it would be unwise, if not improper, for an American to have any official connection with any foreign government during the peace negotiations. . . .

The delegates of China at Paris had a very insecure footing. They had to keep one eye on the government at Peking from which they had credentials that might be withdrawn at any moment at the insistence of Japan, to which their government was financially beholden. The other eye was watching a domestic peace conference, assembling at Shanghai in February, in which factions would contend for political control of the country. In spite of their precarious position, however, the Western-educated Chinese plenipotentiaries, energetic and ambitious, committed their delegation to a far-reaching program. Not satisfied merely to attempt at the Peace Conference to free their people from the servitudes to which they had been committed in 1915 and 1918 by Japan, they undertook to revise as many as possible of the agreements under which sovereign rights had been surrendered to other foreign powers.

The Chinese who resisted Japan had the support of American naval and diplomatic opinion, as well as that of their academic friends. Indeed, the Inquiry recommended that steps be taken at the Peace Conference to modify the special arrangements under which foreigners lived in China and which many of them thought both necessary to their security and beneficial to China. The scholars did not recognize the concessions that Japan received in 1915 and that Chinese spokesmen alleged to have been given under duress. They proposed that the question of Shantung should be settled on its merits, that China regain Kiaochow with compensation to Germany for improvements effected, and that the port of Tsingtao should be internationalized and in no circumstance allowed to remain permanently under the control of Japan.

Encouraged by American professors who had taught them and by assurances of sympathy from influential citizens of the United States, the Chinese nationalists at Paris lost little time in revealing their strategy to American delegates and in seeking their assistance, while their propagandists skillfully stimulated anti-Japanese feeling. The receptivity of the Americans, which was lively from the first, did not suffer from their entertainment at Chinese dinner parties. At a luncheon on January 22, C. T. Wang proposed to three American advisers an arrangement that would return to China all the treaty rights held by Germany and Austria. The Chinese hoped later to do away with the extraterritorial rights of other powers.

When in January the Supreme Council had considered the question of Japan's claims in connection with arrangements for Germany's Pacific islands, Japan's chief spokesman, Baron Makino, asked for the unconditional cession to Japan of all German rights in Shantung province. He justified this demand by the fact that Japanese armed forces had destroyed the German base at Kiaochow and were now in possession there.

At this first formal presentation of Japanese claims, Wellington Koo was permitted, at the insistence of the Americans, to speak for China. Notified only an hour before the Supreme [Council] met on the morning of January 27, Koo hurried to see Lansing, from whom he understood that he could count on the effective support of the United States. He then appeared before the council and asked that it defer action until he could prepare a presentation of China's case.

Immediately afterward Koo called upon Wilson, who showed surprise and distress at the Japanese presentation and suggested that Koo speak plainly to the council about China's desires. The president agreed to endeavor to enlist the support of the British government, although he supposed that its hands were tied by its alliance with Japan. When Koo pressed him to speak in favor of China in the Supreme Council, however, Wilson would go only so far as to say that he had deep sympathy for China and would do his best to help. The crisis in respect of mandates for the Pacific islands precluded involvement in further controversy with Japan at this moment. Wilson did, however, go so far as to ask that the Chinese and Japanese delegates produce copies of the exchanges between their governments in 1915. Here he met with resistance from Makino, who proposed to consult Tokyo.

Koo proved himself fully capable of pleading his country's cause. In a brilliant speech on January 28—his first of many delivered to international congresses—he posed as "spokesman for one-quarter of the human race" and as defender of Shantung, China's "Holy Land, the Home of Confucius." He argued that Germany's occupation of Kiaochow was a transgression against China's integrity, and that to transfer the special rights now to another power would be to repeat the crime. Although grateful to Japan for rooting out the Germans, the Chinese were unwilling to pay their debt of gratitude by selling what they conceived to be "the birthright of their countrymen," and thereby sowing seeds of discord in the future.

In reply Makino insisted that, in accord with the wartime agreements with China, Japan must obtain the German rights directly from Germany before they could be restored to China. The pride of the Japanese was hurt by the imputation that they were not trusted to do justice eventually to China. . . .

The question of Shantung, urgent though it was, was crowded from the agenda of the Supreme Council during the days when the issue with Italy came to a climax. However, on April 25, when Orlando had left Paris, Wilson keenly felt the necessity of preventing another major defection. With Italy and Japan disaffected and Belgium disgruntled, Germany might refuse to sign a treaty and might attempt to form an alliance with Russia and Japan. Wilson reasoned that if the Japanese withdrew from the Peace Conference and the League, they would not then withdraw from Shantung. The president said that the three experts who were delegated to study the matter had reported that it was better for China to act under the wartime agreements of Japan with the Allies rather than in accord with the terms of the Sino-Japanese understandings of 1915 and 1918.

Lloyd George warned that the Japanese were not bluffing in their threat to leave the Peace Conference. At the same time the prime minister said that Great Britain could not think of giving up its special rights in the Yangtse valley if Japan kept privileges in Shantung and was free to carry out a "plan of conquest" by administering and policing railways. He proposed that they make use of the services of Balfour, who suggested that Japan be given the German rights but be asked at the same time to discuss the conditions under which they were to be restored eventually to China. Wilson, at his wits' end, agreed.

"The difficulties here would have been incredible to me before I got here," Wilson confessed in a cable to Tumulty on April 26. Fearing that the League would be wrecked, he had confided to Dr. Grayson the day before that the Italian imbroglio would be "only a tempest in a tea-pot compared with the coming controversy with Japan." His only hope, he said, was to "find some outlet to permit the Japanese to save their face and let the League adjudicate later." In his distress he turned to the American commissioners for advice. House again took the position of a diplomat. Opposing the strong inclination of Lansing and Bliss to rebuff Japan, he argued that it would be a mistake to take any action that might make the Japanese withdraw from Paris. Lansing, who thought, mistakenly, that they were bluffing and were making demands in Shantung that would "restore the shell to China and leave the kernel" in their own hands, urged that the German rights be transferred directly to China, or at least be assumed in trust by the five powers.

In the plenary session of the Peace Conference on April 28, the Japanese still co-operated with the other powers by refraining from pressing, beyond the presentation of a dignified reservation, their desire for a race-equality amendment to the League Covenant. They had made it known through the French press, however, that they were being urged by opinion in Japan to follow the example of the Italian delegates and withdraw from the conference. At the same time a dispatch from Washington reported that Japanese newspapers were intensely hostile both to the League and to the United States and that none believed the American position to be sincere.

Meanwhile, Balfour was carrying out the wish of Lloyd George and Wilson that he take the matter in hand. He was informed by Makino on April 27 that the Japanese government could not sustain both a defeat on the question of racial equality and a rejection of its claims in Shantung. Balfour, learning that Wilson was not disposed to talk with the Japanese until the plenary session on April 28 approved the League Covenant, told The Three on the morning of that day that the Japanese might take drastic action if they were not satisfied in respect of Shantung before they agreed to accept the Covenant without an amendment on racial equality. It was Balfour's understanding that, once Japan had the German rights in Shantung, it would keep only economic concessions without any military control and that it would hand back to China the whole of the leased territory. Wilson remarked that such an arrangement would give China a better position than that held under its treaty with Germany, but his advisers doubted that the Japanese would carry out their professed intention. He himself wished to have these intentions set down in black and white. He conveyed to his European colleagues the substance of a message just received from Tumulty. This asserted that the "designs of Japan" were as indefensible as those of Italy and gave the president an opportunity to "cast another die" similar to the public manifesto that had exacerbated the Italian crisis. The president, however, did not repeat the mistake that he had made in dealing with Italy.

Balfour then addressed a note to Makino, informing him that "The Three" were "quite satisfied" with the arrangement he had proposed. Wilson had been brought to a settlement that was most distasteful to him and was contrary to the recommendations of three of the American commissioners and the advising experts. Indeed, Bliss wrote a vigorous letter to Wilson to state the view of the three dissenters. Balfour and Lloyd George were fearful that the president would be unable to overcome the moralistic presumptions of his advisers and the tug of his own emotions. The prime minister took House aside and asked whether the colonel could not bring his chief to reason; and House then wrote to Wilson in support of the British position.

On April 29 the president talked with Makino and Chinda for an hour about the garrisoning of Tsinen and the guarding of the railway. According to the report that he made to Clemenceau and Lloyd George immediately afterward, Wilson told the Japanese that it was his understanding that Japan, once in possession of the German rights, would restore all to China with the exception of a residential concession and some privileges which did not include those of military occupation of the railway and of instruction of the police. He would oppose any terms that went beyond those of the German lease or seemed to impose Japanese control outside of a domain strictly economic.

The Japanese delegates were forced to listen to close questioning on April 29 by Wilson in the session of the Council of Four. Balfour put emphasis upon the validity of the Sino-Japanese Treaty of September 1918, which was in his view "a voluntary transaction between sovereign states . . . which gave important pecuniary benefits to China." The foreign secretary guided the drafting of a compromise formula that satisfied both Japan's dignity and Wilson's scruples. When the president insisted that the agreement be made public and the Japanese feared the effect of this on opinion in Japan, Balfour suggested the expedient of making a statement in the form of an interview and thus avoiding any impression that Japan was being coerced. In this session Wilson bore down upon the Japanese with a moral fervor that seemed to House ungracious.

Balfour forwarded a compromise text to Wilson for his approval, and he received from the president a version only slightly revised. It was given out as the substance of an interview and was not included in the articles approved for insertion in the treaty with Germany, whereby the German rights in Shantung went directly to Japan. It was released to *Le Temps* on May 5 and endorsed by Japan's foreign minister in a press conference at Tokyo on the seventeenth.

Thus Japan, having been thwarted in its desire for a declaration of race equality and for outright possession of German islands in the Pacific, received in effect all that it demanded in Shantung. But the satisfaction of its people was marred by the suspicious and admonitory tone of the Americans at Paris as well as by the sympathy for the Chinese nationalists that was aggressively asserted by Americans. The Japanese delegates at Paris became even more sensitive to any slights on the part of their Allies, especially in the matter of representation on committees of the Peace Conference. At their request they were given a part in the work of the committees on reparations, new states, and study of the German observations of the peace terms; and in June, Makino was allowed a seat in sessions of the Supreme Council even when the interests of Japan were not being discussed.

In Wilson's opinion the settlement was "the best that could be got out of a dirty past." A defection by Japan might not only break up the Peace Conference but destroy the League of Nations and result in Japanese alliance with Germany and Russia. China must look to the League for protection from encroachments by foreign powers.

At the request of the president, Baker informed the other American plenipotentiaries of the decision and took word of it to the Chinese delegates as they were dining with American friends. According to one of those present, the banquet "became a wake." The Chinese, apprehensive of personal injury when they returned to China, were inconsolable. On May 4 they addressed a protest to The Four, saying that it would be difficult to explain to their people what the Peace Conference really meant by "justice." E. T. Williams, the chief American adviser, confessed that he was "ashamed to look a Chinese in the face." Lansing, Bliss, and White, hoping to reverse the decision, persuaded Williams to campaign publicly against it in a way that would not impugn their loyalty to the president. (They said, according to Williams, "We cannot be responsible. You must be the goat.") Criticism of the Shantung verdict was so widespread, in the United States as well as among the friends of China at Paris, that the president was moved to prepare a brief public statement to explain his position. Apparently wishing to avoid any appearance of a defensive posture, he asked that it not be released as a quotation but used "in some other form for public information at the right time." In his statement Wilson specified the assurances that the Japanese had given and called them "very satisfactory in view of the complicated circumstances." Furthermore, reverting to the vision of a free China that he had revealed to Clemenceau and Lloyd George at the end of their discussion on April 28, he detected, hopefully, "a general disposition to look with favor upon the proposal that at an early date through the mediation of the League of Nations all extraordinary foreign rights in China and all spheres of influence should be abrogated by the common consent of all the nations concerned."

One of the American experts, Stanley K. Hornbeck, lost no time in suggesting that the Chinese now bring up the fundamental question of tariff revision and that of withdrawal of foreign post offices from China. However, when the Chinese formally renewed their plea for a general consideration of the position of foreigners in China, they were told by the Council of Four that this question did not arise out of the war, and therefore it could not be discussed appropriately at the Peace Conference. On May 14 Clemenceau informed Lou Tseng-tsiang that the Supreme Council, recognizing the importance of the questions raised, suggested that they be brought before the League of Nations.

When news of the rebuff at Paris reached China, the political turmoil in that land grew. Dispatches from American officials reported that a "May Fourth Movement" was resulting in violent public indignation and anti-Japanese boycotts in many parts of the country, and a general denunciation of foreigners from which Americans and their president were, for the most part, spared. The political conference that was in session at Shanghai, seeking Chinese unity, was disrupted. American residents in China wired formal protests to their government, and Japanese officials thought them not free from blame for inciting bad feeling. In the Japanese press vituperation against Wilson continued. There was fear among Americans at Peking that a national uprising in China would give Japanese militarists an opportunity to occupy much of the country on the plea of restoring order.

The American delegates at Paris took every opportunity to attempt to mitigate the blow that was dealt to the Chinese nationalists. American officials were asked by the Chinese for counsel as to whether they should put their signatures on the disappointing treaty of peace. House, consulted by Koo, advised that the Chinese sign with a reservation such as they had presented in the plenary session of the Peace Conference on May 6. This was intended to enable their government to ask, at a suitable moment after the signing, for a reconsideration of the decision with respect to Shantung. According to Koo's record, House went so far as to say that Wilson would not object to a Chinese reservation. Lansing told Koo that he could see no legal objection to this course, and that without a reservation the Chinese should not sign.

Emboldened by American advice, the senior Chinese delegate formally notified the Peace Conference on May 26 that, under instructions from his government, China would sign the treaty with a reservation. There was no ruling until June 24, when the secretary general of the conference, speaking for Clemenceau, gave notice that no reservations would be permitted, either in the text of the treaty or outside. The Chinese protested and, notifying the Americans of Clemenceau's verdict, sought their "friendly offices." Wilson, advised by Lansing that any sovereign power could make reservations in signing, put this opinion before the Council of Four. But Clemenceau said that the proposal of China lacked precedent and also awakened fears of establishing one. He was supported by Lloyd George.

Wilson himself was not so indulgent of a Chinese reservation as House had given Koo to believe. The president was chary of setting a precedent that might be used by his adversaries at Washington to justify American reservations. He had informed Tumulty, just two days previously, that it was his "clear conviction" that "the adoption of the treaty by the Senate with reservations would put the United States as clearly out of the concert of nations as a rejection." Despite a personal appeal from Koo on the evening of June 27, the day before the signing of the Treaty of Versailles, the president took no action.

Negotiations continued up to the moment of the signing of the treaty at Versailles on the afternoon of June 28. At the last minute the Chinese delegates notified Clemenceau that they did not "consider themselves qualified to sign the Treaty." At the same time they issued a press statement to the effect that they had been denied justice by the Peace Conference and were submitting their case "to the impartial judgment of the world."

Secretary's Notes of a Conversation Held in M. Pichon's Room at the Quai d'Orsay, Paris, on Tuesday, January 28, 1919, at 11 a.m.

M. CLEMENCEAU said that . . . the Council would proceed to discuss the question of the German possessions in the Far East, together with the Chinese delegates.

As the question of restitution of the fortress had been raised, he thought it useful to read the words of the Japanese ultimatum to Germany, because it had a bearing on the purpose in hand: —

> "Considering it highly important and necessary in the present situation to take measures to remove all causes of disturbance to the peace of the Far East, and to safeguard the general interests contemplated by the agreement of the Alliance between Japan and Great Britain in order to secure a firm and enduring peace in Eastern Asia, the establishment of which is the aim of the said agreement — the Imperial Japanese Government sincerely believe it their duty to give advice to the Imperial German Government to carry out the following two propositions:
>
> 1. To withdraw immediately from Japanese and Chinese waters German men-of-war and armed vessels of all kinds, and to disarm, at once, those which cannot be withdrawn.
> 2. To deliver on a date not later than the 15th September, 1914, to the Imperial Japanese authorities, without condition and compensation, the entire leased territory of Kiauchow, with a view of eventual restoration of the same to China."

Since the occupation of Kiauchow, Japan has been in actual possession. In view of all that had passed between the Governments of China and Japan, Baron Makino thought that China fully realized the import of

Japanese occupation. The friendly interchange of views on this subject had been entered into, and Japan had agreed to restore Kiauchow as soon as Japan had free disposal of the place. Agreements had also been reached with regard to the (leased) railway.

As notes had been exchanged, he thought that a statement of these engagements might be worth the consideration of the members of the Council.

PRESIDENT WILSON asked Baron Makino whether he proposed to lay these notes before the Council.

BARON MAKINO said that he did not think the Japanese Government would raise any objection, but as the request was an unexpected one he would be compelled to ask its permission.

PRESIDENT WILSON asked on behalf of China if Mr. Koo would do likewise.

MR. KOO said that the Chinese Government has no objection to raise.

M. CLEMENCEAU asked both the Japanese and Chinese Delegates to state whether they would make known to the Council the conditions of the restoration agreed between them.

BARON MAKINO said that he would do so, provided his Government would make no objection. He did not think it would. If it were within his own power, he would produce these documents as soon as possible. There was, however, one point he wished to make clear. Japan was in actual possession of the territory under consideration. It had taken it by conquest from Germany. Before disposing of it to a third party it was necessary that Japan should obtain the right of free disposal from Germany.

PRESIDENT WILSON pointed out that the Council was dealing with territories and cessions previously German without consulting Germany at all.

BARON MAKINO said that the work now in hand was one of preparation for the presentment of the case to Germany. It followed therefore that the cession of Kiauchow would have to be agreed upon by Germany before it was carried out. What should take place thereafter had already been the subject of an interchange of views with China.

MR. KOO said that he was very glad, on behalf of China, to have the opportunity of putting the case of his country. He had heard with interest the Dominion speakers, who spoke on behalf of a few million people. He felt his own responsibility was enhanced by the fact that he was the spokesman of 400 millions, one quarter of the human race. The Chinese delegation would ask the Peace Conference for the restoration to China of the Leased Territory of Kiauchow, the railway in Shantung, and all other rights Germany possessed in that province before the war. He would confine himself to broad principles in order not to employ too much of the Council's time. Technical details would be explained in full in a memorandum which he proposed to submit. The territories in question were an integral part of China. There [*they?*] were part of a province containing 3 million inhabitants, of Chinese in race, language and religion. The history of the lease to Germany was doubtless familiar. The lease had been extorted by force. The German fleet had occupied the coast of Shantung and landing parties had penetrated into the interior. The lease had been extorted as a price for the withdrawal of the expedition. The pretext of this proceeding was the accidental killing of two missionaries in the interior of the country in a manner quite beyond the control of the Chinese Government. On the principles of nationality and of territorial integrity principles accepted by this Conference, China had a right to the restoration of these territories. The Chinese delegation would feel that this was one of the conditions of a just peace. If, on the other hand, the Congress were to take a different view and were to transfer these territories to any other Power, it would, in the eyes of the Chinese Delegation, be adding one wrong to another. The Shantung province, in which Kiauchow and the railway to Chinanfu were situated, was the cradle of Chinese civilisation, the birthplace of Confucius and Mencius, and a Holy Land for the Chinese. This province had always played a very important part in the development of China. Economically, it was a densely populated country, with 36 million people in an area of only 35,000 square miles. The density of the population produced an intense competition and rendered the country quite unsuitable for colonisation. The introduction of a Foreign Power could only lead to the exploitation of the inhabitants, and not to genuine colonisation. Strategically, Kiauchow commanded one of the main gateways of North China. It controlled one of the shortest approaches from the sea to Pekin, namely, the railway to Chinanfu which, at its junction with the railway from Tientsing, led straight to the capital. In the interest of Chinese national defence which in time would be organised, the Chinese Delegation would be unable to admit that any Foreign Power had claims to so vital a point. China was fully cognisant of the services rendered to her by the heroic Army and Navy of Japan in rooting out German power from Shantung. China was also deeply indebted to Great Britain for helping in this task at a time of great peril to herself in Europe. China also was not forgetful of the services rendered her by the troops of the other Allies in Europe, which had held in check an enemy who might otherwise have easily sent reinforcements to the Far East and thereby prolonged hostilities there. China appreciated these services all the more because the people in Shantung had also suffered and sacrificed in connection with the military operations for the capture of Kiauchow, especially in regard to requisitions for labour and supplies of all kinds. But, grateful as they were, the Chinese Delegation felt that they would be false to their duty to China and to the world if they did not object to paying their debts of gratitude by selling the birthright of their countrymen, and thereby sowing the seeds of discord for the future. The Chinese Delegation therefore trusted that the Conference, in considering the disposal of the leased territory and other rights held by Germany in Shantung, would give full weight to the fundamental and transcendent rights of China, the rights of political sovereignty and territorial integrity.

BARON MAKINO said that he had listened with great attention to what had fallen from his Chinese colleague concerning the direct restitution of Kiauchow to China. In the statement put forward on the previous day, he had explained the reasons for which the Japanese Government had undertaken the reduction of this German stronghold.

MR. KOO said that the Chinese Delegation did not adopt quite the same view as Baron Makino. He was well aware that Japan after her undertaking in 1914—which he was glad to note had just been renewed by Baron Makino—would not retain the territory.

But there was a choice between direct and indirect restitution. Of the two China would prefer the first. It was always easier to take one step than two if it led to the same place. They had always considered all the Conventions made with Japan as provisional and subject to revision by the Peace Conference. Before becoming a belligerent China had agreed to accept all the conditions made to Germany by Japan.

China's entry into the war, however, had completely altered her status. None of the previous arrangements precluded China either from declaring war on Germany, or from being represented at the Peace Conference. Nor could they preclude her now from demanding from Germany direct restitution of her rights. China's belligerency had in itself put an end to the leases obtained by Germany in Chinese territory. Furthermore, there was a clause in the lease to the effect that Germany could not transfer her rights to another power.

(The meeting then adjourned.)

Hankey's and Mantoux's Notes of a Meeting of the Council of Four

President Wilson's House,
Paris, April 22, 1919, 4:30 p.m.

I. President Wilson said that the Chinese Plenipotentiaries knew the interest he felt in the Kiauchau-Shantung settlement. On the previous day he had a Conference with the Japanese representatives, and this morning they had come to confer. M. Orlando, unfortunately, could not be present. Since he had last seen Mr. Koo, he had carefully read the documents, from which he gathered the following was the chain of events.

Before China entered into the war, there had been an exchange of Notes. He thought in 1915 (Mr. Koo said it was the 25th May). In that exchange of Notes, the Japanese Government had said that when the German rights in Kiauchau were transferred after the war to Japan, Japan would return them to China. The Chinese Government had taken note of this. Subsequently, there had been a further exchange of notes, and he believed, also a treaty although he had only seen Notes, in which the Japanese Government laid down certain conditions. The Chinese Government had accepted these conditions. Great Britain and France (Mr. Lloyd George said that this had occurred between the two exchanges of Notes between China and Japan) had entered into a similar but not identical agreement with Japan to the effect that they would support the claims of the Japanese Government on the Continent and on the islands North of the Equator. In the case of the British Government it had been on the understanding that Japan supported her claim to German islands South of the Equator. Hence, Great Britain and France were in much the same position in the matter.

MR. LLOYD GEORGE explained that at that time the submarine campaign had become very formidable. Most of the British torpedo-boat-destroyers were in the North Sea, and there was a shortage of those craft in the Mediterranean. Japanese help was urgently required, and Japan had asked for this arrangement to be made. We had been very hard pressed, and had agreed.

PRESIDENT WILSON then read extracts from the exchange of Notes printed on page 62 of the Official Claim of China for direct restitution to herself of the leased territory of Kiauchau, etc., circulated by the Chinese Delegation:

> "When, after the termination of the present war, the leased territory of Kiauchau Bay is completely left to the free disposal of Japan, the Japanese Government will restore the said leased territory to China under the following conditions."

He then read the following reply of the Chinese Foreign Minister, in which, after rehearsing the whole of the Japanese Note, he had said "In reply, I beg to state that I have taken note of this declaration." He then read an extract from page 82, namely, exchange of Notes dated September 24, 1918:

> "The Japanese Government, mindful of the amiable relations between our two countries and out of a spirit of friendly co-operation, propose to adjust all the questions relating to Shantung in accordance with the following articles.
>
> 1. Japanese troops along the Kiauchow-Chinan railway, except a contingent of them to be stationed at Chinanfu, shall be withdrawn to Tsingtau.
> 2. The Chinese Government may organise a Police Force to undertake the policing of the Kiauchow-Chinan railway.
> 3. The Kiauchow-Chinan Railway is to provide a reasonable amount to defray the expense for the maintenance of the above mentioned Police Force.
> 4. Japanese are to be employed at the Headquarters of the above-mentioned Police Force, at the principal railway stations, and at the Police Training School.
> 5. Chinese citizens shall be employed by the Kiauchow-Chinan Railway Administration as part of its Staff.
> 6. The Kiauchau-Chinan Railway, after its ownership is definitely determined, is to be made a Chino-Japanese joint enterprise.
> 7. The Civil Administration established by Japan and existing now is to be abolished.
>
> The Japanese Government desires to be advised of the attitude of your Government regarding the above-mentioned proposal."

To this the Chinese Minister had replied:

> "In reply I have the honour to state that the Chinese Government are pleased to agree to the above articles proposed by the Japanese Government."

The Chinese Delegation would see, President Wilson continued, the embarrassing position which had been reached. Mr. Lloyd George and M. Clemenceau were bound to support the claims of Japan. Alongside of them the Chinese had their exchange of notes with Japan. He reminded Mr. Koo that when urging his case before the Council of Ten at the Quai d'Orsay, he had maintained that the war cancelled the agreement with the German Government. It did not, however, cancel the agreement between China and the Japanese Government, which had been made before the war. What he had himself urged upon the Japanese was that, as in the case of the Pacific Islands, the leased territory of Kiauchau should be settled by putting it into the hands of the Five Powers as Trustees. He did not suggest that Treaties should be broken, but that it might be possible, in Conference, to bring about an agreement by modifying the Treaty. He also proposed to them that all Governments should renounce the special rights they had acquired in China, so as to put China in a position free from the special limitations which had been imposed upon her. The Japanese were not willing to have Kiauchau handed over to the Five Powers, and the British and French Governments were embarrassed by their Treaties. When he pressed the Japanese for explanations of the meaning of their agreement, they had replied that the exploitation of two coal-mines and one iron-mine had not proved a successful venture, and were now bound up with the railway. They stated, however, that they would withdraw the civil administration; that they would maintain troops only on the termini of the railway; and that if a general agreement was reached, they would withdraw their extraterritoriality. They urged that they wanted a community of interest with the Chinese in the railway, and the only reserve they made was for a residential district in Kiauchau.

MR. KOO said that the Treaties of 1915 and the subsequent exchange of Notes were the outcome of the 21 demands which Japan had made on China and were all part and parcel of one transaction. He hoped he had made this clear before the Council of Ten. He felt that the Treaties and Notes which had been exchanged after Japan had delivered an ultimatum stood outside of the regular procedure and course of Treaties. They dealt with matters arising out of the war.

MR. LLOYD GEORGE asked what ultimatum he referred to.

PRESIDENT WILSON asked if Mr. Lloyd George had never heard of the twenty-one points.

MR. LLOYD GEORGE said he had not.

MR. KOO said that in January 1915 after the capture of Kiau Chau that port had been opened up to trade; China then asked Japan to withdraw her troops from the interior of the province. The Japanese took occasion to treat this note as though it were an unfriendly act and shortly after sprung on China twenty-one demands divided into five groups—for example, that China should accept Japanese advisers; that they should give up railway concessions in which Western Powers were concerned, and he would draw Mr. Lloyd George's attention to the fact that Great Britain was concerned. China was put in an extremely embarrassing position. She resisted and resisted and only gave up when she was absolutely compelled to. On the 7th May the Japanese sent China an ultimatum in regard to the majority of demands giving China only 48 hours within which to accept; otherwise Japan would consider herself free to take such steps as she thought fit to enforce them. This caused absolute consternation to the Chinese Government which eventually had to submit to force majeure.

MR. LLOYD GEORGE asked if they had not appealed to the United States of America.

PRESIDENT WILSON said they had and the United States had intervened in regard to the infringement of sovereignty and political independence. The whole transaction, however, had been kept extremely secret and the United States only learnt of it in a roundabout way.

MR. KOO said that secrecy had been imposed upon China by Japan under severe penalties. It had been said that Japan had informed the Allied Governments and the United States Government that there had been only 11 Demands; but actually 21 Demands had been made on China. The Chinese Government felt that the Treaties and Notes exchanged as a result of these demands followed by an ultimatum were on a different footing from the ordinary. China had always endeavoured to carry out to the letter all engagements made in good faith. These, however, had been made against China's free will, and the same applied to the notes exchanged in the previous year. For the last four years since they had captured Kiauchau, Japanese troops had penetrated far into the province of Shantung, where there was a population of 36,000,000 people. This had been very uncomfortable for the general population, and the results had been disturbance and trouble. The Chinese Government had protested, and asked Japan to withdraw her troops who were stationed 250 miles up the railway, but they had refused and had established civil administration bureaux in the interior of Shantung and extended their control even over the Chinese people by levying taxes on Chinese people and asserting judicial power over them. The feelings of the Chinese people against the extension of Japanese control were so strong that the Chinese Government felt constrained to take some immediate step to induce Japan to withdraw her troops and remove the civil administration bureaux, the object being to relieve the tense situation until the question could be finally settled at the Peace Conference.

MR. LLOYD GEORGE said that it looked that by the Treaty with China, the Japanese Government would get more than the Germans had had. He asked Mr. Koo which he would prefer—the Treaty with Japan, or the transference to Japan of the German rights?

MR. KOO said that the situation was so difficult that he felt he must speak very frankly. The Japanese position was so close to China, especially in Manchuria, where they occupied a railway which was connected with Pekin, that merely to transfer German rights would create a very serious situation. With the Japanese on the Manchurian railway, and the Shantung railway, Pekin would be—at it were—in a pincers.

PRESIDENT WILSON pointed out that the Japanese claimed that the administration of the Shantung railway would be a joint one, and they proposed to withdraw the Japanese administration.

MR. LLOYD GEORGE said that Mr. Koo had not quite answered his point. Supposing the Great Powers had to decide (and this really was his position since he was bound by a Treaty) between Japan inheriting Germany's rights in Shantung or exercising the rights under the treaty with Japan, which would China prefer? He pointed out that Great Britain was only bound by the rights which Japan inherited from Germany.

PRESIDENT WILSON said that if Japan inherited the German rights, it would involve her retaining the leased territory. He thought Mr. Lloyd George's point was that possibly Japan was claiming greater rights than Germany had exercised. As the British and French Governments had to support the Japanese claim to what Germany had had, they wanted to know whether China would be better off according as Japan could exercise the rights that Germany had or those that she obtained by her Treaty.

MR. LLOYD GEORGE agreed that this was the point, and said the real question was whether the Treaty with Japan was better for China than Germany's rights.

(At this point there was an interval to permit the Chinese plenipotentiaries to confer.)

MR. KOO said that he had now consulted his colleague. He could make no choice, because both alternatives were unacceptable; he would merely compare them. The Treaty and Notes with Japan provided for restoration of the Leased Territory to China on certain conditions, but such restoration would be only nominal. Between the two, he thought that the German rights were more limited than the rights claimed by

Japan under her Treaty and Notes with China. Even mere succession to the German right, however, would create a grave situation for China's future. In claiming direct restitution of German rights, he was not asking for any compensation or remuneration for China as a result of her entry into the war, but only for what was necessary for peace in the Far East. The experience of the last three years made it so clear what the Chinese position would be if Japan was allowed either to succeed to the German rights in Shantung or to retain the rights she claimed under her treaty with China. It was an uncomfortable position both to the Chinese people and the Government. He was not in the least exaggerating, but only saying what was necessary to explain the situation.

PRESIDENT WILSON said that M. Clemenceau and Mr. Lloyd George would bear witness that he had put the Chinese case as well as he could to the Japanese Delegation in the morning. He had emphasised the great need of trust and friendship between Japan and China, which he regarded as essential to peace in the Far East. He had urged that China should be free and unfettered to carry out her development. What he asked now was only a means of getting out of a position that was extremely difficult. In this Conference the United States of America was the only power that was entirely unbound. Great Britain, France, China and Japan were all bound by Treaties. They were bound to keep these Treaties because the war had largely been fought for the purpose of showing that Treaties could not be violated.

MR. LLOYD GEORGE suggested that in the exchange of notes of September 1918, China might have stood out.

MR. KOO said that the exchange of notes in 1918 was the result of the Shantung Treaty, made in consequence of the 21 demands. It was part of the same transaction.

PRESIDENT WILSON said that the exchange of notes had grown out of the previous agreement. He looked for the Shantung Treaty.

MR. KOO said that it was on page 59 of *China's Claim for Direct Restitution of Kiaochow*, etc.

PRESIDENT WILSON read the following extracts from the treaty and said that China had then had to accept and had had no other choice:

> "*Art. 1—The Chinese Government agrees to give full assent to all matters upon which the Japanese Government may hereafter agree with the German Government relating to the disposition of all rights, interests and concessions which Germany, by virtue of treaties or otherwise, possesses in relation to the Province of Shantung.*

"Art. 2 — *The Chinese Government agrees that as regards the railway to be built by China herself from Chefoo or Lungkow to connect with the Kiaochow-Chinanfu railway, if Germany abandons the privilege of financing the Chefoo-Wehsien line China will approach Japanese capitalists to negotiate for a loan.*"

Mr. LLOYD GEORGE said he would like to have the two positions examined by British, French and American experts, and to learn their views as to which course would be best for China.

M. CLEMENCEAU said he had no objection.

Mr. LLOYD GEORGE said that it was also only fair that China should be given more time to consider this question. This seemed to be the only alternative there was to acquiescing in the Treaties between China and Japan. Great Britain and France, however, were not bound by this latter Treaty, but only by their own arrangements with Japan. . . .

PRESIDENT WILSON then read the following extracts from the 21 Demands on page 52 and 53 of the Chinese Document.

Group IV.

"*The Chinese Government engages not to cede or lease to a third Power any harbour or bay or island along the coast of China.*

Group V.

"Art. 1. — *The Chinese Central Government shall employ influential Japanese as advisers in political, financial, and military affairs.*

"Art. 3. — *Inasmuch as the Japanese Government and the Chinese Government have had many cases of dispute between Japanese and Chinese police which caused no little misunderstanding, it is for this reason necessary that the police departments of important places (in China) shall be jointly administered by Japanese and Chinese or that the police department of these places shall employ numerous Japanese, so that they may at the same time help to plan for the improvement of the Chinese Police Service.*

"Art. 4. — *China shall purchase from Japan a fixed amount of munitions of war (say 50% or more of what is needed by the Chinese Government) or that there shall be established in China a Sino-Japanese jointly worked arsenal. Japanese technical experts are to be employed and Japanese material to be purchased.*"

PRESIDENT WILSON recalled that there were other demands designed to exclude other Powers from the commercial and industrial development; (Mr. Koo said, on page 52.).

PRESIDENT WILSON read Article 1 of the Group III as follows:

"The Two Contracting Parties mutually agree that when the opportune moment arrives the Hanyehping Company shall be made a joint concern of the two nations and they further agree that without the previous consent of Japan, China shall not by her act dispose of the rights and property of whatever nature of the said Company nor cause the said Company to dispose freely of the same."

MR. KOO pointed out that the Hanyehping Company was the largest coal and iron mining Company of China, situated in the Yangtze Valley. He requested the reading of Article 2 which, he said, was even more serious.

PRESIDENT WILSON read the following:

"Art. 2—The Chinese Government agrees that all mines in the neighborhood of these owned by the Hanyehping Company shall not be permitted, without the consent of the said Company, to be worked by other persons outside the said Company; and further agrees that if it is desired to carry out any undertaking which, it is apprehended, may directly or indirectly affect the interests of the said Company, the consent of the said Company shall first be obtained."

MR. LLOYD GEORGE asked whether China had agreed to this Article.

MR. KOO said that the Chinese Government had had to accept most of the 21 Demands with slight modifications. That was why China was seeking some redress.

PRESIDENT WILSON asked if the following point of view would make any appeal to the Chinese Plenipotentiaries? Hereafter whatever arrangements were made both Japan and China would be members of the League of Nations, which would guarantee their territorial integrity and political independence. That is to say, that these matters would become the concern of the League and China would receive a kind of protection that she had never had before and other nations would have a right which they had never had before to intervene. Before it had been, comparatively speaking, none of our business to interfere in these matters. The Covenant, however, laid down that whatever affected the peace of the world was a matter of concern to the League of Nations and to call attention to such was not an hostile but a friendly act. He, himself, was prepared to advocate at the Council of the League and at the Body of Delegates that the special positions occupied by the various nations in China should be abandoned. Japan declared that she was ready to support this. There would be a forum for advocating these matters. The interests of China could not then be overlooked. He was stating this as an element of security for China in the future if the powers were unable to give her what she wanted now, and he asked the Chinese Delegates to think the matter over. While there was doubt as to the Treaty and Notes between China and Japan, there was no doubt whatsoever as to the agreements entered into by France and Great Britain. Hence, even if the agreements between them and Japan were abandoned, these two Governments were bound to support Japan in getting whatever rights in Shantung Germany had had. Hence, the question which the Chinese Plenipotentiaries had to consider was, would they prefer to retain the rights which Japan had secured in their treaty with her or would they prefer that Japan should inherit the German rights in Shantung.

MR. KOO said that he could not lay too much emphasis on the fact that the Chinese people were now at the parting of the ways. The policy of the Chinese Government was co-operation with Europe and the United States as well as with Japan. If, however, they did not get justice, China might be driven into the arms of Japan. There was a small section in China which believed in Asia for the Asiatics and wanted the closest co-operation with Japan. The position of the Government, however, was that they believed in the justice of the West and that their future lay there. If they failed to get justice there, the consequential re-action might be very great. Further, he wished to suggest that the validity of the arrangements was questionable owing to the following facts: (1) They arose out of the war: (2) China had subsequently come into the war herself: (3) New principles had now been adopted by all the nations as the basis of the peace and the agreements with Japan appeared to be in conflict with them. Consequently, in thanking the Supreme Council for hearing the views of the Chinese Delegation, he wished to state the great importance of attaining a peace which could be relied on to endure for 50 years instead of a peace so unjust that it would only sow the seeds of early discord.

PRESIDENT WILSON said that these were serious considerations, but he would not like Mr. Koo even personally to entertain the idea that there was injustice in an arrangement that was based on treaties which Japan had entered into. The sacredness of treaties had been one of the motives of the war. It had been necessary to show that treaties were not mere scraps of paper. If treaties were inconsistent with the principles on which the peace was being formed, nevertheless we could not undo past obligations. If that principle were accepted, we should have to go back and France would have the treaty of 1814 and there would be no end to it. He would not like to feel that because we were embarrassed by a treaty we were disregardful of justice. Moreover, the unjust treatment of China in the past had not by any means been confined to Japan. He hoped that the quandary in which the Powers were would be stated to the Chinese people. He hoped that it would be shown to them that the undoing of the trouble depended on China uniting in reality with other nations, including the Western Nations. He felt absolute confidence that the opinion of the world had the greatest sympathy for the realm of China. The heart of the world went out to her 400 millions of people. Much depended on the state of mind of these 400 million people. Any statesmen who ignore their fortunes were playing a dangerous game. But it would not do to identify justice with unfortunate engagements that had been entered into.

MR. KOO said he believed prevention to be better than cure. He thought that it would be better to undo unfortunate engagements now, if they endangered the permanence of the future peace.

MR. LLOYD GEORGE said the object of the war was not that. The war had been fought as much for the East as for the West. China also had been protected by the victory that had been won. If Germany had won the war and had desired Shantung or Pekin, she could have had them. The very doctrine of the mailed fist had been propounded in relation to China. The engagements that had been entered into with Japan had been contracted at a time when the support of that country was urgently needed. He would not say that the war could not have been won without this support. But he could say that Kiauchau could not have been captured without Japanese support. It was a solemn treaty and Great Britain could not turn round to Japan now and say "All right, thank you very much. When we wanted your help, you gave it, but now we think that the treaty was a bad one and should not be carried out." Within the treaties he would go to the utmost limits to protect the position of China. On the League of Nations he would always be prepared to stand up for China against oppression, if there was oppression. China was a nation with a very great past and, he believed, with a still greater future. It would, however, be of no service to her to regard treaties as Bethmann von Hollweg had regarded them, as mere scraps of paper to be turned down when they were not wanted.

M. CLEMENCEAU said that Mr. Koo could take every word that Mr. Lloyd George had said as his also.

PRESIDENT WILSON asked whether assuming for the sake of argument that the engagements were unfortunate nevertheless they had been entered into for the salvation of China, because they had been entered into for the salvation of the world, of which China was a part. In fact, it would be said that the very engagements were instruments for the salvation of China.

MR. KOO said they had been designed apparently to meet a situation in Europe and not in the Far East.

MR. LLOYD GEORGE pointed out that if Germany had won the war in Europe, she would have won it in the Far East also. The world would have been at her feet.

M. CLEMENCEAU agreed.

PRESIDENT WILSON pointed out that the German project was not only domination from Hamburg to Bagdad but also the control of the East. Germany knew China to be rich. Her objects were mostly material. The Kaiser had been the great exponent of what was called the "Yellow Peril." He had wanted to get France and Great Britain out of the way and afterwards to get everything else he could. One result of the war undoubtedly had been to save the Far East in particular, since that was an unexploited part of the world.

MR. LLOYD GEORGE said that he wished to consider the question further before arriving at a decision.

PRESIDENT WILSON asked the Chinese Delegates also to give further consideration to the question and hoped that it could be taken up soon again.

(The Chinese Representatives then withdrew.) . . .

The Japanese delegation to the Peace Conference. Seated from left: Baron Nobuaki Makino, Marquis Kimmochi Saionji, and Viscount Sutemi Chinda. (Woodrow Wilson Papers Project, Photographs Series, Mudd Library, Department of Rare Books and Special Collections, Princeton University Library)

PART

V The Abortive Quest for Human Rights

W. E. B. Du Bois

The Case for African Liberation

William Edward Burghardt Du Bois, an African-American with a Ph.D. from Harvard who served as director of publicity and research for the National Association for the Advancement of Colored People (NAACP), sent the following memorandum to President Wilson's personal secretary shortly after the end of the war. His polite, deferential request that Wilson meet with a delegation of black leaders to discuss the topic of Africa's right of self-determination in Paris received no response. A similar petition from a young Vietnamese nationalist in Paris named Ho Chi Minh on behalf of

From W. E. B. Du Bois, "Memoranda on the Future of Africa" [Submitted to Woodrow Wilson on November 27, 1918], *The Papers of Woodrow Wilson*, Vol. 53, 236-238. Copyright © 1986 by Princeton University Press. Reprinted by permission of Princeton University Press.

self-determination for his people met a similar fate. It was evident that Wilson's conception of self-determination was restricted to the regions of the world inhabited by white Europeans.

William Edward Burghardt Du Bois to Joseph Patrick Tumulty, with Enclosure

Sir: New York November 27, 1918

In consultation with Mr. George Foster Peabody, I have been working for some months on the question of the African colonies. The enclosed memoranda [sic] has been drawn up and received the assent of numbers of leading colored men, as expressing our ideas.

We want to get this memoranda before the Peace Conference and before the conscience of the world, and we are convinced that the best way to do this is to present the matter formally to the President.

I write to ask if the President would receive before he sails a small delegation of representative colored men, including Dr. R. R. Moton of Tuskegee, and others, to lay this memoranda before him. We would take but a few moments and confine ourselves to a short statement, which could be submitted before hand.

I realize, of course, how very busy the President must be, and I only ask because I understand that this is a matter in which he has great interest, and I am thinking that perhaps it would be helpful for him to have in this form the expressed opinion of Negro America.

I am, Sir,   Very sincerely yours,   W. E. B. Du Bois

Enclosure

Memoranda on the Future of Africa
By W. E. B. Du Bois

1. The barter of colonies without regard to the wishes or welfare of the inhabitants or the welfare of the world in general is a custom to which this war should put an end, since it is a fruitful cause of dissension among nations, a danger to the status of civilized labor, a temptation to unbridled exploitation, and an excuse for unspeakable atrocities committed against natives.

2. It is clear that at least one of Germany's specific objects in the present war was the extension of her African colinies [colonies] at the expense of France and Portugal.

3. As a result of the war, the Germany [German] colonies in Africa have been seized by the Allies, and the question of their disposition must come before the Peace Conference. Responsible English statesmen have announced that their return to Germany is unthinkable.

4. However, to take German Africa from one imperial master, even though a bad one, and hand it over to another, even though a better one, would inevitably arouse a suspicion of selfish aims on the part of the Allies and would leave after the war the grave questions of future colonial possessions and government.

5. While the principle of self-determination which has been recognized as fundamental by the Allies cannot be wholly applied to semi-civilized peoples, yet as the English Prime Minister has acknowledged, it cannot [can] be partially applied.

6. The public opinion which in the case of the former German colonies should have the decisive voice is composed of:

    a. The Chiefs and intelligent Negroes among the twelve and one-half million natives of German Africa, especially those trained in the government and mission schools.

    b. The twelve million civilized Negroes of the United States.

    c. Educated persons of Negro descent in South America and West Indies.

    d. The independent Negro governments of Abyssinia, Liberia, and Hayti.

    e. The educated classes among the Negroes of French West Africa and Equatorial Africa and in British Uganda, Nigeria, Basutoland, Nyassaland, Swaziland, Sierra Leone, Gold Coast, Gambia and Bechuanaland, and the four and one-half millions of colored people in the Union of [South] Africa.

    These classes comprise today the thinking classes of the future Negro world and their wish should have weight in the future disposition of the German colonies.

7. It would be a wise step to ascertain by a series of conferences the desires, aspirations and grievances of these people and to incorporate to some extent in the plans for the reconstruction of the world the desires of these people.

8. The first step toward such conferences might well be the chief work of the movement to commemorate the three hundredth anniversary of the landing of the Negro in America.

9. If the world after the war decided to reconstruct Africa in accordance with the wishes of the Negro race and the best interests of civilization, the process might be carried out as follows: the former German colonies with one million square miles and twelve and one-half millions of inhabitants could be internationalized. To this could be added by negotiation the 800,000 square miles and nine million inhabitants of Portuguese Africa. It is not impossible that Belgium could be persuaded to add to such a state the 900,000 square miles and nine million natives of the Congo, making an International Africa with over two and one-half million square miles of land and over twenty million people.

10. This reorganized Africa could be under the guidance of organized civilization. The Governing International Commission should represent not simply governments but modern culture — science, commerce, social reform, and religious philanthropy.

11. With these two principles the practical policies to be followed out in the government of the new states should involve a thorough and complete system of modern education built upon the present government, religion and customary law of the natives. There should be no violent tampering with the curiously efficient African institution of local self-government through the family and the tribe; there should be no attempt at sudden "conversion" by religious propaganda. Obviously deleterious customs and unsanitary usages must gradually be abolished, and careful religious teaching given but the general government set up from without must follow the example of the best colonial administrators and build on recognized established foundations rather than from entirely new and theoretical plans.

12. The chief effort to modernize Africa should be through schools. Within ten years twenty million black children ought to be in school. With[in] a generation young Africa should know the essential outlines of modern culture and groups of bright African students could be going to the world's great universities. From the beginning the actual general government should use both colored and white officials and natives should be gradually worked in. Taxation and industry could follow the newer ideals of industrial democracy, avoiding private land monop[o]ly and poverty, promoting cooperation in production and the socialization of income.

13. Is such a state possible? Those who believe in men; who know what black men have done in human history; who have taken pains to follow even superficially the story of the rise of the Negro in Africa, the West Indies, and the Americans of our day know that the wide-spread modern contempt of Negroes rests upon no scientific foundation worth a moment's attention. It is nothing more than a vicious habit of mind. It could as easily be overthrown as our belief in war, as our international hatreds, as [our] old conception of the status of women; as our fear of education [educating] the masses, and as our belief in the necessity of poverty. We can, if we will, inaugurate on the Dark Continent a last crusade for humanity. With Africa redeemed, Asia would be safe and Europe indeed triumphant.

Carole Fink

The Protection of Ethnic and Religious Minorities

The idea of protecting the rights of minority groups threatened by their government was first codified in an almost entirely forgotten set of "minority treaties" that were signed at the Peace Conference along with the peace treaty with Germany. Professor Carole Fink of the Ohio State University, a leading international historian who has undertaken an intensive study of this long-neglected subject, identifies the sources of these protective guarantees and demonstrates how they were applied (with minimal success) to the ethnic and religious minorities inhabiting the nations of East-Central Europe.

On June 28, 1919, just moments after the German government signed the Treaty of Versailles, Roman Dmowski and Ignacy Paderewski, the two representatives of the government of Poland brought into existence on that day, were ushered into an adjacent room where they also signed

From Carole Fink, "The Paris Peace Conference and the Question of Minority Rights," *Peace and Change: A Journal of Peace Research*, Vol. 21:3 (July 1996), pp. 273–288. Reprinted by permission of Blackwell Publishers. Footnotes omitted.

a treaty with the Allied and Associated Powers. Most of the treaty's clauses pertained to routine and fairly innocuous economic, financial, postal, transit, and commercial obligations that were to be undertaken by the new Polish state. Perhaps the only controversial item was an agreement to assume a portion of the former czarist debt, insisted upon and inserted at the last minute by the otherwise friendly French government. It was instead the first twelve articles of the Polish treaty, pertaining to minority rights, that drew the most attention.

Article 93 of the Versailles Treaty with Germany had stipulated that Poland would be bound by specific clauses to protect its racial, religious, and linguistic minorities. For six long weeks in May and June of 1919 a special peace conference committee had hammered out the twelve articles that Poland signed under protest on June 28. Woodrow Wilson had proposed this initiative; David Lloyd George had reluctantly agreed; and the peace conference president, Georges Clemenceau, had signed an extended letter to the Polish premier, Paderewski, justifying the Minority Treaty. The treaty was heralded as ushering in a new era of international involvement in minority rights. How had this come about? Why had the peacemakers taken this step? What was the significance of the "Little Versailles Treaty" for Poland, its minorities, for Europe, and for this century?

Certainly, international protection of minorities was scarcely new. Since the mid-seventeenth century, diplomats had routinely inserted specific clauses in treaties that assigned governments responsibility for the protection of religious minorities. For example, in 1814, the Congress of Vienna had been confronted with the fate of German Jews (which it chose to ignore) and that of the Poles about to be redivided among Prussia, Russia, and Austria (to whom the assembly directed pious hopes that they grant tolerance and protection to their minority subjects). The Congress of Aix-la-Chapelle in 1818 received a petition on behalf of Jews in czarist Russia; the Congress of Paris in 1856 directed its gaze toward Jews and Christians in the Ottoman Empire; and the Congress of Berlin in 1878 dealt with the status of Jews in Romania, Serbia, and Bulgaria.

Yet such nineteenth-century conventions largely failed. Consequently, oppressed and discontented minorities added an extremely volatile element to international relations. The self-professed defender of slavdom and orthodoxy in St. Petersburg used the plight of Balkan Christians to interfere in the Ottoman Empire; independent Balkan governments persecuted non-Christians; and fleeing minorities created a disconcerting swell of refugees flooding Western Europe and the

United States. The liberal Western powers were reluctant to take action to compel Romania to enfranchise its Jewish citizens or to persuade Russia to reduce its state-sanctioned intolerance. For the oppressed the options were protests and sporadic revolt, nationalist and socialist agitation, and, increasingly, emigration to other states and continents.

West European Jews were alarmed at the oppression of their co-religionists in the East. As it happened, the Jews of the Ottoman Empire gained an articulate defender in the Alliance Israélite Universelle. Based in Paris, this right hand of the Quai d'Orsay assisted its compatriots' cultural and religious development and prudently fought the worst abuses. British and American Jews, ranging from Zionists to assimilationists, sent considerable aid and support to the East, tried to help the massive numbers of impoverished refugees, and worked to stave off immigration restrictions and waves of anti-Semitism.

However, throughout the nineteenth century there were no concerted international efforts to quell the oppression of minorities. In this heyday of European imperialism, international anarchy, and national economic protectionism, internal politics were largely deemed a domestic matter. Moreover, it seemed reckless, futile, and even hypocritical to interfere in the East given the notoriety of France's Dreyfus Affair, England's Irish problem, and America's segregation of its black population. Russia's humiliating treatment of the Jews, even those with foreign passports, went largely ignored in London and Paris, its partners in the Triple Entente. In 1911, the United States, stung by the prejudicial treatment of one of its citizens, denounced its trade treaty with St. Petersburg; and in 1913, the State Department made a vain attempt to pressure Romania on behalf of its Jewish population. But Washington's gestures were a rare recognition that rights denied in one place affected those elsewhere and also violated a basic international code. And so the "wretched refuse" continued to flee to the West, provoking nativism and anti-Semitism from all segments of society, from workers to right-wing racists, and the international community concentrated on its unprecedented arms build up to maintain a fragile great-power balance.

World War I was an unexpectedly bitter and extended struggle, unprecedented in its violence and damage, unparalleled in its revolutionary consequences. During the prolonged stalemate, both sides probed their enemies' weak points. Using nationalism as a weapon, they encouraged their opponents' minority populations to revolt. The Germans applied this subversive policy in Russia and Ireland, the Entente in Eastern Europe, and the British in the Near and Middle East. Nineteen seventeen marked the peak of such strategies among the great powers. Lenin and Wilson, from widely different perspectives, endorsed the principle of self-determination. The war-weary Entente encouraged the emigré "national committees" whose aim was to dissolve the Habsburg monarchy. And Britain, on the eve of Allenby's capture of Jerusalem, endorsed the Zionists' claim to a homeland in Palestine.

Nevertheless, for the vast number of people of the Russian, Habsburg, Hohenzollern, and Ottoman Empires, the Great War offered little relief from pogroms and state restrictions of minority rights. Especially endangered were the Jews in Galicia, wedged between huge warring armies and victims of violence and plunder. Many took flight. Despite generous help from their kin in Western Europe and the United States, their situation worsened. As disparate nationalities prepared to clamor for statehood after the war, Jewish organizations across the entire political spectrum were determined that the next peace would ensure decent treatment for their coreligionists as well as other minorities and would recognize some sort of Jewish national identity.

The sudden collapse of the Central Powers forced the victors to clarify their vague and often contradictory wartime plans. The Allies, tempered by Wilson's idealism (as expressed in his Fourteen Points) clothed their territorial and economic demands in humanitarian garb: the "ethnographic principle" would justify not only the return of Alsace-Lorraine to France and Schleswig to Denmark but also the enlargement of Poland and the reduction of Austria-Hungary and Turkey to create or expand their client states. Those to be sacrificed to the Allies' more practical economic and strategic desiderata—such as the Germans of Poland and Bohemia, the Hungarians of Slovakia and Romania—would hopefully fall under the protection of the new League of Nations. Strongly promoted by Wilson and the liberal internationalist, Lord Robert Cecil, this League, it was expected, would establish and maintain universal principles of justice among all nations. But those who put their faith more in realpolitik than in high principles would dominate the peace conference.

How did the Minority Treaty come about? Traditional historiography has credited and blamed Woodrow Wilson, who promoted a free and independent Poland (Point 13), but who also, under the powerful influence of American Jewish leaders, proposed special clauses for minority protection. This is the historical version of Wilson who strong-armed the Allies, assuaged German protests, placated the Jews, outflanked the Bolsheviks, and convinced the Poles to sign.

But this is a simplistic analysis. In the winter and spring of 1918–19 there were a multitude of elements that interacted to lay the groundwork for the Polish Minority Treaty. In this breeding ground for the great political and economic transformation of the early twentieth century, there were all sorts of human contingencies as well as a host of direct and historical forces—visible and latent—which created this novel instrument, with its cautious generosity toward minorities, its judicious encroachment on state sovereignty, and its timid advance in a major realm of international supervision.

The peacemakers were about to create a belt of new and enlarged states, the *cordon sanitaire*, between defeated Germany and Bolshevik Russia, all to be fledgling democracies and League of Nations members. However, it soon became apparent that all of the *cordon* would contain considerable numbers of minorities who would, paradoxically, be victims of the "self-determination" of their new masters.

The minorities issue came to the fore only eleven days after the armistice. On November 22, 1918, a huge pogrom erupted in Lemberg (Lwów), the former capital of Austrian Galicia. Immediately after Polish troops captured the city, they attacked the Jewish quarter. Three full days of beating, rapes, looting, and murder followed. The world press, informed by German, Austrian, Jewish, and neutral sources, recorded the outrages. Almost overnight, the image of a martyred Poland—carefully cultivated by the Polish National Committee and the famed pianist Paderewski—was obliterated by the gruesome stories from Lemberg.

Less than a month later, the first meeting of the American Jewish Congress took place in Pittsburgh, Pennsylvania. Representatives of American Zionism coupled their goals for Palestine with a "Bill of Rights" for the millions of endangered Jewish minorities of Eastern Europe. Shaken by the events in Lemberg, the Allied governments sent stiff warnings to Polish leaders that their case at the peace conference would be prejudiced by continued violence. Warsaw authorities, however, denied that pogroms had occurred and accused Jews, Germans, and Bolsheviks of maligning their honor.

During the opening months of the Paris Peace Conference, the minorities question was not raised. Wilson's main preoccupation was to create a League of Nations. But as the Allies deliberated over the fruits of their victory, the spreading violence in Eastern Europe created new "facts." The Poles, Czechs, and Romanians began seizing their neighbors' territory under the banner of fighting the communist menace and swelled the numbers of their involuntary minority populations.

In March 1919, the delegation of the American Jewish Congress arrived in Paris and assumed leadership over the already assembled Comité des délégations juives auprès de la conférence de la paix. The Comité, much to the chagrin of the assimilationist-oriented French and British Jewish representatives, insisted that the Jews of Eastern Europe constituted a distinct nationality which required protection of its language, education, and culture as well as its faith. The proposals for Jewish autonomy in Eastern Europe were endorsed by Germany and by the excluded Bolshevik regime. Not surprisingly, the "Big Three" opposed political or cultural autonomy; Britain, France, and the United States had strong domestic as well as diplomatic reasons for resisting the creation of a "state within a state."

In March 1919, the Poles launched a new eastward campaign against Belorussia and Lithuania and at once new pogroms were reported. On April 5 in Pińsk, thirty-five Jewish civilians were shot by Polish soldiers who had broken into an authorized meeting and arrested everyone present. A few days later, when the Poles captured Vilna, hundreds of Jews were beaten and scores killed. Once more the world press was filled with news of Polish barbarism and with editorials demanding minority protection. Germany, working with Jewish organizations, provided the grim details to journalists. Giant protest meetings sprang up in Western and neutral capitals; questions were asked in parliaments; and the problem of minority rights leaped to front-page status.

The peacemakers were forced to respond. What were the consequences of the new borders about to be established? Could unwillingly conquered peoples be assimilated? Or, if persecutions continued, would they flee abroad and, if so, where? (The United States was moving toward restrictions on immigration; and the prospective Jewish homeland in Palestine was, at best, an uncertain destination.) Moreover, the incidents in Lemberg, Pińsk, and Vilna challenged the very basis of Wilsonianism: that a people granted self-determination would be peaceful and grant justice to its ethnic and religious minorities. Under the banner of militant anticommunism, Poland's eastward, southward, and northward expansion was creating a new empire, characterized by indiscriminate oppression. By fomenting instability in the region, a bloated Poland conjured up the nightmare of a German-Bolshevik rapprochement that could destroy the as-yet-unwritten peace settlement. The resurrected Polish realm would indeed be a multinational state of only two-thirds Poles and significant Ukrainian, Jewish, White Russian, Lithuanian, and German populations.

At Wilson's urging and his partners' acquiescence, the Paris Peace Conference on May 1, 1919 took the initiative that previous great-power statesmen had assumed, so vainly, after past wars. The victors created a Committee on New States to draft a Polish Minority Treaty which would be the model for all the new and enlarged states of Eastern Europe. Meeting almost daily and in secret, the committee conferred with Jewish leaders, East European statesmen, and legal and political experts from the U.S., British, and French delegations. The committee created a document, and a doctrine, laced with compromise that nevertheless revolutionized the history of minority rights.

The "Minority States" as they were to be called did not accede easily to this procedure. On May 31, there was a single plenary meeting between the Big Three and their associates to discuss the treaties. No Jewish, German, or Ukrainian minority representatives were present. Romania's premier Ionel Bratianu launched a vehement attack against this threatened violation of state sovereignty. Paderewski was more subtle and more moderate. But Wilson rejected all the protests by insisting that the great powers "cannot afford to guarantee territorial settlements which they do not believe to be right, and they cannot afford to leave elements of disturbance unremoved which they believe will disturb the peace of the world." The Big Three had little doubt about their *right* to dictate rules of political conduct, despite their minimal military and political presence in Eastern Europe. The collapse of four empires, the threat of German revanchism and Bolshevik expansion—combined with the emergence of vulnerable dependents and unconstrained new masters—had forced upon the victors unwonted and unwanted power and responsibility.

The Allies were shocked by the intensity of the East Europeans' resistance; and they were discomfited by Poland's ominous silence and nonresponse to the draft minority treaty. The new and enlarged states of Eastern Europe would undoubtedly require extended aid and supervision; yet their compliance and cooperation were essential to make the new order function. The French seemed to know precisely what sort of Eastern Europe they wanted: a strong, pro-Allied barrier separating the Germans and the Soviets. The British, as suspicious of France's hegemonic impulses as of German and Bolshevik threats, rued the absence of Allied unity and strength to impose order in Eastern Europe. And Wilson, battered by bad health, bleak political news from home, and the growing disaffection of those around him, bowed to pragmatic solutions.

The Polish Minority Treaty as signed on June 28, 1919, consisted of twelve articles, about two pages of text. With minor modifications, the same provisions appeared in the treaties with Czechoslovakia, Romania, Yugoslavia, Greece, Austria, Hungary, Bulgaria, and later with the new Baltic states of Latvia, Lithuania, and Estonia. Finland was exempt, as was Italy (which had been awarded ethnically mixed areas of the former Habsburg Monarchy). Except for special provisions which would affect the partitioned province of Upper Silesia, Germany was also not forced to sign a minority treaty. As Paderewski charged, and Wilson acknowledged, the system made an invidious distinction between "new, inexperienced governments" and older, more settled states—although Greece was thirty years older than "great power" Italy, and a half-million Slavs would remain under German rule.

The core of the Polish Minority Treaty (and of all the others subsequently signed) lay in Articles 1–8, which were deemed "fundamental laws" overriding any previous legal codes, legislation, or edicts. Determined to prevent a repetition of Romanian or czarist-era persecution, the Allies insisted that Poland pledge to assure "full and complete protection of life and liberty to all inhabitants . . . without distinction of birth, nationality, language, race, or religion"—thus creating an environment in which foreigners as well as Poles could function freely. Moreover, in a phrase echoing the American Constitution, "all inhabitants . . . . [were to] be entitled to the free exercise, whether public or private, of any creed, religion, or belief whose practices are not inconsistent with public order or public morals."

Then came the knotty question of citizenship, which had consumed hours and jars of ink. The Jews and Germans, fearing the expulsion and spoliation of those who had taken flight or served in one of three armies during the war, pleaded for an August 1914 date to determine residency. The Poles insisted on as late a date as possible in order to eliminate as many non-Poles as possible. The result, a compromise which satisfied no one and produced a half-decade of lawsuits, gave automatic citizenship to residents on the signing date of the treaty, to those born to "habitual residents," and to those born on Polish soil who were not nationals of another state. However, the agreement left a large grey area of German colonists and Russian-Jewish settlers which filled the court dockets for years.

Article 7 contained the basic civil, political, and cultural rights insisted upon by the American and West European Jews: all Poles were to be equal before the law and enjoy identical rights as citizens and workers. Notwithstanding the establishment of Polish as the national language, minority tongues could be freely used in private intercourse, commerce, religion, and the press, at public meetings, and before the courts. But all claims for national-cultural autonomy were rejected in the text. Contrary to the aspirations of the Germans, Jews, and Ukrainians, non-Poles were not recognized as distinctive national groups but were identified under the legally innocuous title of "Polish nationals who belong to racial, religious or linguistic minorities." Clearly the Allies had no intention of weakening Poland by exaggerating its multinational character, even in the cultural realm.

Article 8 dealt the deathblow to German and Jewish hopes for political autonomy. Minorities were to be permitted to establish, manage, and control (at their own expense) *private* charitable, religious, and social institutions as well as schools and other educational establishments without interference from the government—and to use their language and exercise their religion freely. Article 9 specified that Poland was obliged in areas heavily populated by minorities to set up schools at public expense, but only *primary* schools and with the Polish language equal to the minority tongue. To make their very limited intent perfectly clear, the Allies restricted German-speaking schools to "that part of Poland which was German territory on August 1, 1914."

Articles 10 and 11, pertaining specifically to the Jews, were undoubtedly due to the efforts of the Comité des délégations juives and to the uproar over the violence. Article 10 permitted Educational Committees, appointed *locally* by the Jewish communities, "to establish and manage schools and to use their native language therein." This was a small victory for Yiddish, which was now recognized as a separate language. But it represented a crushing defeat for Jewish nationalism by foreclosing a *national* Council. Moreover, all public instruction above the primary level was to be conducted exclusively in Polish. Because Poland's Jews lacked the resources to create a private-school system and a patron across the frontier, Jewish learning and culture were threatened by this ban on public support to Jewish higher education. Article 11, the Sabbath clause, exempted the Jews from performing any acts that violated their Sabbath, except for their military obligations. But the crucial issue of Jewish Sunday trading was ignored.

The heart of the Polish Minority Treaty was its guarantee clause, Article 12, which assigned responsibility for enforcement to the Council of the League of Nations. Since history had proven the great powers' reluctance or inability to halt the persecution of minorities, the Allies turned this burden over to the as yet unborn League. The League Council was to "take such action and give such direction" as needed in dealing with violations of treaty provisions. Differences of opinion between Poland and the Council were to be adjudicated by the World Court, whose decision was to be final.

The guarantee clause fell far short of the hopes that minorities would have direct access to the League. Their fate would once again be in the hands of disinterested great powers. Neither Wilson nor his colleagues were prepared to grant the Jews or any other minority the status of a recognized entity within a League of sovereign states. And neither Wilson nor his colleagues wanted to give any minority encouragement to remain forever separate within a nation-state.

*   *   *

Nobody liked the minority treaty. In fact, its authors neglected to publish it, and the agreement remained a mysterious instrument for several years. The minorities put a good face on their setback. The Poles, although resentful, ratified the treaty more in gratitude for continued Allied support for their war in the East than in good faith. In Paris, the Committee on New States proceeded to draft minority clauses which were imposed on the recalcitrant Romanians, Yugoslavs, and Greeks, on the more compliant Czechoslovaks, and on defeated Austria, Hungary, and Bulgaria.

In 1920, the League of Nations reluctantly assumed its responsibility to Eastern Europe's minorities. The Council established a formal procedure which openly favored the new states over their minority populations. Minority petitions were to adhere to strict terms of acceptability; publicity was restricted; and complaints were to be handled mainly by "friendly" negotiations between the Geneva bureaucracy and officials of the accused government. Thus, in subsequent years, few petitions reached the Council, whose members largely supported minority assimilation, and were reluctant to embrace minority cases and confront a fellow government.

There was considerable criticism of the League's ad hoc and secretive minorities procedures. (These were far more restrictive than the mandate system, which included a permanent commission and annual public reports.) In only rare instances were cases involving the Jews of Eastern Europe heard in the halls of Geneva. On the other hand, once Germany joined the Council in 1926, the German minority in Poland—especially in the partitioned province of Upper Silesia—deluged the League with attacks on the Warsaw regime. Germany's proposals of 1929 to expand the League's minorities work were thwarted by the British and

French and by League officials. At this dire moment of economic depression and political radicalization, the German minorities began looking away from Geneva for a champion.

The advent of the Third Reich altered the picture entirely. Hitler, who had no interest in the League or in the intricacies of minority rights, exited Geneva, unchallenged, in October 1933. Poland, in the wake of its sudden rapprochement with Berlin, unilaterally renounced its hated minority treaty in September 1934. Bonfires were lit throughout the country to celebrate the end of international servitude, and there was no response by the signatory powers.

* * *

In reviewing the Polish Minority Treaty, one must discard old myths. It represented not simply a Wilsonian invention, a Jewish victory, or a Polish defeat. Wilson would indeed have preferred a more general minorities-protection clause in the League of Nations Covenant, but he was thwarted by Japan's demands for, and Britain's reservations about, a global declaration of minority rights. Jewish representatives from the United States, Britain, and France, with their rival personalities and ideologies, undermined their opportunity to achieve significant gains for their coreligionists in Eastern Europe; and Polish Jewry, scarcely consulted, was even more deeply divided among its Zionists and nationalists, socialists and assimilationists. Moreover, Poland scarcely collapsed before the Allies; Paderewski's smooth words and dogged intransigence reaped vital concessions.

The Polish Minority Treaty in 1919 grew out of historical and practical necessity at a confusing and dangerous moment of victory. The Allies, against their political scruples, were forced by egregious violence and public clamor to take steps to compel the new states to treat their minorities equitably. Poland in the spring of 1919, menaced by a recalcitrant Germany and a hostile Soviet Russia, accepted a form of external control in return for economic and military aid to expand its borders eastward.

At the heart of the Allies' calculations was the unspoken assumption that mistreated minorities, blocked from emigrating, might turn to the Bolsheviks or to Germany and destabilize the peace. The Polish Minority Treaty was designed to grant a minimal number of basic rights, to foster loyal citizens, and to prepare the way for assimilation. It was also a way of controlling a weak expansionist Poland and promoting its internal consolidation. No statesman in 1919 was prepared to grant group or national rights to minorities, something almost universally considered dangerous to a state's stability.

Nevertheless, the Polish Minority Treaty represented a genuine accomplishment. Its basic idea, as Wilson announced on May 30, 1919, was both pragmatic and idealistic: to allow peoples to stop injustice and achieve an acceptable level of security. But conditions in Eastern Europe differed markedly from the West, where smaller, largely assimilated, and generally patriotic minorities enjoyed broad-ranging possibilities for education, professional advancement, and personal security. In Eastern Europe the legacy of war, poverty, and intolerance strengthened the currents of political radicalism, violence, and separatism.

The Jews and the other minorities of Eastern Europe emerged from the Peace Conference with a scrap of paper that America, its Allies, and the League were reluctant to redeem. It is no accident that after World War II the United Nations refused to reestablish specific mechanisms for the international protection of minorities and has focused on the more general category of human rights. The end of the Cold War and the intensification of minority problems in almost all the successor states to the former communist regimes of Eastern Europe and the USSR have rekindled considerable interest in minority treaties. As statesmen ponder this remedy, the previous history of such efforts should be carefully examined.

Paul Gordon Lauren

The Denial of Racial Equality

While the appeals by W. E. B. Du Bois and Ho Chi Minh on behalf of the non-Western peoples fell on deaf ears, the Eurocentric prejudices of the peacemakers were dramatically revealed by the controversy that erupted when the Japanese delegation introduced an amendment to the League of

From Paul Gordon Lauren, "Human Rights in History: Diplomacy and Racial Equality at the Paris Peace Conference," *Diplomatic History*, Vol. 2, No. 3 (Summer 1978), pp. 257–277. Reprinted by permission of Blackwell Publishers. Footnotes omitted.

Nations Covenant affirming the principle of racial equality in world affairs. As the following article by Professor Paul Gordon Lauren of the University of Montana demonstrates, the Japanese proposal (which was strongly supported by representatives of non-European peoples) provoked staunch opposition in the American, British, and Australian delegations, which prevented its adoption.

The great and the small who assembled at Paris in 1919 were, for a short period of time, the arbiters of the world. Their decisions influenced the globe and their peace conference was appropriately described as "the clearing house of the Fates." Added to the silent influences of the dead from World War I were the tumultuous demands of the living who had survived. Individuals, pressure groups, political parties, states, empires, and races met to vie with each other over both spoils and principles. Although some thought that they were only cleaning up the folly of an exhausted civilization gone mad, others sincerely believed that they were creating an entirely new era where respect for basic human rights would rule supreme.

To the hopeful, this was to be a world of a "new" diplomacy different in its origins, objectives, and methods from those of the past. They believed that respect for individuals and countries could be guaranteed in large measure by the participation of states and peoples heretofore excluded from that traditional "inner sanctum" of high international politics. This development had been foreseen shortly before and during the war when many people throughout the globe spoke of the necessity for emancipation and equality. At Paris, the point was stressed even further. Indeed, the peace conference itself struck many contemporaries as a dramatic visual representation of the new age. W. E. B. Du Bois, the Negro leader from the United States, excitedly described the gathering as "THIRTY-TWO NATIONS, PEOPLES, AND RACES. . . . Not simply England, Italy, and the Great Powers are there, but all the little nations. . . . Not only groups, but races have come—Jews, Indians, Arabs, and All-Asia." Another observer in Paris described the conference in the following words:

> *Chinamen, Japanese, Koreans, Hindus, Kirghizes, Lesghiens, Circassians, Mingrelians, Buryats, Malays, and Negroes and Negroids from Africa and America were among the tribes and tongues forgathered in Paris to watch the rebuilding of the political world system and to see where they "came in."*

This was something unknown in the annals of diplomacy, and to the Japanese the time appeared particularly ripe to insist that all delegates now support the principle of racial equality—at least among the influential nations of the world.

It is hardly surprising that the Japanese should have been concerned about the issue of equality among races in international relations. In the years before and during World War I racial prejudice reached new intensity. These were the early days when publicists sought to elaborate on the slogans of "The White Man's Burden," "Nordic Superiority," and "The Yellow Peril," among others. While some proclaimed that Asiatic control of territory surely would result in "racial retrogression," others spoke contemptuously of "those whose skins are black, yellow, or red." Another author asserted that the world would be safe only if the Japanese would "stay in their place"—"one in which they do not greatly intensify and so embitter the struggle for existence of the white man." These statements were accompanied by "scientific" studies of skull types, bone structures, speech patterns, and skin color designed to "prove" the superiority of one race over all others in the world.

For Japan the foreign policy manifestations of this prejudice had been serious. Severe immigration restrictions strongly embittered diplomatic relations with the United States, Canada, and Australia. Various laws in California segregated Japanese children from public schools and prohibited their parents from ownership of real property. Discriminatory judgments at the Hague Court of Arbitration grated against the sensitivities of Japan. Businessmen and professionals from Japan complained of maltreatment and humiliation when they traveled abroad. The most offensive feature of all these practices, as expressed by the Japanese Foreign Ministry, was that the citizens of Japan were subject to discrimination while those aliens of white origin were not. During the First World War, allies and enemies alike portrayed the Japanese as threatening, scheming, slant-eyed creatures. Complaints went unheeded—particularly those to the United States. Indeed, according to Asian specialist Akira Iriye, "The self-conscious antagonism between Japanese and Americans came to a climax during World War I."

One of the reasons for this intensified antagonism was the continuous and vocal insistence by Japan that action be taken to end these violations of human rights. A great deal of publicity was given, for example, to a 1915 speech made by Premier Shigenobu Okuma. Here he announced that discrimination was not simply a problem between Japan and the United States. "It is of far deeper meaning and wider scope," he said, "being an expression of the racial prejudice lying at the bottom of the affair." Okuma continued:

> *It is, in fact, no exaggeration to say that from its satisfactory solution will date the harmonization of different civilizations of the east and the west, thus marking an epoch in the history of human civilizations.*
>
> *If, on the other hand, the solution be proved unattainable, one must then forever despair of the possibility of harmonizing the different thoughts and systems of cultures of different races. In this sense the importance of the problem is universal.*

The premier concluded his speech by saying that "inferiority must end" and declaring that Japan "plans to gain equality."

The opportunity to gain such equality appeared after World War I when Japan emerged on the side of the victors. Long resentful that their country's stunning action in the Russo-Japanese War had never received the recognition in international politics that it deserved, Japanese leaders now determined that their recent military victories would never be ignored or pushed aside. Startling successes against German possessions in the Far East, occupation of Russian maritime provinces, burgeoning industrial strength, and loyalty to treaty obligations with the Entente would guarantee them a place among the Great Powers at the peace conference. Here they could press for their demands: transfer of German rights in Shantung; possession of those islands in the South Seas occupied by Japanese naval forces during the war; and of particular importance, recognition of the principle of racial equality.

Japanese press opinion appeared to be absolutely unanimous on stressing the necessity for their representatives to insist on this matter of human rights. The *Hochi* declared that "discrimination is humiliation and therefore an injustice to the people discriminated against," and demanded that the Japanese delegates "not fail to have the matter brought up" at the conference—"and solved properly." The *Yorozu* announced that "now is the time to fight against international racial discrimination." "Barring all else," stated the *Nichinichi*, "Japan must carry through her point on this score [of racial discrimination]." "As to the terms of peace," said the particularly outspoken *Asahi*, "Japan should insist on the equal international treatment of all races . . . not only for Japan but for all the countries of Asia." "No other question," it continued, "is so inseparably and materially interwoven with the permanency of the world's peace as that of unfair and unjust treatment of a large majority of the world's population." The Japanese mission, therefore, was to vindicate "the wrong suffered by other races than the white."

The prospects of achieving this mission and the other objectives at the peace conference seemed excellent to the Japanese. All the leading victorious powers already had recognized Japan's special interests in Shantung—the British, French, and Italians with the London Declaration of 1915 and later in an exchange of notes in 1917; the Americans with the Lansing-Ishii Agreement of 1917; and even the Chinese with the Peking Treaty of 1915 and an exchange of notes as late as September 1918. For the Japanese, the acceptance of this demand simply was "a foregone conclusion." On the racial equality issue, she was also confident. President Woodrow Wilson's many inspiring speeches had created beautiful images of a future world. One particular war message, in the words of one careful contemporary observer, "went most forcibly home to the Japanese mind." This was the speech in which he announced:

> *Only a peace between equals can last. Only a peace the very principle of which is equality and a common participation in a common benefit. The right state of mind, the right feeling between nations, is as necessary for a lasting peace as is the just settlement of vexed questions of territory or of racial and national allegiance. The equality of nations upon which peace must be founded, if it is to last, must be an equality of rights. . . .*

Since this was the same man that was now about to lead much of the peace conference, there seemed to be little to fear. As one paper stated, "If the discrimination wall is to remain standing, then President Wilson will have spoken of peace, justice, and humanity in vain, and he would have proved after all only a hypocrite."

The confidence of the Japanese was heightened even further by the quality of their delegation. Marquis Kimmochi Saionji was a former premier and a leading statesman of the country whose prestige was unmatched. Baron Nobuaki Makino was a former minister for foreign affairs and a leading member of the *Gaiko Chosaki*, or Foreign Affairs Advisory Council, and highly respected. They were to be assisted by Viscount Sutemi Chinda, His Imperial Majesty's ambassador at London. The public reaction to this choice was enthusiastic and these men were hailed as simply ideal, unequaled in prestige, and highly qualified to achieve Japan's objectives. The *Asahi* looked forward "with great expectations" and declared: "The country cannot have a better set of men to represent it on so momentous an occasion as the great peace conclave, and it would expect that its success at the conference will be proportionately great." Together, they were described as "one of the most perfectly organized delegations in Paris."

For all these reasons, the Japanese delegates set sail "amid banzais" and "deafening cheers" from the public who completely expected them to achieve great success. Lest they forget their mission, however, the leading Tokyo newspaper, *Asahi*, issued one last piece of advice to the delegation on their way to the Paris Peace Conference:

> *Above all our Peace Envoy must not forget to persuade the Conference to agree to the relinquishment of the principle of racial discrimination, which if allowed to exist would continue to be a menace to the future peace of the world. Fairness and equality must be secured for the colored races who form 62 per cent of the whole of mankind.*

Upon arrival at Paris, the Japanese delegates immediately, carefully, and methodically began to push for the principle of racial equality. They quickly determined that the best opportunity for success lay in the League of Nations Commission. This was the body charged with the special tasks of creating a new organization to promote international reconciliation and of delineating the fundamental principles on which it operated. They knew that Wilson personally attached overwhelming importance to the work of this commission and to the drafting of the Covenant for the league. He had specifically expressed concern about the rights of religious, national, and racial minorities in this context. It was with great confidence, therefore, that the Japanese approached the American delegation to solicit support for their plan to include an explicit statement of racial equality in the Covenant of the league.

Makino and Chinda were received on 4 February by Wilson's close friend and advisor Colonel Edward House. Rather than provide immediate and unconditional assurances of support on this racial equality principle, however, House hesitated. He stated that he, of course, deplored prejudice ("one of the serious causes of international trouble" and one that "should in some way be met"), but that he would advise caution. The Japanese, he suggested, should prepare two resolutions: one that would state what they desired and the other comprising the minimum they would accept. The first of those, as described by House, was "discarded at once." Wilson then modified the second proposal and returned it to Chinda for consideration. According to the Japanese, Wilson's amended suggestions for the equal treatment of races "was practically meaningless."

This conflict opened the first round of a tremendous controversy over the principle of racial equality at the Paris Peace Conference. The Japanese had expected that for reasons of both pragmatism and principle this matter of basic human rights could not be denied them. They quickly discovered, however, that when dealing principally with the Americans, British, and Australians, domestic politics and prejudicial attitudes about race stood in their way. The Japanese knew that Wilson was subjected to strong political pressure at home on the matter of immigration; but perhaps they were not aware that, despite his many wartime speeches on principle, he was also the southerner who had introduced segregation into federal departments, who had told a group of Negroes, "Segregation is not humiliating but a benefit, and ought to be so regarded by you [colored] gentlemen," and who had written that because Orientals "do not blend with the Caucasian race" he supported the exclusion of "coolie immigration." Prime Minister William Hughes of Australia unashamedly had proclaimed his views to the world and had campaigned for years on a strident platform that included the statement: "Our chief plank is, of course, a White Australia. There's no compromise for *that*. The industrious coloured brother has to go—and remain away!" Similarly, the official attitude of the British was expressed by Foreign Secretary Arthur Balfour to House in a conversation recorded by another member of the American delegation:

> *Colonel House handed me a pencil memorandum which he showed to Mr. Balfour, commencing with the proposition taken from the Declaration of Independence, that all men are created equal. Mr. Balfour said this was an eighteenth century proposition which he did not believe was true. He believed it was true in a certain sense that all men of a particular nation were created equal, but not that a man in Central Africa was created equal to a European.*

Confronted by these kinds of attitudes among their "close allies," the Japanese decided to appeal to the League of Nations Commission as a whole. On the evening of 13 February, Baron Makino defied House's stereotype that "the Japs never speak," and rose to make a formal statement. He began by saying that prejudices had been a teeming source of troubles and wars throughout history and that they may become even more acute in the future. The problem, he recognized, was of "a very delicate and complicated nature, involving the play of deep human passions," but that human rights could not be denied simply because of one's race. People throughout the world were demanding that they be treated on an equal footing, particularly now that under the proposed League of Nations they might be required to lay down their lives to protect those of another race or nationality. For these several reasons, said Makino, political and moral integrity required that all delegates use the golden opportunity offered by the new league to go on record supporting the following amendment:

> *The equality of nations being a basic principle of the League of Nations, the High Contracting Parties agreed to accord, as soon as possible, to all alien nationals of States members of the League equal and just treatment in every respect, making no distinction, either in law or in fact, on account of their race or nationality.*

This statement presented the Japanese position on racial equality. In the words of one observer, it "struck fire at once."

The response of the British delegation to this speech was quick. Lord Robert Cecil, who represented the empire on the league commission (and who had told House earlier that, with reference to any Japanese clause on racial equality, "the British would not agree to it at all, probably not in any form"), stated that there already had been "long and difficult discussion" about this matter. He expressed sympathy and hope for future toleration, but said that in this case, the issue was "highly controversial" and would create "extremely serious problems." Cecil therefore thought it wiser to postpone discussion altogether. Wellington Koo, representing China, considered this response offensive and announced that he was "profoundly interested" in the question and was "in full sympathy" with the spirit of the proposed amendment. The importance of this move was not lost as the lines began to be drawn in this controversy. As a member of the American delegation wrote: "In this great question of world policy, it is highly significant that the Chinese, though suspicious of the Japanese in every other way, came here to their support." In order to avoid a headlong clash, Colonel House proposed a delay in discussion. Nevertheless, on the next day when President Wilson read the completed and printed Covenant to a plenary meeting of the peace conference, there was a deliberate omission of any mention of a racial equality clause. That evening Wilson left Paris for Washington. Refusing to be silenced, Baron Makino announced that Japan would resubmit her proposition at the earliest opportunity.

During the month of Wilson's absence from the Paris Peace Conference, the question of racial equality did not sleep. Indeed, after the plenary session meeting, the issue went public. No longer would the matter of discrimination be confined to private conversations and secret commission meetings. Now all of the delegates were aware of the Japanese proposal and, even more disruptive, so were their respective publics at home. This aroused passions on both sides of the controversy and directly affected negotiations. To reach a just and equitable resolution in this context, said Baron Makino to the correspondent of the *New York Herald*, "all people must be prepared to do a little hard thinking, and to have enough courage to part with many prejudices we have inherited from our ancestors, among which are racial prejudices."

The Japanese pushed hard on this matter. Pressure mounted from legislative and public meetings protesting "the badge of shame" imposed by the white race against the colored races of the world. Individuals wrote articles in several languages stressing the importance of human rights in international relations. Private citizens in Japan formed the Association for the Elimination of Racial Discrimination. The Japanese press went even further. A significant article in *Asahi*, for example, compared the mission of Japan with that of Britain at the 1815 Congress of Vienna. It noted that then the British were the only ones courageous enough to face strong opposition and fight for humanity and justice by opposing the practice of slavery. The paper concluded:

> *Now the question of racial discrimination occupies today precisely the position which that of slavery did then. . . . Japan being the leading colored Power, it falls on her to go forward to fight for the cause of two-thirds of the population of the world. Japan could not fight for a nobler cause. . . . Japan must endeavor to make the Peace Conference leave behind a glorious record of putting an end to an inhuman and anti-civilization practice as did the Vienna Conference a hundred years ago.*

"The contention against racial discrimination," wrote *Nichinichi* bluntly, "must be insisted upon to the last."

The Japanese delegates understood perfectly well, however, that any successful resolution on human rights would come not from words in the press but rather from careful and exacting negotiations with the other representatives in Paris. Here the key still rested with the Americans, British, and Australians. Time after time Makino and Chinda arranged private meetings with individuals and with groups, and "drafted amendment after amendment in the hope of finding one that would satisfy the other Allies." Nevertheless, they met with continued opposition. Hughes, with his policy of "Slap the Jap," publicly insisted that he would "not deviate an inch" from his position. In secret conversations with the British delegation, he warned that Australia would oppose the entire League of Nations if a clause on racial equality were included in the Covenant. "Hughes insists that nothing shall go in, no matter how mild and inoffensive," recorded House in his diary, and noted that he even threatened to appeal deliberately to racial prejudices and "raise a storm of protest not only in the Dominions but in the western part of the United States." Great Britain, for its part, submitted legal arguments to the other delegations explaining why different states and races could not be considered as equal. At home, English publications continued to reinforce existing images with statements such as: "The Japanese are five feet high, brown in color, they have swivel-shaped eyes, and they eat raw fish."

Frustrated in their negotiations with the Australians and British, the Japanese turned increasingly to the Americans. Indeed, according to House's former secretary Stephen Bonsal, they called "almost every day." Each time the colonel was kind but firmly refused to make any concessions at all. Anticipating that such discussions might prove to be fruitless, the Japanese determined to appeal directly to Wilson himself. On 4 March, the day the president left Washington to return to the peace conference, Viscount Ishii, the ambassador of Japan to the United States, handed him a memorandum concerning racial equality. He politely thanked Wilson for his "sympathy and support" in the past but cautioned that should this provision "fail of general recognition the Japanese Government do not see how a perpetual friction and discontent among nations and races could possibly be eliminated." Ishii informed the president that Japan would not deviate from this objective. He concluded that any support or positive suggestions on this matter would be received "with great pleasure."

Not satisfied with this personal appeal for assistance on the racial equality principle, Ishii made a public address before the Japan Society in New York on 14 March. Hoping to generate public support and perhaps put pressure on Wilson, he stressed that a great war for international justice had just been fought with races fighting "side by side" and asked, "Why should this question of race prejudice, of race discrimination, or race humiliation be left unremedied?" Ishii stated that the injustice of denying human rights should be considered independently of the politically sensitive issue of labor and immigration. The one, he said, was principally economic in nature, whereas the other was a matter "of sentiment, of legitimate pride, and of self respect." The Japanese government, announced Ishii explicitly, would not use this principle of racial equality as a wedge to insert more immigrants into the United States. On the following day, the *New York Times* noted that "not only the remarks of the Ambassador but also the earnestness with which he uttered his plea developed immediate interest among statesmen and diplomats." It seemed clear, said the paper, that Japan was "making a definite stand on the race discrimination issue."

The reaction to this well-publicized speech was quick. Western senators in the Capitol expressed fear over Japanese intentions. A movement started in the California legislature to pressure Wilson through statements like those of Senator J. D. Phelan, who declared that "equal rights cannot be accorded to Oriental peoples without imperilling our own national existence and destroying western civilization." Fearing that a racial equality clause might be written into the Covenant, the San Francisco Board of Supervisors even sent a resolution to Washington and Paris strongly opposing such action. On the other side, Japanese residents from Hawaii sent telegrams to the American delegation urging support for this principle of human rights. Americans were "very sensitive of race problems," editorialized the *Asahi*, but must be reminded of their own Declaration of Independence which contained "unmistakable guarantees of justice and equality alike to all mankind." In addition, thirty-seven private organizations in Japan banded together to form the Conference for the Equality of the Races and explicitly warned the council at Paris that unless they abolished every racial hinderance and disqualification, "all conferences of peace, alliances, and leagues of nations can build only on sand."

Sensing this strong reaction and meeting continued resistance in the negotiations, Makino and Chinda decided to submit a revised amendment. In order to facilitate approval they pared down their initial proposal to a less offensive statement merely asking support for "the principle of equality of nations and just treatment of their nationals." It was obvious, in the phrase of one scholar, that the "word 'race' was studiously avoided." A bitter debate opened within the Japanese delegation when several members deplored this omission as "a miserable compromise." "It is absolutely meaningless," said one angry delegate. "Stick to equality [of race] or nothing. Let us be honest with those who oppose us, even if they fear to be honest with us." The reasonableness of this milder amendment appeared to guarantee approval. In the event that there might be any question, however, Makino announced at a press conference that if Japan lost on this matter she might refuse to join the League of Nations itself. "We are not too proud to fight but we are too proud to accept a place of admitted inferiority in dealing with one or more of the associated nations," he said. "We want nothing but simple justice."

The final decision on the racial equality and "simple justice" issue came swiftly on 11 April. In the words of one of the participants, this "was indeed a day of battle!" On this date the League of Nations Commission met again under the chairmanship of Wilson in a final session that lasted until nearly one o'clock in the morning. The president had just finished a vigorous fight for a special reservation clause stating that nothing in the Covenant would affect the validity of the Monroe Doctrine. (The Americans had been so adamant on this point that House threatened "to ride over" any opponents, saying that "they could go to Hell seven thousand feet deep" because the clause "was going to be put through the way it was.") Although strongly opposed by the French, who protested against this special privilege, the American reservation had been passed with the support of the Japanese. Now it was their turn. All of the delegates were aware of the new amendment from Japan. Moreover, they already had prepared their fixed positions on what was described as "the burning question" and one "so filled with explosives." Makino had insisted that the Japanese were "not too proud to fight." Hughes had stated to the Associated Press that Australia was unalterably opposed to the proposal "in any form." Cecil had received instructions to support the dominions and to place the British vote against Japan. Only Wilson refused to reveal his decision in advance.

In the midst of this hostile atmosphere, Makino rose to make his speech. Here, as he had done on so many other occasions, he calmly but firmly renewed the Japanese plea for human rights and racial equality — a matter "of great moment and concern for a large part of mankind." The whole purpose of the league, began Makino, was "to regulate the conduct of nations and peoples toward one another, according to a higher moral standard than has reigned in the past, and to administer justice throughout the world." In this regard, the wrongs of racial discrimination have been, and continue to be, the source of "profound resentment on the part of large numbers of the human race," directly affecting their rights and their pride. Many nations fought in the recent war to create a new international order, he said, and the hopes of their nationals now have risen to new heights with victory. Given the objectives of the league, the wrongs of the past, and the aspirations of the future, stated Makino, the leaders of the world gathered in Paris should openly declare their support for at least "the principle of equality of nations and just treatment of their nationals." Upon concluding his speech, Makino sat down before a stunned, silent audience. The presentation "was admirably done," recorded one member of the American delegation, "and it seemed to me that they had the support of the entire room." Others described it as "cogent" and "impressive," "dignified," "strong," "admirable," and "most embarrassing" to those who opposed the Japanese position. By all accounts, Makino's speech was a persuasive, moving performance.

After the initial shock had passed, Cecil addressed the assembled delegates and delivered what was described as a "pathetic speech" and "a deliberate evasion of the issue." He announced that he personally agreed with the Japanese proposal and position on human rights, but regretted that he was "not in a position to vote for this amendment." The words were not precise and he feared that if approved they would "open the doors to an immense controversy and to an intrusion into the domestic legislation of states." The rest of Cecil's speech betrayed his own perplexity and embarrassment. When finished, in the words of one listener, he "sat silent with eyes fixed on the table, and took no part in the subsequent debate."

Chinda replied immediately to the objections raised by Cecil "in the strongest public language yet used by Japan on the issue." Japan, he stated, had not explicitly raised the issue of race and immigration. The now-modified amendment asked for nothing more than a formal recognition of the principle of equality of nations and the just treatment of their nationals. Support of this simply would "signify that all the members of the League should be treated with equality and justice." Rejection, on the other hand, clearly would indicate "that the equality of members of the League is not recognized." This principle, he concluded, was of great importance and the national aspirations of the people of Japan were depending upon its adoption. Prime Minister Vittorio Orlando of Italy also spoke in favor of this statement on human rights. Equality was a question that perhaps ought not to have been raised, he said, but once raised, their was no other solution except that of adopting the amendment. Senator Leon Bourgeois of France urged adoption and argued that it would be impossible to reject this proposal that embodied "an indisputable principle of justice." Further statements of support came from the representatives of Greece, Czechoslovakia, and China. It appeared that a majority would vote for the Japanese proposal and that it would pass.

Then Wilson, as chairman of the session, decided to act. He had just been handed a note from House that warned bluntly: "The trouble is that if this Commission should pass it, it would surely raise the race issue throughout the world." In the words of Birdsall, "Wilson took the hint." The president started a lengthy statement that began, "Gentlemen, it seems to me that it is wisest that we should be perfectly candid with one another in a matter of deep importance like this." He stated his hope that "national differences and racial prejudices" would be "forced as much as possible into the background" at this juncture in history, for "the burning flames of prejudice" surely would "flare out in the public view." This, said Wilson, he wanted to avoid at all costs. The principle of the equality of nations was already an implicit, fundamental feature of the league, he declared, and it was not necessary to state it explicitly in the Preamble of the Covenant and thus cause controversy. "I offer these suggestions with the utmost friendship, as I need not assure my Japanese colleagues," Wilson concluded, "and with a view to the eventual discussion of these articles."

The delegates from Japan were swayed neither by these assurances of friendship nor by promises of "eventual discussion." Makino said that he did not wish to continue an unprofitable discussion, but on this matter of principle he was representing the unqualified opinion of his country. Therefore, he could not avoid the necessity of asking the commission to make a definite decision, and toward this end, he had the honor of asking his fellow members to vote upon the amendment as stated. Wilson was forced by this request to call for an official vote. The vote was taken, and the results indicated eleven out of seventeen in favor of the Japanese proposal—a clear majority.

Confronted with this result, Wilson suddenly declared from the chair that the amendment was not adopted, for it had failed to receive the unanimous approval of the entire commission. This announcement shocked the majority of the delegates, for they knew perfectly well that on two other occasions (both of which were of concern to Wilson), the unanimity "rule" had not applied at all. F. Larnaude, the French legal expert, quickly brought this to the attention of the commission and stated that a majority had voted for the amendment. When questioned, Wilson admitted this fact but said that in this case there simply were "too serious objections on the part of some of us" to have it inserted in the Covenant. "I am obliged to say," he concluded, "that it is not adopted." Makino, in great disappointment, asked that the vote be recorded "for the record."

The decision on the Japanese amendment in Paris quickly made headlines. In the United States the *Sacramento Union* announced in bold letters on the front page, "PEACE DELEGATES BEAT JAPAN'S PROPOSAL FOR RACIAL EQUALITY," and the *San Francisco Chronicle* declared, "JAPAN DENIED RACE EQUALITY." Those who supported the proposal, on the other hand, were shocked. They described the decision as "outrageous," "a snub and humiliation," and "deplorable." Among the Japanese press, the *Nichinichi* stated its belief that with this failure of the human rights provision, the league now would be made "a medium for provoking racial hatred and jealousy that will lead to friction and hostilities" throughout the world. The *Kokumin* observed that the delegates "have dared to invite the ill feeling of 1,000,000,000 colored people, and have made their countries the living exponents of a way to destroy the League of Nations." Even the moderate *Japan Times*, which catered mostly to white Europeans and Americans, editorialized in the following words:

> A historic and august congress of the representative white peoples has now formally refused to admit and accept the principle of equality of the non-white people with themselves. It is sincerely to be lamented that this action of the League of Nations Commission will most probably result in erecting a perpetual barrier against a harmonious comingling of the races toward which the world tendency has been thought to have been moving. . . .
>
> The population of the white people in different quarters of the world is calculated at seven hundred millions, while the non-whites number eleven hundred millions. The fact that those two groups are now sharply divided on account of the white people formally refusing to admit the other races on a footing of equality can only tend to accentuate racial prejudices which will far from realize President Wilson's ideal for a lasting peace of the world.

After Wilson's ruling, but before the Covenant was printed in its final form, in the words of one observer, "the Japanese did all that was humanly possible to secure correction of this injustice." In this effort they failed. Nevertheless, Makino refused to be silenced and he rose again to speak at the final plenary session of the League of Nations Commission. Here he reaffirmed his deep conviction that the race question was still "a standing grievance which might become active at any moment." He explicitly stated that Japan wanted nothing more than to set forth a guiding principle for future international relations, not to encroach on the internal affairs of any nation. Makino then reviewed the whole history of the proposed Japanese amendment: how it had been introduced, how it had met with resistance, how it had been modified in order "to conciliate the viewpoints of different nations," and how even the mild amendment had been rejected "although it obtained, may I be permitted to say, a clear majority in its favor." He announced that as a result, Japan now wanted to return to the original proposal and to declare itself in favor of the principle toward all alien nationals of "equal and just treatment in every respect, making no distinction, either in law or in fact, on account of their race or nationality."

Makino declared that since the opposition was so strong he would not press for the adoption of his proposal at this moment. Nevertheless, he concluded,

> *I feel it my duty to declare clearly on this occasion that the Japanese Government and people feel poignant regret at the failure of the Commission to approve of their just demand for laying down a principle aiming at the adjustment of this longstanding grievance, the demand that is based upon a deep-rooted national conviction. The Japanese Government and people will continue in their insistance for the adoption of this principle by the League in the future.*

As one correspondent described it, "The League of Nations was being born without a racial or national equality hair on its head."

The weeks and months following the historic decision on the principle of equality at the Paris Peace Conference were filled with emotional recriminations, hostile warnings, and a few solemn reflections. Some in Japan blamed "the indolence, timidity, and incompetence" of their once-praised delegates, and argued that had they been firm, "they would have never brought on themselves the failures which now darken their record." Others accused the prejudices and "paralyzed conscience" of the "so-called civilized world" of the Anglo-Saxons. Still others placed the blame squarely on the shoulders of specific individuals—Cecil, Hughes, and particularly Wilson, who used one voting arrangement for his own positions and another for those of everyone else. Warned one paper, "The majority of mankind will yet have occasion to make President Wilson regret his mistake in the unfair decision he made in adopting the minority opinion in rejecting the [equality] principle." Anger was expressed in other editorials as well, which threatened an "awakening of the colored peoples of the world against the white." The failure to support the principle of equality at Paris, stated the *Yorozu*, was like "wrapping explosives in a wet rag."

Several critics of the Japanese tried to ignore these expressions of indignation and anger by claiming that Japan had not been serious about the racial equality issue at Paris. That is, that the human rights issue simply had been a bluff at best or a camouflaged counter in bargaining at worst. The argument was made that Japan neither expected nor intended to win on the matter of equality, and that she therefore had tried to use a problem that she knew to be embarrassing to the Anglo-Saxons in order to extract concessions on the Shantung Peninsula. The response from the Japanese was immediate. A spokesman for the delegation firmly asserted that there was "absolutely no truth in this allegation." He accurately stated that the introduction of the racial equality clause had been decided upon well before the delegates left for Paris, when no one in Japan entertained any serious anxiety or foresaw difficulty on the Shantung question. In addition, the fate of the equality clause had been decided on during the 11 April meeting, long before the issue of Shantung was before the Council of Four. And, finally, despite the failure of the league commission to support the principle of equality, the Japanese had declared their support of the league publicly two days before the final decision on Shantung. The spokesman concluded:

> In the minds of the Japanese delegates, the justice of their contention on these two questions was so patent that never for a moment did it enter their mind that such tactics as insinuated were necessary.

This opinion was confirmed confidentially by Western sources as well and, in the words of one observer, the force of the Japanese argument "pulverized" the critics.

The factor that seemed to hurt the Japanese most, however, was not the criticism of supposed motives or tactics but rather the failure on the part of those from the West to appreciate the importance of their efforts for human rights. As one contemporary described it, they "had neither time nor thought" for this matter. The peacemakers not only refused to adopt the principle of racial equality, but—perhaps even more telling—refused to recognize that this issue was of intense concern to many peoples throughout the world. There were, without question, many immediate and monumental problems competing for attention at Paris and demanding solutions. Nevertheless, at the peace conference, Japan was regarded by friends and critics alike as "the standard-bearer of the colored cause" and as the leader of a great historic mission to advance human rights. Spokesmen described the racial equality issue as being "of absolute importance" and as "one of the most, if not the most, important international problems confronting us today." This matter, however, was seldom reported in the Western press, not followed carefully in official transactions, and largely ignored by those responsible for negotiations. . . .

Suggestions for Additional Reading

More than in any other modern war, the conditions of the armistice that was signed on November 11, 1918, influenced the peace settlement that was to follow the end of hostilities. For a brilliant analysis of the armistice by the dean of French diplomatic historians, see Pierre Renouvin, *L'Armistice de Rethondes, 11 Novembre 1918* (Paris, 1968). Arthur Walworth's *America's Moment, 1918: American Diplomacy at the End of World War I* (New York, 1977), traces the flurry of diplomatic activity between Washington and the enemy capitals. Stanley Weintraub, *A Stillness Heard Round the World: The End of the Great War: November 1918* (New York, 1985) is an evocative recreation of the public mood at the end of the war. Bullitt Lowry, *Armistice 1918* (Kent, Ohio, 1996) is the only recent monograph to exploit the French, British, and American archives.

Ever since the end of the peace conference that officially terminated the Great War, the deliberations in Paris and the agreements that they produced have been subjected to intense scrutiny. Disillusioned participants in the Parisian drama of 1919 hastened to record their objections to the final outcome. John Maynard Keynes's *The Economic Consequences of the Peace* (London, 1919) was the first in a long series of works by youthful members of the British and American delegations who criticized what they regarded as the betrayal of President Wilson's principles in the peace treaties. Whereas Keynes's criticism was mainly directed at the individual statesmen, Harold Nicolson's *Peacemaking, 1919* (London, 1933) denounced the disorganization and incoherence of the peacemaking procedures.

Those who had fashioned the new international order chimed in, with varying degrees of confidence, in defense of their diplomatic handiwork. André Tardieu, *The Truth About the Treaty* (Indianapolis, 1921) was a no-holds-barred endorsement by French Prime Minister Georges Clemenceau's right-hand man who had played a central role in fashioning Franco-American compromises on territorial and security issues. Clemenceau's *Grandeur and Misery of Victory* (New York, 1930) was a bittersweet reminiscence of his vigorous efforts to protect France's vital

255

interests in the face of sustained opposition from his Anglo-American interlocutors. David Lloyd George, *The Truth About the Peace Treaties* (2 vols., London, 1938) represented the British prime minister's defense of the Versailles system that was crumbling even as he wrote. George A. Riddell's *Lord Riddell's Intimate Diary of the Peace Conference and After, 1918–1923* (London, 1933) includes juicy tidbits of gossip about the high and the mighty offered up by Lloyd George's press agent, crony, and golfing companion.

President Wilson's physical collapse in the autumn of 1919 prevented him from recording his version of the events in Paris. But he encouraged Ray Stannard Baker, his press secretary in Paris, to produce an authorized history of the conference. Baker's *Woodrow Wilson and the World Settlement* (2 vols., New York, 1922–1923) was a ringing defense of the American president's diplomacy and an implicit criticism of the European allies for their self-serving policies. Two other prominent members of the American delegation offered more nuanced appraisals of their chief's diplomacy: see Robert Lansing, *The Peace Negotiations, A Personal Narrative* (Boston, 1921) and Edward M. House and Charles Seymour, eds., *What Really Happened at Paris* (New York, 1921).

A number of reliable general histories of the peace conference have appeared since the last official documents from the period (those of the French government) were declassified and opened to researchers in the early 1970s. Arthur Walworth, *Wilson and His Peacemakers: American Diplomacy at the Paris Peace Conference, 1919* (New York, 1986) is a magisterial, multiarchival study that sometimes loses sight of the forest for the trees. By contrast, Alan Sharp, *The Versailles Settlement: Peacemaking in Paris, 1919* (London, 1991) is a brief, crisp, lucid summary of the principal issues at the peace conference. Pierre Miquel, *La Paix de Versailles et l'opinion publique française* (Paris, 1972) treats the interplay of French domestic politics and the deliberations of the peacemakers in the French capital.

The best studies of the principal participants include Jean Baptiste Duroselle, *Clemenceau* (Paris, 1988); David Watson, *Clemenceau: A Political Biography* (London, 1974); and Antony Lentin, *Lloyd George, Woodrow Wilson and the Guilt of Germany: An Essay in the Pre-History of Appeasement* (Baton Rouge, 1984). Inge Floto's *Colonel House in Paris: A Study of American Diplomacy at the Paris Peace Conference, 1919* (Aarhus, 1973) and François Monnet's *Refaire la France: André Tardieu* (Paris, 1993) are probing studies of Wilson's and Clemenceau's principal collaborators, respectively.

The decision-making process at the highest levels has been carefully analyzed in Howard Elcock, *Portrait of a Decision: The Council of Four and the Treaty of Versailles* (London, 1972). The verbatim record of the Big Four's deliberations is conveniently presented in Arthur S. Link, ed., *The Deliberations of the Council of Four (March 24–June 28, 1919): Notes of the Official Interpreter Paul Mantoux*, 2 vols. (Princeton, 1992). Seth P. Tillman's *Anglo-American Relations at the Paris Peace Conference of 1919* (Princeton, 1961), based largely on American sources, remains the most comprehensive treatment of the complicated relationship between the American and British peace delegations. M. L. Dockerill and J. D. Goold, *Peace Without Promise: Britain and the Paris Peace Conference, 1916–1920* (London, 1981) relies on British records. Klaus Schwabe, *Deutsche Revolution und Wilson-Frieden: Die amerikanische und deutsche Friedensstrategie zwischen Ideologie und Machtpolitik 1918–1919* (Düsseldorf, 1971), translated in a condensed form as *Woodrow Wilson, Revolutionary Germany, and Peacemaking, 1918–1919: Missionary Diplomacy and the Realities of Power* (Chapel Hill, 1985), is a thoughtful study of German-American relations at the end of the war and during the conference.

The role of technical experts in the planning for the peace settlement has received insufficient attention from scholarly specialists. Laurence E. Gelfand's *The Inquiry: American Preparations for Peace, 1917–1919* (New Haven, 1963) remains the definitive study of the American specialists' activities. A more recent study of the role of the political intelligence specialists attached to the British Foreign Office in preparing for the peace settlement is Erik Goldstein's *Winning the Peace: British Diplomatic Strategy, Peace Planning, and the Paris Peace Conference, 1916–1920* (Oxford, 1991).

On the exceedingly complex subject of German reparations, John Maynard Keynes, *op. cit.*, provoked a spirited response from other participants in the reparation imbroglio in Paris. Bernard M. Baruch, an American specialist on reparation matters, issued a prompt defense of the compromise against Keynes's critique in *The Making of the Reparation and Economic Sections of the Treaty* (New York and London, 1920). Louis-Lucien Klotz, the French finance minister and chairman of the Reparation Commission, presented his government's case in *De la guerre à la paix* (Paris, 1924). Useful compendia of documents related to reparations are to be found in Phillip M. Burnett, *Reparation at the Paris Peace Conference from the Standpoint of the American Delegation* (2 vols., New York, 1940) and Etienne Weill-Raynal, *Les Réparations allemandes et la France,* 3 vols; vol. 1: *Des Origines jusqu'à l'institution de l'état des payements (novembre 1918–mai 1921)* (Paris, 1947). More recent studies that challenge Keynes's indictment of the reparation settlement include Marc Trachtenberg, *Reparation in World Politics: France and European Economic Diplomacy, 1916–1923* (New York, 1980) and Stephen A. Schuker, *American "Reparations" to Germany, 1919–1933* (Princeton, 1988). Modified and updated versions of the orthodox critique of the reparation requirement appear in Peter Krüger, *Deutschland und die Reparationen, 1918–1919* (Stuttgart, 1973) and Bruce Kent, *The Spoils of War: The Politics, Economics, and Diplomacy of Reparations, 1918–1932* (Oxford, 1989). Robert Bunselmeyer, *The Cost of the War, 1914–1919: British Economic War Aims and the Origins of Reparation* (Hamden, Conn., 1975) exposes the harshness of anti-German rhetoric in Great Britain at the end of the war but does not demonstrate its effect on British policy at the peace conference.

The influence of the Bolshevik revolution and the Russian civil war on the peace conference was exhaustively treated in Arno J. Mayer, *Politics and Diplomacy of Peacemaking: Containment and Counterrevolution at Versailles, 1918–1919* (New York, 1967) and John M. Thompson, *Russia, Bolshevism, and the Versailles Peace* (Princeton, 1966). Michael J. Carley, *Revolution and Intervention: the French Government and the Russian Civil War, 1917–1919* (Kingston and Montreal, 1983) probes France's unremitting hostility to the new Soviet state before and during the peace conference. Betty Miller Unterberger, *The United States, Revolutionary Russia, and the Rise of Czechoslovakia* (Chapel Hill, 1989) addresses the complex question of the Wilson administration's policy toward the fledgling Bolshevik regime.

The difficulties related to the drafting of the new frontiers in Europe are addressed in Harold I. Nelson, *Land and Power: British and Allied Strategy on Germany's Frontiers, 1916–1919* (London and Toronto, 1963); Kay Lundgreen-Nielsen, *The Polish Problem at the Paris Peace Conference: A Study of the Politics of the Great Powers and the Poles, 1918–1919* (Odense, Denmark, 1979); and Dagmar Perman's still definitive study, *The Shaping of the Czechoslovak State: Diplomatic History of the Boundaries of Czechoslovakia, 1914–1920* (Leiden, 1962).

For an astute analysis of the origins of the American plan for the League of Nations, see Thomas J. Knock, *To End all Wars: Woodrow Wilson and the Quest for a New World Order* (Princeton, 1992). Lloyd Ambrosius's *Woodrow Wilson and the American Diplomatic Tradition: The Treaty Fight in Perspective* (Cambridge, England, 1987) traces the tragic fate on Capitol Hill of Wilson's prescription for world order. George W. Egerton, *Great Britain and the Creation of the League of Nations: Strategy, Politics, and International Organization, 1914–1919* (Chapel Hill, 1986) examines the British contributions to the League idea (for which the American president took much of the credit). David Hunter Miller, the legal adviser to the American peace delegation, recorded the day-by-day negotiations that produced the League's constitution in *The Drafting of the Covenant*, 2 vols. (New York, 1928).

The acrimonious conflict over the postwar political status of the Rhineland has received a great deal of scholarly attention. Jere C. King, *Foch versus Clemenceau: France and German Dismemberment, 1918–1919* (Cambridge, Mass., 1960), written before the French records were available, has been superseded by more recent works. See Walter A. McDougall, *France's Rhineland Diplomacy: The Last Bid for a Balance of Power in Europe* (Princeton, 1978); David Stevenson, *French War Aims Against Germany, 1914–1919* (Oxford, 1982); and Jacques Bariéty, *Les Relations franco-allemandes après la première guerre mondiale* (Paris, 1977). A still useful summary of the then mayor of Cologne, Konrad Adenauer's, ambivalent posture toward Rhenish separatism and its French sponsors during the peace conference may be found in Karl Dietrich Erdmann, *Adenauer in der Rheinlandpolitik nach dem Ersten Weltkrieg* (Stuttgart, 1966).

The first comprehensive study of the peace settlement in the colonial world was Quincy Wright's classic work *Mandates Under the League of Nations* (Chicago, 1930). For more recent treatments based on a wide range of sources, see Christopher M. Andrew and A. S. Kanya-Forstner, *France Overseas: The Climax of French Imperial Expansion, 1914–1924* (London, 1981). Elie Kedourie, *In the Anglo-Arab Labyrinth* (London, 1976) is based on British Foreign Office and India Office sources, and may be supplemented with David Fromkin, *A Peace to End All Peace: Creating the Modern Middle East, 1914–1922* (New York, 1989). Melvin E. Page, ed., *Africa and the First World War* (New York, 1987) and Brian Digre, *Imperialism's New Clothes: The Reparation of Tropical Africa, 1914–1919* (New York, 1990) are useful treatments of the redistribution of the German colonial empire in Africa.